PRIME TIME

PRIME TIME

A BOLD NEW NARRATIVE FOR LIFE AFTER 60
AND A ROADMAP FOR RE-INVENTING YOUR FUTURE

DR. MARIE MORGAN

DELGADO STREET PRESS

SANTA FE, NEW MEXICO

Published by Delgado Street Press, LLC

Santa Fe, New Mexico

Hardback ISBN: 979-8-9998534-0-0
Paperback ISBN: 979-8-9998534-1-7
eBook ISBN: 979-8-9998534-2-4
Audiobook ISBN: 979-8-9998534-3-1

Disclaimer: This is a work of nonfiction that includes fictionalized characters created from the author's experiences. All characters, including the six main characters and the author of the Foreword, are composites with fictitious names to prevent association with any actual persons, living or dead, and are intended to represent common post-retirement experiences.

Permissions:

Excerpt from *Theory U: Leading from the Future as It Emerges* by C. Otto Scharmer (SoL, The Society for Organizational Learning, 2007), "Morning Practice," reprinted with permission of the author.

Essay "Three Keys to Innovation, Creativity, and Transformation" by Kelly Wendorf, EQUUS, reprinted with permission.

"Circles of Coherence Guidelines," adapted from The Presencing Institute. Licensed under Creative Commons Attribution-ShareAlike 3.0 (CC BY-SA 3.0).

Author: Marie Morgan
Editor: Bessie Gantt
First edition: January 2026
Printed in the United States of America
10 9 8 7 6 5 4 3 2 1

For information on bulk purchases, permissions, or rights, please visit:
https://www.delgadostreetpress.com
https://www.MarieMorganPrimeTime.com

CONTENTS

Foreword

A moment of coincidence introduced me to *Prime Time*.

After a career in Silicon Valley, I retired early at sixty-two. I was in Santa Fe for a week to visit the MEA Ranch and explore what might come next. The weekend before the retreat, I wandered into a gallery opening and ran into my cousin. We had not seen each other in a decade. She squealed. I laughed and then buried her in a hug. She asked what had brought me to Santa Fe, and when I explained, she told me she had someone I needed to meet. We agreed I would join a group at her home the following evening.

I had believed retirement would bring me relief and freedom after an intense career that was all strategy and execution of other people's goals. The relief came, but the "freedom" started to feel almost bottomless. I'd always had a company's mission as my starting point and compass. Now I had nothing.

At dinner, my cousin introduced me to Marie, who soon asked me, "How does it feel now?" I told her the freedom felt almost overwhelming. When she told me about *Prime Time*, I said, "This is just what the doctor ordered." Then I had to grin… my cousin Himari is a doctor.

At the end of the evening Marie handed me a brief note she had penned. With an encouraging smile, she said, "This will help you begin."

Over the next month, slowly and reflectively, I made my way through the book that you're holding now. It helped me name an inner voice that had been keeping me from exploring new options with an open mind. It helped me recognize a certain "gift" I had always taken for granted at work. Opportunities opened up that I could never have imagined.

That chance dinner conversation was the spark, but the fire is all mine. I am determined to find new places to use my gift again, with joy and purpose—on my own terms.

If you're feeling like I was—free but unmoored, relieved yet restless—I hope this book sparks new possibilities for you., as it did for me. I want to share the hope I now feel for my future. That's why you're reading this letter.

I asked Marie to share that "way to begin" note with everyone.

You can download it now at

https://www.mariemorganprimetime.com/begin/

Print it out. Tuck it in your journal or tape it on your mirror. Write whatever comes to you, and you will be on the way to creating *your own* Prime Time.

Michael Tanaka

Mountain View, California

THE INTRODUCTION YOU DO NOT WANT TO SKIP

*I don't know what I expected retirement
to be, but this definitely is not it.*

—ANNE, A RECENTLY RETIRED PROFESSIONAL

I was checking in with my friend Anne on Zoom, and I asked her, "How's it going?"

"I don't know what I expected retirement to be, but this definitely is not it," she said to me, almost in a whisper.

Her response was simple, but it echoed across the Rocky Mountains to me, because thousands of baby boomers are thinking this right now. I've heard this same message in my interviews for this book. I hear it anecdotally nearly every time retirement comes up in my personal relationships, and also in my career in leadership development and management consulting.

Some retired professionals are thriving on the promise of an "eternal vacation," but this book is not for them. I am writing for the larger-than-expected number who are quietly restless or frankly lost. They are not finding their groove in travel or hobbies—the main goals the culture tells them they should have. Something is missing, but they can't articulate what that is. Some grieve the loss of responsibility or authority that used to define them. Some were so expert in their field that they never developed deep interests in other areas. Others miss most their wide-ranging professional friendships. And some long to make a difference in a new way but have no idea how to go about it.

A professor who was about to retire told me she knew she had a lot more to give, but without the structure of the university, she could not see how to do that. A retired surgeon could see no transfer of his skills into volunteering. A chief financial officer, retired for six months, was cooking regularly for his grandchildren, and cherished it because he had spent so little time with his own young children. But he realized this couldn't be his life for the next twenty years. The people I've met and interviewed have encouraged me to write this book. They speak of an elusive longing, from a quiet tug to a hunger, for something they cannot quite name. They are seeking help untangling their dilemma. These stories are all around us, in a thousand different forms. Across our society they carry delight and confusion, inklings and panic, adventure and devastation.

One retired attorney said she had recently realized that "keeping herself entertained," as she put it, was not giving her sufficient reason to get out of bed each morning. She had just read that seniors without a compelling purpose in their lives are much more likely to develop dementia, and that worried her… a lot. I knew how she felt because I've been there too. More on that in a moment.

Every story is unique, but a pattern emerges: The myth of retirement that our grandparents lived by has become unhelpful. Being told to stay home and relax, travel a little, then sit on the porch until we die—that doesn't work for us. We need to talk about what's not working, why this invisible trap is so powerful, what is so different now from past generations, and, most important, what we can do about it.

My hope is to help retired professionals searching for something more, or something different, to finally find the words—a name for the problem. Then we'll frame it so we can find a way forward, placing this seismic shift in historical terms so readers can see and feel, "I'm not the only one."

I will offer clear steps for how to get from here to a new "there" that is unique for each person. Finally, we'll explore how the baby boom generation can once again reshape society, making it more life-giving for those who follow behind us.

We are embarking on a journey, an adventure together to explore our own Prime Time.

Why "Roadmap"?

The subtitle calls this book *A Roadmap for Reinventing Your Future*. But we're not talking about the GPS on a phone, where you type in a destination and follow a single blue line. What we need is more like the old multi-page atlas we once carried on long road trips—or the detailed USGS topographic maps tucked in a backpack. With those, we could see the whole territory: the places we'll never visit, the detours we never imagined, the empty stretches between towns, and the tangled beltways we might choose to avoid. A good map helps us name the lay of the land and talk with fellow travelers—pointing out an arroyo, a mesa, or a bayou.

Most important, these maps shape how we experience the journey. Our inner maps—the mental models and stories we carry— literally create the world we know. When we redraw the map, new possibilities appear; when we shift our focus, new pathways open. This *Prime Time* Roadmap won't dictate a destination. It will open up more possibilities than we can find alone and help us draw new mental maps for a future we create one day at a time.

How We Will Survey the Landscape and Take Stock of the Challenges

I have structured this book differently from what you may expect in order to give you an up-close-and-personal experience. After we identify the problem and how we can reframe it, I will introduce you to six fictional characters based on my interviews and my work with clients. I myself will also be a character in the story, as a facilitator for the group of six. You will have the benefit of seeing how a small group can effectively work through the material, and glimpse how different people naturally see issues differently. In the group I use the same insights, techniques, and exercises that I use with real-life clients. For clarity, when I speak to the group, my words are in quotes. Without quotes, I speak directly to you, the reader.

In chapter 1, I will define "the problem that has no name." By identifying in more detail what people are experiencing, we can go a long way toward finding solutions. And learning that we are not the only ones experiencing this problem is tremendously freeing. The examples I offer will also help the reader who asks, "Is this book for me?"

Chapter 2 outlines several forces that we are up against:

- The weight of consumer culture's expectations and what we can do about it
- Our generation's unexpected longevity and what that means personally
- The oppression of an outdated narrative and some encouraging alternatives

In chapter 3, I introduce our six "guides," the fictional but entirely real characters who go through a transformation process together. I describe the same ideas, methods, and techniques that I use with my own clients. These six characters not only embody many of the dilemmas readers experience, but they show how a small group, working on solutions together, can be the "secret sauce" that delivers surprising results far beyond—or faster than—what one person can accomplish in isolation. (At the end of chapter 3, I describe in more detail why and how to study this book in a group. Feel free to skip ahead to consult that section if finding or forming a group is even slightly interesting for you. I promise you will gain worlds more value from this book working through it in a group.)

In phase I, and throughout the book, "highlights" at the end of each chapter provide key teaching points from that chapter to review and reinforce what you have learned. Exercises at the end of each chapter give you journal prompts and other ways to integrate each chapter's ideas into your own life. Using the book as a workbook as you read will help create actual results in your life, beyond just acquiring interesting knowledge.

Phase II shifts from problem to solutions. I spell out two proven methods: a carefully orchestrated series of steps, processes, and methodologies that work together with a certain synergy to bring you to a new and different path for your life than you had previously imagined. This will help you get past both the internal and external obstacles that tend to block us from creative alternatives for our lives. These are not quick fixes. These tools are designed for readers who want to do the work, but these are breakthrough methods that deliver unexpected insights and changes. I have had clients stop me on the street years later and say, "You changed my life." I have confidence in the methods I'm offering you.

With these tools in your kit bag for the journey, phase III takes a deep dive into who you are as a unique person. Becoming able to hear your calling includes practicing the skills you learned in phase II and reflecting on your unique gifts, talents, values, and interests, but unlike many books on the topic of retirement, I will urge you to reach deeper inside yourself. You are here for a reason, and we are on this journey together to help you discover it.

Most professionals I have worked with, or spoken with informally, will acknowledge that they have *Superpowers*. I have chosen this term for that special something we do so well it feels easy. When we are using our Superpower, we are in the zone. I believe that if we can find a new setting to practice our Superpowers, our Prime Time life will become far more satisfying. The challenge, my interviews have shown, is that people often need some help learning to imagine such a scenario. First, I ask you to claim your Superpowers. Then, using your curiosity, passion, and confidence in shaping your future, you can both hear and step into your calling.

Phase IV is all about taking specific action on what you have heard and learned up to this point. Reading and learning are necessary, but living your actual life differently will require taking steps in the real world, and I provide guidance for those action steps.

After this very personal and applied process, we "stand up on the balcony" in chapter 10 to look at the significant effects we can have on our society as we embark on this journey together. A movement is a collection of a lot of individuals moving in the same direction at the same time. I am inspired by the possibilities. I hope you will be too.

I promise that if you faithfully apply your mind and energy to the exercises as we go, review the highlights to be sure you understand each one, and then take to heart the possibility that your life can become decidedly more purposeful and satisfying, you will hear your new calling and discern a path going forward. You will start living your Prime Time. If you find a small group to work on the journey together, this can all come together more quickly and may even be more fun to work through. As I mentioned earlier, you will find a more extensive discussion of both why and how to form a group at the end of chapter 3.

The data are clear: On this path you are likely to live longer, but, more importantly, you increase your chances to live with better health, a sharper mind, more friends, and deeper satisfaction. You will have choices that weren't available when you had to conform to your employer's needs and demands. You can be your own boss. Choose your own hours, your own cause…or wild endeavor. These could be the most gratifying decades of your life. This is your Prime Time.

How I Was Called to Write This Book

In the 1990s I had an executive coaching and leadership development practice in Portland, Oregon. Previously I had earned a doctorate combining psychology and spirituality, focusing especially on how we change as we go through adult developmental stages. The question that has most intrigued me throughout my adult life is, "How do we create containers where people can truly change?" By "containers" I mean any safe setting where people intentionally gather to share stories, explore mutual concerns, and learn together. In 1999 I joined my husband for eighteen months during his consulting contract in New York City. When we returned to Oregon, I took a year's sabbatical to study art and design full-time before I returned to my consulting practice.

In 2006 an entrepreneur offered to move us to Santa Fe so my husband could assist his high-tech group in building their company. We had already decided to retire to Santa Fe "someday," so it was an easy decision. I knew that Santa Fe was too small a city to support my executive coaching, organizational development, and leadership consulting practice, but at age sixty-four the word "retirement" had never crossed my mind. Santa Fe is an art capital, so without much thought I imagined I would somehow morph into an artist.

Once in Santa Fe, several people we met encouraged me to start a "house church," a living-room-sized alternative congregation for people from various traditions who considered themselves "recovering" from that faith. I had a seminary degree and had been ordained as a minister when I was forty, so I took on the role of spiritual leader—an experiment I led for a decade. This group was basically a half-time commitment, but I needed a different head space for my art. I moved my art practice to a studio, which gave me both more physical space and, significantly, a more focused inner state. Later I moved to a different studio with a storefront gallery. But despite the blessings of these settings, I never felt I was getting to the heart of making meaningful art. I even applied for and was accepted into a masters' program at Pacifica Graduate Institute, seeking to find more "soul" in my art.

Fortunately, I realized before that program began that I was asking the wrong question. I had started with "art" and asked how I could make *it* more meaningful, more "soul-full." As promising as the program was, studying depth psychology and ancient myth linked to the arts, it was not going to be the path to what I was actually searching for. This was an "out-there" question. Instead, I needed to ask an "in-here" question. David Whyte calls it starting "close in." Start with what is most meaningful, most soulful to yourself, and then ask how that might best be expressed.

Even after changing my perspective, I felt at a loss for where to turn next. I could feel an ache. An emptiness. Something deep within me that was not being expressed. A deeper longing. Something that wanted to emerge. For decades I had been helping others to journal, pray, meditate, read, and reflect on how to develop their leadership skills and gifts. In a blinding flash of the obvious (a BFO), I applied everything I could think of to my feelings of emptiness and longing, including much of what you will read in this book. Then, one day, sitting on my couch, gazing at the snow-topped Rocky Mountains to the east, it all came together in my mind.

With my leadership clients I like to use the term BFO. You might have heard it called an epiphany. I almost named this book *Epiphany*. Epiphanies can come in a flash, but they also can come in what I call a slow epiphany, a likely path for you in this book. That day, however, mine came fast.

I realized that my Superpower is an almost psychic ability to see the talents and abilities of others—often before they can recognize these themselves—and to help that person grow into that potential. My Superpower is insight and guidance. My Superpower is *not* in art. Nor can I even today visualize how my Superpower might look if I made it into art. I am creative, and I can make interesting stuff— paintings, sculpture, interior design. But art is not my Superpower. Helping people become their best selves is what I naturally do best.

So that afternoon, on the couch staring at the mountains, I could look back and see my twenty-year path, a wandering, looping path, to where I was now, finally realizing who I wanted to be when I grew up.

Then it hit me: "Surely I can't be the only one. Surely others are also looking for a deeper and more meaningful retirement." I also recognized that since I was in excellent health, and my mother and her father had both lived to age ninety-four, I probably still had another decade or two to do this new thing. I realized I needed to sell my studio and gallery and find a way to help retirees develop more meaningful lives.

I started interviewing people across the country, informally at first, then sourced by Facebook ads and extensive networking. When I inquired what people were thinking on this subject, I quickly learned that they could not articulate it. I found people feeling listless, aimless, missing their profession, or growing frustrated with the trial-and-error method of self-discovery. They just knew they were unsatisfied, feeling adrift, mourning the loss of the joy and productivity of their careers, or just depressed and feeling useless. And they also knew they didn't want to spend decades wandering in those futile circles. I began more serious research. I came across stunning longevity findings: Our generation is going to live decades longer than previous ones. More inquiries led me to working professionals in their sixties who were terrified about retiring, creative people who nevertheless could not visualize a retirement where they could be deeply and usefully engaged.

I could clearly see I needed to write a book. I needed to help people identify and name the problem so they could begin an intentional search for something different. Write a book, then help people through the process. That was the calling. And I also could see that day, as the afternoon waned and our Sangre de Cristo Mountains turned purple, that I already had many of the tools to help people do that. The same tools that had helped my business clients hear a calling and claim their Superpowers in their careers could help retirees like myself find their new calling in their Prime Time.

Fictional Characters, Real Truth

We will accompany the book's six characters as they learn new practices and gentle disciplines that strengthen their inner navigational guidance systems. Although some sections may read like a psychological novel, the book also includes a Sourcebook (a more boring word is "appendix.") and group study guide that allows friends or newfound fellow searchers to meet in a group with defined how-to steps week by week.

Readers naturally want to know what is true, what is fiction. *This account is entirely truthful fiction.* The characters are made up, but they are carefully representative of the many people I have met and interviewed. Shirley, Himari, Martina, Paul, Samuel, and Alicia are composites of the many dynamics, both psychological and social, that retired professional baby boomers are experiencing. (You will find a list of characters in the Sourcebook's chapter 3.) Michael Tanaka, who wrote the Foreword, is also fictional, based on two actual people.

The ways the fictional characters react in this setting are entirely true to how I have seen real people respond to their own issues and circumstances. I have been trained in and worked extensively for decades with the inner character methodology featured in chapter 4, seeing clients in both individual and group settings. The leaps of insight and the dawning awareness are quite real. (Please note that the method in chapter 4 is not intended as a substitute for therapy.)

Editors often encourage authors to share personal stories. The reason one character is named Shirley is that my mother, always intent on keeping me safe when I would dream up yet another scathingly brilliant project or adventure, would say to me, "*Surely* you don't think you are going to _____?!" In a book that dares us all to stretch into new unimagined places, the irony seemed only fitting.

The material is designed to stimulate your imagination. Contrary to popular myth, we are not all supposed to match. Think about it. There are lemurs and ladybugs, giraffes and gorillas, platypuses and peregrine falcons. We aren't all supposed to be doing the same thing, especially not in retirement, and even though we sometimes imagine we'd be more comfortable if everyone looked like us and did what we do, wide variety is healthy for the human spirit.

But I Need to Find a Job…

A note for those millions who must keep working for pay well into their "retirement" years: I hope this book will help widen the perceptions and assumptions employers have about older workers. We have a national labor shortage, and more seniors can benefit from this shortage when more employers recognize the enormous talent pool in older workers. If employers can encourage more job sharing and flexible hours, and a dozen other creative adaptations, we all win. I wish I had the expertise to offer additional help in finding those needed paying jobs, but that search will have to be aided by others with different skills than I have to offer. If this book can in any way ease that search, I'll be glad it has served a useful purpose. Chapters 6 and 9 may help expand visible options, chapter 7 can help clarify Superpowers, chapter 4 can help readers see how we sometimes get in our own way, and chapters 4 and 5 show a way to expand a grounding personal daily practice.

This last point leads me to one additional element of this book.

A Spiritual Dimension

My approach here includes a spiritual thread. I use the terminology "connecting with Source." My doctorate is from a Jesuit school of theology, but here I am decidedly *not* writing about dogma, beliefs, or traditional religions. In adopting the word "Source," I have carefully selected a term that I hope is as neutral as possible yet still carries profound meaning.

Our search is about learning to listen in a deeper way than the secular world can teach. It is about attuning to *our own* deeper wisdom and touching into the greater wisdom. I respect whatever spiritual or historic traditions my readers may bring to this experience. Having no spiritual tradition is fine too. I just ask that each participant, including the skeptics, trust their own ability to listen in this (possibly new) way and try the processes we will practice to connect with Source or inner wisdom as we go. Amid all the noise that our culture puts out, I am inviting readers to practice a profound kind of listening, a profound type of silence, that can transform not only our lives but the culture itself.

Application to Your Own Life

This book is carefully designed as a self-*help* book, not only as a self-*inform* book. It is easy to get caught up in the momentum of reading "to see what happens next," but I enthusiastically encourage you to do the exercises as you go along. Some are embedded in the narrative, and every chapter has assignments at the end. Think of yourself as a member of the group in the story and join in their journey with your own discoveries.

You will find three levels of exercises. Most of the exercises involve personal reflections that you will want to enter into a journal. If you do not already have a journal or blank book, obtaining one before you start chapter 1 will help you gather momentum. Decorated or leather covers are fun and memorable, but any spiral or three-ring notebook will work. The vital step here is to gather all your thinking, explorations, and questions *in one place*. You will be amazed how revisiting an earlier passage can evoke new insights on a later day. Also, you will want to be able to reference earlier observations as you progress along your path.

1. The simplest exercises are indicated by an occasional nudge: **Your Turn** . You will be doing these exercises along with the characters. These prompts are embedded in the text as you go. I encourage you to pause and do each exercise as described. I truly understand the temptation to skip ahead with well-intentioned thoughts to "come back

later." I promise you will get more out of each section if you *apply* what you are reading to your own life, specifically and intentionally, as you read.

2. The second level of exercises are at the end of each chapter. As with the first level, you will find the book far more useful if you pause to do that chapter's action steps before moving on to the next chapter. Each chapter builds on what you learned in previous chapters, and if you haven't yet fully applied a chapter, the next chapter will not be as meaningful nor as useful to you. You owe it to yourself to make this a *workbook*, not just a "readbook."

3. The third way to apply the material to your own life comes in the Sourcebook at the end of the book. Here you will find deeper and more extensive exercises, organized by chapter number. I also offer deeper dives into certain subjects (see "Additional Reading").

Because this isn't just a book to read, it's a journey to live, you will also find at the end of each chapter a section called Prime Time Milestones. These serve as your check-in points. They're not tests or to-do lists, just a place to pause and notice what you've learned, what's shifting, and how you want to move forward. You can record these reflections in your journal. You don't have to get it *right*—just aim to get it *real*. What you see or feel may surprise you, and the steps you are ready to take may be smaller—or bolder—than you imagined. It's a way to measure how much more *you* you're becoming.

Group Discussion of Exercises

If you are meeting with a group to study the book together, you may decide as a group which exercises you want to share aloud once they are completed. If you find a certain exercise challenging—hard to come up with a response or hard to deal with emotionally—I encourage you to bring up those difficulties, if not all the specifics, with your group. Often we are not the only one feeling a certain way, and wrestling with the difficulties together is one of the most effective ways to learn, grow, and change.

Where We Go from Here

I promise this book will change your life. If you take the process—and yourself—seriously, devote some time to it, do the exercises over the course of weeks or months, allow yourself to become something of a contemplative, and, if possible, dare to seek out a few friends on a similar search, I promise you, you will come out in a different place. A place where you can live longer, stay healthier with your mind more alert, encounter challenges with more resiliency, discover a whole new level of meaning, and have fun doing it. You *can* live a new life in your Prime Time.

I have an additional goal for this book.

"We are out to shift the paradigm of retirement," I told a new neighbor last week. I hope this book will change the mental pictures each generation holds for what retirement looks like. If we are going to spend twenty-five to forty years of our lives living it, let's give ourselves a lot more choices. And a lot more freedom to *imagine* it differently, so we can *live* it differently. Let's reinvent retirement. Let's create a new narrative and write ourselves into the story in ways no one has ever thought of before. After all, it's our Prime Time!

When Will You Start?

Imagine that you are twenty-five years old. You say to yourself, "I think I'll just hang out, relax, and see what turns up over the next thirty years." You would then be fifty-five. Do you find this acceptable? This is the plan that our current culture recommends for retirees. Start at sixty and you'll be ninety. Will you stand for that non-planning? Or will you choose a more purposeful, intentional path? If you are up to the challenge, now is the time to start. If you are a CPA or have an MBA, calculate your metaphorical lost-opportunity cost. Not a pretty sight.

Now is better.

I look forward to joining you in the circle of dialogue and the adventure to create your own Prime Time.

Dr. Marie Morgan

Santa Fe, New Mexico, the Land of Enchantment

Exercises: Making It Real

1. **Journal Reflection:** Before you opened this book, how would you have described what you thought retirement was supposed to be? What did it typically look like in your mind's eye? Be as specific and detailed as you can in your journal. There are no wrong answers—this is just a "before" snapshot for your own use for your "magazine article" on remodeling your life. At the end of chapter 10, you can look back and compare your before and after snapshots.

2. **Journal Reflection:** What are the primary reasons you chose this book? What do you hope to find or solve or discover? Do you have specific learning goals? Write in as much detail as you like. If you have particular questions that you hope this book will answer, write these down. You can check back as you progress through the book and see how you are answering them.

3. **Action Step:** I've already encouraged you to start your own learning journal. If, *by some remote chance* you have not yet done that, now is the time—really. And if you grabbed a scrap of paper to jot down notes during this introduction, just tape those notes into your new blank book, and you are on your way to your Prime Time.

Prime Time Milestones

Take a breath. Pause. What are you noticing at this point in the journey? As you reflect, write your thoughts in your journal.

Insight. I see something new…

Sample response: *This stage of life might not be the winding down I thought it was. Maybe it's actually a beginning—with its own kind of power.*

Shift. I feel something changing...

Sample response: *A little flicker of curiosity is waking up in me. Maybe there's more awaiting me here in this new stage than I realized.*

Step. I'm ready to try...

Sample response: *I'll stay open to seeing this book not just as information, but as a mirror—and maybe a map.*

Intention. What brought me here? What would I like to get out of this book?

Write one sentence, even if it changes later.

Sample response: *This intention will help me notice what matters most as I move through the pages ahead.*

PHASE I

Prime Time:
A Seismic Shift

CHAPTER 1

The Problem You Can't Name
But Cannot Ignore

*What's wrong with me? I should feel grateful… and
I am… but each morning, I really don't know what
to do with myself. My life feels like a whole dinner
of watercress. Nothing satisfies. Am I crazy?*

—HELEN, A RETIRED ATTORNEY

Helen was just ten minutes into our first meeting when she revealed these feelings to me. She had come to me when she learned I was researching a book on reinventing retirement. She explained that a year had passed since she retired from a prosperous law practice and she had run through her "when I finally have time" list. Then she hit a wall. The activities her friends were into, such as being a museum docent and master gardener, bored her. Their suggestions to her fell flat. "They just didn't engage my spirit," she told me. By the time another friend recommended Helen call me, she realized she was starting to get depressed, and that scared her. She had always been "the dynamo" to everyone who knew her. Now she wanted me to tell her what was wrong with her.

I asked if she by any chance had a name for what she was experiencing. "No idea," she answered. "Haven't a clue. No one I know has ever been through something like this." I doubted that, based on my many interviews. But I also knew almost no one talked about it, so how could Helen know? She thought she was the only one.

"This is a common but mistaken theme among my clients," I told her. I could see this would take some convincing.

Richard, another client of mine, took two years to charge through his bucket list. Then one day he returned from a tropical fishing trip, unpacked his equipment, and stared at the empty bags. "What's the point?" he heard himself say out loud. He was a bit surprised to hear his own voice, then he just stood and listened to the words echoing through his head. It was true. On the last three trips he had felt inklings of the question, but he pushed them aside. Now this question was all he could think about.

He had literally kept a written bucket list, and this trip was the last item on that page. Now what? He had been avoiding the blank space. Now, hearing his own voice, he knew it was time to face whatever that meant. And he knew he had never encountered anything quite like this before.

As a gifted high school athlete, a runner, he had always had a tangible goal in front of him. His years at Cornell and then his MBA program had been the same. That first "real" job and then he was "on the track," as he called it: "the track called life." When he sold his company, he was so eager to get to his bucket list, it didn't occur to him to think beyond it. Now here he was. No more races that he could think of. Or at least no more that seemed to make sense.

At our first meeting, after hearing his story, I asked him, just as I had asked Helen, "Do you have a sense of where this question is coming from or why you might be feeling this way?" He too had no idea.

"You mean the seeds of my discontent?" he asked me with a slight grin. "No. If I knew, I probably wouldn't be here. I like to think

I can figure out just about any problem, but this is such a blank page. It's a little disconcerting." He paused for a long minute, then slowly explained to me, "They used to tell me I was 'coachable' back at Cornell... that this was my strength. That's probably the only reason I am here today."

Four Themes

Helen and Richard represent just two of many stories of retired professionals today. You will hear more of them throughout this book. Widely varying circumstances but common themes start to appear. Even though Helen and Richard (and everyone else) are going through retirement with widely different circumstances, at least four particular themes begin to emerge. First, as I immediately assured both Richard and Helen, *they are not the only one* feeling this way.

A second theme is the *silence*. This dilemma among retirees just isn't talked about. Or wasn't talked about, but that is already changing, to everyone's benefit. Trying to solve it in isolation is the least effective path. My initial reason for writing this book was to give people something concrete to discuss, to get the issues out into the open.

You've probably already noticed the third theme: our culture *does not yet have a name* for these feelings and these dilemmas. Naming a problem allows it to be seen. Before that, a person just feels a vague discomfort, or worse, an acute cognitive dissonance. We must name and describe this dynamic because having no words for a strong feeling only leads to frustration and self-blame. We have outlived the usefulness of the concept of "retirement." A trivial example would be if we all still said, "Dial me up," when we wanted someone to phone us. Put simply, the entire algorithm is antiquated—more on this in a moment. Historically, we see that naming has power. Major cultural shifts can happen when people finally put words to previously invisible but strongly felt realities. *The Feminine Mystique* comes immediately to mind. Naming "burnout," "gaslighting," and "Me Too" also opened the way for solutions.

As I worked with Helen and Richard, I needed to explain a fourth theme or pattern because I knew they were unaware of it: *The problem is systemic*, not just personal, and not their fault, as I assured them. In chapter 2 we will discuss this in greater detail, but I wanted to take the pressure off Helen and Richard because I could feel their self-blame and their wondering, "What am I doing wrong with my life?" The culture is sending us outdated messages about what retirement *should* be. This is a huge systemic problem that goes unmentioned. It is quite simply an antiquated model for retirement.

An Antiquated Model for Retirement

The concept of retirement was invented when people worked long and exhausting jobs then quit when their bodies wore out. Stepping away made sense. They were encouraged to relax and enjoy life for a few years. Then they died. Today, as we discuss at more length in chapter 2, we baby boomers are expected to live into our nineties and some beyond. That can mean a thirty-year time block. As one client said to me, "That's an awful lot of golf."

The instructions we have been given by the culture—what we are expected to do—is to take an eternal vacation. But this coding of our operating system is outdated. This hidden program is also archaic because it relies on the core message that consumer culture powerfully crafted in the 1950s: "What you buy will make you happy, and if you feel unhappy, buy more." Most people I talk to realize this is a false promise, and that friendships and meaningful activities are far more satisfying. But the message persists that keeping ourselves entertained—mainly with what we can purchase—is just "what you do" when you retire.

The power isn't just in finding a name for the dilemma. What matters is that we create a specific and detailed map of the current terrain so we can then carve new paths in this longevity wilderness.

Real power comes in fully understanding the symptoms and obstacles we face—so we can find new solutions.

We must start with how we think about the future, our future. This is our Prime Time. We are standing on the edge of a profoundly different world view regarding aging, that is, for the years beyond sixty or sixty-five or whenever we leave our paid careers to create a new life. Prime Time isn't just about rejecting the old model for retirement. It is about coming to understand what really matters to us, shaping new experiences accordingly, and stepping into that new future as we create it.

Once we start thinking in the Prime Time framework, everything changes. We become active players, no longer passively accepting the antiquated story.

The Categories of Our Dilemmas

We can identify several categories or ways of thinking about the dilemmas we encounter after we leave our professions behind. Exploring them here at the outset will help form a comprehendible map of what we are facing. We will discuss each category in depth as we move through the book and your journey.

Missing Structure

Marsha's first words to me were, "I'm in a panic! I'm embarrassed to admit that, but once I stop teaching my MBA students, I literally cannot picture what I will do. I'm afraid that without the semester's rhythms, without students to show up for, without the challenge of creating new curricula, I'll just sit on the couch and rot!"

As we talked, I could see that she, like so many with careers in large institutions, had her day, her months, her years, even her worldview constructed by that entity. Although she had been entrepreneurial in inventing new, relevant courses, she could not seem to transfer that creativity to the redesigning of her own life.

I explained to her that we could go through a systematic process of identifying how the skills she already had would help her meet this challenge. That day, she remained skeptical. And worried. A totally normal response.

Louisa faced a similar dilemma. As a science professor at a major university, she depended on her lab and her graduate students to form the foundation for the most exciting part of her life. "I love science. I'm not ready to give that up," she told me, "but the university can only supply lab space to emeritus faculty for so long. I don't know what I'll do after that." She had worked in that building for decades. Her list of awards was pages long. But now she was going to need to solve a different kind of problem. She, like Marsha, was going to have to learn an entrepreneurial mindset, if she was going to continue her Superpower for the anticipated decades that her health would allow.

Loss of the structure that our careers provide can leave a huge hole in our sense of who we are and what we can do going forward.

Missing Identity

Jack and I were chatting casually, catching up on how his week had gone. He'd been retired from a career in cardiology for two or three years, and he was still unsure what to do next. I asked him how his golf game had gone on Tuesday. "Oh, OK, I guess…" He trailed off. I asked if he liked golf. "No, not really, but isn't that what you're supposed to do when you retire?" His words saddened me, but they weren't unusual—they echoed the unspoken expectation our culture hands to nearly everyone at this stage.

Having an intensely demanding career leaves many of us without an alternative identity. It is not uncommon to have no hobbies or wider interests in reserve. One retired medical specialist had had the chance to go to Juilliard instead of medical school, so while he chose the medical profession, he still had his love and talent for piano to feed his spirit through the years. He had a ready-made sense of self the day after he retired from medical practice. He now gives recitals (with great food) twice a year in his home, and this gives him a program to plan, pieces to work on, string players to rehearse with. And because of his love for the art and his high level of expertise in this alternative medium, a sense of purpose and calling seem to be built in. He had something to look forward to all those years.

But for people like Jack, who don't have a lifetime of alternatives to draw from, it takes more diligence and dedication to discover a new identity. Particularly for those who knew their career goal from a young age, they have never before had to face the question, "Who am I?" It takes a commitment to intentional exploration, often over a period of months or even years, to pry out of their unconscious, and out of their environment, that new thing that excites them— something they can become and thrive on.

A note on gender differences: More men than women I have spoken to seem to struggle with this identity issue. When I ask men—and also women—about this, they often attribute it to women having stronger parallel roles throughout their careers— wife, mother, caregiver, family events planner, remodeling manager, even logistics strategist. Women seem to have more to draw on once the career position disappears. But if other identities follow women into their Prime Time years, they still face other challenges.

Missing Friends and Networks

Ellen thought she had her retirement all planned out. As a single woman, an outgoing person, and a pharmaceutical sales rep, she had lots of friends and knew a lot more people beyond the friends she socialized with. But she was getting a little burned out with the pace, so she took a retirement package. At that point she had managed to purchase some rural land with a small house on it. She had dreams of fixing it up a little—it didn't need a lot—and settling in with the three-foot stack of novels she was dying to get into, her two dogs…and the silence. In her mind it felt like heaven. A reward well earned.

She assured a few dubious friends that this dream would be "enough." But as the second year came to a close, she started to get restless. She had done all the remodeling she could afford. She had finished the last book on the stack and had ordered a dozen more from Amazon. But the novelty was wearing off. And she was missing her friends. She tried calling them but soon discovered that, since most of them were still working, they really didn't have time to do as much or as many things as she was hoping for. And some of them, even at her old company, didn't even manage to return her calls.

She woke up to a pattering rain one gray morning and felt lost. Her first instinct was to talk it through with a friend, but that was part of the problem. Who would that be? She tried some online searches and wondered if Meetup was still a thing. She was also clear the "finding a husband thing" was not the answer her friends had once urged. Her loneliness issues would need a different approach.

She started attending retreats and conferences in subjects she had some interest in, including species loss, reforestation, and permaculture. She was also hoping to meet new potential friends with common interests, so she tried a cooking class. Someone told her about my work with people in her situation. The first day she called me, we talked for an hour and she admitted that she needed some kind of larger purpose in her life, not just "more things to do," as she had first believed. She had taken for granted her career providing cancer treatment drugs, and now she would have to discern what else mattered deeply to her. I explained that the process could take a while, but she said she had all the time in the world. Whatever it took, she was in.

We also discussed some ways she could start to build a new network of friends. As she began to uncover her deeper interests, I alerted her to watch for clues about where to find new kindred spirits. As she spent time with them, I assured her, they would lead her to deeper answers for her new life that she would never have stumbled upon on her own.

Navigating Timing That Is Beyond Our Control

Another category of dilemma retired professionals face has to do with time itself.

My new client, Jorge, had been planning to retire in two years, so when his job ended suddenly, it was particularly upsetting. "My staff and I came in to work one morning," he told me, "to find an email that told us the company was closing operations in our state and our jobs all ended that day at noon. Now I have to recalibrate. It's been four months—I've needed that long to adjust my nervous system to the initial shock. And to mourn. I really loved my job. Now I need to make some decisions—plan my future—but on a much shorter notice than I ever expected. I still feel overwhelmed. I know I need help with this."

I explained to him that, although some clients come to see me two years before their retirement date, many come two or three years after it happens. Among the latter, some have learned the guitar or remodeled the garage into a studio or traveled to their list of dream locations, but now they've hit what we call the "What now?" wall. I assured him he was not too late to begin the process.

As Jorge described his background in law, his early interest in debate, and his deep experience in seeing both sides of complex issues and being able to speak coherently to both sides, I assured him I could see he had great potential to create a new path. I caught a glimpse of his Superpower, even if he could not see it yet. He had his work cut out for him.

That same week Nathan, who had been retired for nearly a decade, described his former career as fitting him "like a suit too tight to allow a full breath." He loved the freedom to be the full self that retirement had brought after a lifetime of public service. He was thriving on learning to paint in watercolor for the first time. He told me the most exciting part of art was learning to *see* differently. But he had spent his career in public policy in the disabilities world, and he was still feeling, in spite of those new hobbies, the need to make a difference once again "in some small way," as he put it. He wanted to begin an intentional search for what that refashioned calling might be. For Nathan the discovery process was a leisurely reflection on new possibilities.

Timing "is what it is," and each timeline brings its challenges and promises. It is important to take care not to assume that there is something "wrong" with whatever shows up in our lives. There will be a gift embedded in each challenge, if we have eyes to see.

The Conspiracy of Silence

"I hate to complain," LuAnn began. "I have so much." LuAnn was about to wade into a largely unacknowledged dilemma that dissatisfied retirees face today.

"I know. I do understand." I tried to reassure her. "You are unhappy and unsettled about your retirement, but everyone else *seems* to be doing fine with it. You feel as if because no one else ever talks about it, they must not have a problem."

"Yes!" she continued. "And I feel guilty about feeling this way. There are people starving and living on the streets right here in our city, and here I am complaining about my comfortable middle-class existence. If it weren't your job, Marie, I'd be embarrassed to even bring this up, but—" She paused and stared out the window. "But if it is your job, then I suppose I can't be the only one feeling this way!" She brightened at her own sudden realization.

I continued with my encouragement. What's important at the beginning of this journey of exploration is that you recognize and be reassured that you are *not the only one* to feel this way. Each person who takes a chance and mentions a bit of their dilemma faces the possibility that the listener will not understand, but this is survivable. I asked her about other career risks she had taken in the past, and she soon realized that she could, in fact, handle this one.

"I can see now," she admitted, "that only when we start talking about this openly will we be able to start working out creative solutions."

Finding a Purpose

Greta plopped down in the chair in my office, crossed her long legs, and rolled her eyes. It was our third meeting, and she slapped her journal on the table beside her, glaring at it.

"I did the assignment you gave me," she said, "and it was really annoying."

I appreciated her honesty. I nodded, encouraging her to elaborate.

"You asked me to ponder why I thought I was here on the planet. How should I know? You asked me to try to capture what I thought my purpose was *during my career*. That was a lot easier. As a management consultant my purpose was always to help my clients accomplish their highest goals. I worked primarily with founders of medium-sized companies, and I was fortunate to mostly deal with companies that were founded on high ideals. So I didn't have to worry about purpose. Their purpose was my purpose. I was good at what I did, so I was able to pick and choose and only work for ethical companies."

"Greta," I began, "I appreciate your being willing to at least struggle with these questions. I can assure you that a lot of retired professionals haven't had to give much thought to why they have done what they did at work because the job itself hands you a compelling purpose. Now you get to choose your own."

"Thanks," she said, with irony in her voice. "That's quite a gift." Then slowly she finally smiled. "Actually, I suppose it is a gift to be able to choose what I want to live for. A lot of people are just getting by. Staying alive, providing for their families, pretty much fills their days. I guess I need to learn how to even think about the question before I can come up with my own answer."

I promised her that the process we were starting together—represented now in this book—would assist her not only in discovering a purpose of her own, but also coming to understand it as her calling. It is a process that our consumer culture and our retirement culture have failed to teach us. Now we have a new opportunity to discern new answers.

Trying to Solve It Alone

My client Serena shared her frustration with me at a high pitch: "When I try talking with some of my peers about this, they don't understand my problem. If they love travel or their volunteer committees, I get a lot of blank stares. I need a certain amount of human interaction. I want to think out loud every now and then. Working alone on this isn't getting me there. But then what can I do? I feel like I *should* be able to figure this out!"

I nodded, hoping she would feel understood. She took a deep breath and calmed a bit.

I said, "You are pointing out something few people realize. I call it a hidden enemy. We feel like we need to figure these things out *all by ourselves*. It is a holdover from the great American myth of rugged individualism. And it really is a myth. Apart from a few pioneers who lived out on the prairie with no one within fifty miles, most of our ancestors depended heavily on their families, their neighbors, and their communities to keep life moving along."

Serena smiled tentatively. "I get you. I grew up in a strong community. I know what you are talking about."

"Even today," I said, "while we pretend we are individuals, independent and self-sufficient, we nevertheless care more about keeping our connections with one another than we do about truth. So we keep quiet about our deepest pain and disappointments. Keeping the do-it-myself myth alive can hold us back from growing into our best selves. And it keeps us lonely when we believe the fiction that we are the only one who feels the way we do."

"You're right," Serena said. "Where did I get that idea? It still just seems like I *ought* to be able to figure it out for myself. This will be hard to shake off."

"For now," I told her, "it is enough that you recognize that reaching out for help, and possibly also helping others, might be a smarter path."

Falling into the Trap of Trial and Error

In the years I have been interviewing and working with professionals over sixty, I have overheard a recurring piece of advice that seems to be embedded in common speech. It often goes something like this: "You just have to take the time to do trial and error. You pick something and go do it for a while. It doesn't work out, so you go try something else."

I appreciate that this is what the person giving this advice has done, but it is bad advice. As they have looked around, they haven't seen anyone modeling any other way, so they think this is the *only* way. And they recommend it to others, even though it is not particularly effective. The truth is, random and unexamined trial and error will often lead to years of frustration and disappointment. And there *is* a better way.

It's not that we don't want to try new things, it's that we usually fail to critically analyze what worked for us and what didn't—and why. "Why" is important. Toward the end of chapter 9 we will discuss how to creatively critique our experiments, but at the outset I encourage my clients not to assume that just charging out and trying different things will solve the deeper questions.

There Is No One-Size-Fits-All Approach

The final category we will identify here regarding our dilemma is simply the fact that our situation is complex, not one-size-fits-all. One single stereotype for "retirement" is no longer helpful. The existing retirement system was designed to ensure financial survival, and even today most retirement counseling speaks to that goal. Furthermore, most books on retirement today address either financial planning or they prompt the reader on how to find more interesting things to do to occupy their time. Readers are encouraged in a generic way to "stay active." These approaches are useful, to a point, but they fall short. They are a mismatch for the realities of our time. Retirement as we have known it has a design flaw. It fails to address at least three real, current needs: our upcoming longevity, the spirit-hunger created by our consumer values, and our longing for deeper meaning. It fails to address these because it was built for a world that no longer exists.

Hundreds of lives, like the stories illustrated here, speak to the rich variety of expertise, experience, and even Superpowers that retired professionals bring to the table today. Now is our Prime Time to rewrite the narrative for what it means to be "retired."

In the next chapter, we will discuss four important situations and concepts that will help equip us to create new scenarios: a past movement that can instruct our future, the current realities of longevity, some assumptions about the eternal vacation model of retirement, and a new way to define our future.

Each situation, reframed, brings new opportunities. Living in Prime Time means life as we have never known it before.

Highlights

Recurring Themes – Among retirees from varying backgrounds and circumstances, the same themes appear again and again:

- **The feeling that you are the only one going through this.** Countless other people are in the same situation and face the same dilemma. You are not alone. You are not the only one experiencing this or feeling this way.
- **Silence around the topic.** No one is talking about this! Trying to solve this in isolation will not work nearly as well as starting a conversation and getting the issues out in the

open. This book and starting a group to work through it together are a great start.

- **Lack of a name for the dilemma.** As it is, we don't have a word, a recognizable concept that people immediately can identify with and rally around. We can instead start contemplating the future face of this situation: our *Prime Time*.

- **The systemic nature of the dilemma.** This is not a personal problem. Society over time developed a model of retirement that is now outdated and no longer relevant. We aren't "wrong" or "deficient" or "abnormal" for not being able to conform to this model. We are not alone. We can be part of a social movement to change the model as we change our own lives.

The Categories of Our Dilemmas – People seem to find themselves in one—or more—of the following categories in terms of what is particularly bothering or scaring them about life after their professional career:

- **Missing structure.** Whether it's time and scheduling or place and organization, many of us have had careers that ground and direct us. Over the years, our days and calendars and habits revolve around the institution or company, and it's daunting to consider having to do this for ourselves without these exterior structures.

- **Missing identity.** Some people are lucky enough to have a passion or a talent for something outside of their career that they immediately tap into once they retire. But for many others, especially those with demanding careers, they may not have had the time or even the need to think about their identity beyond their profession. Asking "Who am I?" for the first time since you were young can be disconcerting, and to answer that question takes a commitment to self-exploration that can take time and deep introspection.

- **Missing friends and networks.** Similar to the identity situation, work often provided us with networks of friends and associates. Even if we didn't socialize after work with them, just knowing a lot of people with similar interests provided a built-in sense of community. When all this suddenly seems to evaporate, it can be disconcerting, even devastating. Finding and rebuilding these networks takes a dedicated effort that most people are unprepared for.

- **Navigating timing that is beyond our control.** When the job ends unexpectedly, or we imagine we "should" have something figured out by a certain time and it's not happening, timing itself can seem troublesome. But we have a say in what we believe about timing and can ease the stress by attending to our unconscious assumptions. In short, "going with the flow" can ease the journey.

- **The conspiracy of silence.** We are social beings, and we unconsciously take our cues from others throughout the day. So when people aren't discussing something that we struggle with, we assume no one else experiences the problem. Until we can find kindred spirits who share our feelings, it is vital to grasp and accept that we are not the only one, even with evidence to the contrary.

- **Finding a purpose.** When a sense of purpose was built into our jobs, the sudden vacuum can be unsettling. Even bewildering. It may require a leap of faith at first to believe that pursuing an intentional process—such as the phases laid out in this book—will eventually unearth a new sense of "what we are doing on the planet."

- **Trying to solve it alone.** Americans who travel to other cultures are sometimes surprised at how others rally together as a community to get things done. Our sense of individualism in the U.S. runs deep, even while it is invisible to us. For redesigning our lives, it takes a conscious effort to override the sadly isolating assumption that "I should be able to figure this out by myself." Asking for help, seeking out kindred spirits, is a much smarter strategy.

- **Falling into the trap of trial and error.** People who have tried trial-and-error tend to recommend it to others, even if it has not been a particularly effective way to make forward progress. There are better methods. (See chapter 9.)

- **There is no one-size-fits-all approach.** It is so tempting to wish for a simple fix. But we are complex beings with complex lives, and the beauty is, we have many more choices than a simple fix can offer. Once again, we are in charge of our expectations, and we can welcome the richness of what we can create.

- **Bonus concept.** After we retire, it is sometimes too easy to focus on what we miss. See the <u>Sourcebook for Chapter 1</u> for a list of "Reframed Freedoms" in retirement,

Exercises: Making It Specific

1. **Journal Reflection:** Start your own map by naming the problem. In your journal, reflect on which of the categories of retirement dilemmas or situations sounds like you. For example, is it loss of structure, or of friendships? Identity? Or sense of purpose? Or is yours something else? If several feel familiar, try to identify which one you feel is most acute. You may have your own name for a different challenging situation. Whatever appears real in your own life, record it here. This is all part of naming the problem— for you personally. Also, read "Reframed Freedoms" in the <u>Sourcebook for Chapter 1</u>.

2. **Journal Reflection:** Start to think about priorities. You do not need to decide right now, but make some *preliminary* notes in your journal about which of these categories *might* be a priority for you to focus on, and why it seems important. Record any strong feelings that emerge. This is for your eyes only. Keep an open mind because new perspectives will

emerge in coming chapters, but "notes for now" is a good starting place.

Prime Time Milestones

Take a breath. Pause. What are you noticing at this point in your journey? As you reflect, write your thoughts in your journal.

Insight. I see something new...

Sample response: *I'm not imagining this unease. There's a real gap between what I was promised about retirement and what I'm experiencing.*

Shift. I feel something changing...

Sample response: *Relieved. I'm not alone. There's a name—or at least a shape—to what I've been feeling.*

Step. I'm ready to try...

Sample response: *I'll name one thing that feels off for me, and allow myself to wonder what I might want to change.*

Chapter 2

What If the Story of Retirement Is All Wrong?

To subvert, or not to subvert: that is the question—
whether 'tis nobler in the mind to suffer the slings and
arrows of the dominant paradigm, or to take arms
against a sea of norms and, by opposing, end them.

—The author, taking liberties with Shakespeare

The first explosion rattled our windows and made me jump. My cream golden retriever, Maddie, leaped to her feet from a dead sleep and ran to lean into me. Her whole body was shaking. It was 11:30 p.m. on New Year's Eve, but she had no way of understanding that. My dog vocabulary being rather limited, I couldn't explain it to her. So I gave her a slow full-body rub and told her in a soothing voice that it was going to get worse before it got better, and that for some neighbors this was their idea of fun. I rambled on for a long while, figuring that my tone mattered more than my syntax.

The way Maddie felt on New Year's Eve can serve as a metaphor for how we feel about retirement: We don't fully understand what is happening to us. We lack perspective because people rarely talk about the downside of giving up a rewarding career—or even the costs of giving up a career that has worn us out. The cause of the feelings we described in chapter 1 doesn't have a simple explanation like, "It's just New Year's Eve." And no one can offer the reassurance that "it will all be over in an hour and you can go back to sleep."

One goal for this book is to help you find your way into "a new year" where you can discover the best way to live a satisfying, fulfilling, and meaningful life for the next decade or three.

To get there, let's stretch the metaphor. Maddie was "unconscious" to my explanation about how fireworks work. She could not understand that I held different assumptions about how long the fireworks would last or that they would not enter our house. Our culture has taught us certain assumptions about retirement—let's call them unconscious assumptions—but they no longer fit our current reality. I'll explain each one in detail; meanwhile, here is a summary:

> We are expected to leave the workforce, find a hobby, maybe travel a bit, then slowly get feeble and die, usually not long after we retire. We are supposed to be delighted at not working and thrilled with our "eternal vacation."

Before we discuss the assumptions embedded here, however, we need to notice how unconscious assumptions work. Until we learned about germs, people assumed sickness came from bad air (miasma). To avoid illness, they tried to avoid foul smells. A similar example: doctors once assumed illness resulted from an imbalance of bodily "humors" (blood, phlegm, black bile, and yellow bile) and bloodletting was a common treatment.

More recently we assumed that intelligence and brain capacity were fixed at birth, with little room for change. Now modern neuroscience has revealed that the brain is highly plastic. It can rewire itself through learning, experience, and even after injury. In these and many more examples, our perceptions are shaped by our beliefs, but new information can cause us to notice and then rethink our fundamental assumptions.

A Similar Case of Hidden Assumptions: Feminism

"Do you remember Betty Friedan's book *The Feminine Mystique*?" I asked my daughter last year. She had not yet been born when it was published in 1963, so I wasn't sure how she would answer.

"Sure. We read it at college in a women's studies class," she said. "Wasn't it what sparked the feminist movement? I mostly think of Gloria Steinem as the voice of the movement, but I believe Friedan's book came first."

I had Googled the book that afternoon, just to refresh my memory. When I read a synopsis, I was stunned. It was déjà vu all over again. It's as if that whole movie of the sixties and seventies is being replayed today, but instead of centering on women's issues, it's those of retirees.

My daughter squinted, looking quizzical as I told her what I'd discovered.

"It's not an exact replay," I explained to her, "but the similarities today are chilling."

She looked at me expectantly.

"First of all, retirees don't talk about the problem. And the problem has no name. That's exactly what Friedan was saying about the housewives of the 1950s. Today a whole lot of us who had professional careers are either vaguely dissatisfied with retirement life or we're wondering, 'What am I doing on the planet?' or we're secretly depressed."

"Is the feeling equally widespread?" my daughter asked.

"I'm not saying everybody, but there are more retirees than we realize who are hungry for more meaning in their lives. And they're not talking about it. I know I've been in that category. There were days I loved going to the studio, but more often I wondered, 'What's the point?' But I said nothing to anyone about this."

"OK, I'm tracking so far," she said. "I'll put a check mark next to problem with no name that no one talks about. What else about your déjà vu?"

"*The Feminine Mystique* talks about housewives in the 1950s being unhappy despite material comforts. Today I would reframe that just slightly. The reality today is that we as retirees–and a lot of younger people too—realize that materialism is not the answer to a satisfying life. The messaging to buy our happiness seems orders of magnitude more pervasive than in 1963 when *Mystique* was published, and the middle class owns a lot more stuff. But we certainly aren't orders of magnitude happier."

She said, "So we can check off the box that Friedan's 'materialism isn't the answer' is just as true for retirees today. What's next on your list?"

"The media are always an easy target, but they show up in these parallels too. Friedan called out the magazine editors for making sure that housewives were always depicted as happy and content and the few career women featured were shown as unhappy. Today retirement images are often beaches, margaritas at sunset, and golf."

"Don't forget pickleball." She laughed. "OK, so retirement is portrayed as affluent and relaxing. Period. Except in the memory care unit ads. In those, the adult daughter is the one portrayed as happy." She rolled her eyes. "Is there more?"

"This one is going to sound like a meta-generalization, I confess, but the whole expectation our consumer culture holds about retirement today is that we relax, kick back, and just keep ourselves entertained. Oh, and be sure to keep spending money. The problem I see is that no one expects us to be enterprising or trying to solve serious problems once we quit full-time work. Friedan was all about calling out the post-war expectation that women would return to the home from staffing the war-support industries and confine themselves to housekeeping and mothering."

"I see what you mean," she said. "Either way, meaningful work in the world, paid or not, was, and is, off the table—not on the agenda. I know some sixty-five-year-olds keep working, but I hear you saying that the point here isn't whether the work is paid or not. The point is finding a meaningful place to contribute, using your talents and experience."

She thought about this for a moment, then continued. "It's ironic that Friedan argued for women having the same right as men to have meaningful work that drew on all their talents and interests, and now in retirement, *men*—along with women—are tacitly being denied that same opportunity."

"Yes, it is ironic," I said. "Some institutions and companies have a mandatory retirement age, but it isn't just the law we're talking about. It's the social expectations. And what worries me is that those expectations are contagious. Unfortunately, too many retirees learn not to expect much *of themselves*. Think of it as a learned helplessness."

My daughter pondered this. "Are there any other parallels?"

"I have one more comparison between retirement assumptions and *The Feminine Mystique*. It's an ancient theme: biology is destiny. In the 1950s the cultural assumptions said that a woman's role was determined by her biology—wife and mother were the only proper roles. Today it happens to men and women equally with aging. When we turn sixty-five, a magic wand passes over our heads that says now, reaching this age, we must quit the energetic pursuit of our goals in the world and instead simply find ways to keep ourselves entertained for the rest of our days. We see exceptions in the media, of course, marathoners in their seventies or eighties, ninety-year-olds lifting weights. Nevertheless, because of our chronological age, we assume, sometimes even unconsciously, that we must set aside all our skills, interests, and even work friendships and take up travel and hobbies, or childcare again, as our only purpose for living. All because of biological age. How is that any less arbitrary than decisions based on gender?"

"You're right," she said. "The comparisons *are* eerie."

"But I believe there is reason for hope." I felt myself jumping up on my soapbox, but continued anyway. "It will take a lot of effort by a lot of people to point out these unconscious assumptions, rewrite the narrative for our culture, and reshape our future. The power is in what we carry around in our own heads—what we believe we can do if we choose to. New assumptions about what is possible."

I reminded my daughter, who was born during the early spread of feminism, that the seismic shift in attitudes and assumptions had happened in just a decade. Not that all the battles for opportunity and equality had been won, but the vital first steps toward real change were taken. At least we were questioning assumptions and challenging the paradigm.

She said, "That's what has to happen again right now for boomers, isn't it? I hope you can get it done before I get to sixty-five."

Reality Changes Our Assumptions about Longevity

The Stanford University Center on Longevity has published an extensive report on their research titled *The 100-Year Life Is Here. We're Not Ready.*[1] I could cite lots of statistics, but the essence of the story is that we as a group, the baby boomers, are going to live a lot longer than any generation before us ever has. And those born today will commonly live beyond one hundred.

When I give workshops, I ask participants to turn a blank page to landscape format.

You can do this too as you read this.

Your Turn

At the upper left corner of your page near the edges, draw a 1-inch horizontal line. This short line represents (roughly to scale) your first 22 years of life. Make a visible dot at each end of the line. Write 0 and 22 under the dots.

Then extend this line to represent ages 22 to 52. (This line will be proportionally longer than the first line.) Add a dot at the end and write 52 below it. Now add a short line taking you from 52 to 62, adding a dot and the number 62 under that dot.

Finally, draw your line the same length again as your 22 to 52 line, to represent 62 to 92. Draw a little star to represent your current age on your line. For example, I am 82 as I write this; my mother and grandfather both lived to 94, and I expect to outlive them, so my line needs to be a little longer than the average I've asked you to draw. I put my star at 82. You can extend your line farther if you expect to live beyond 92.

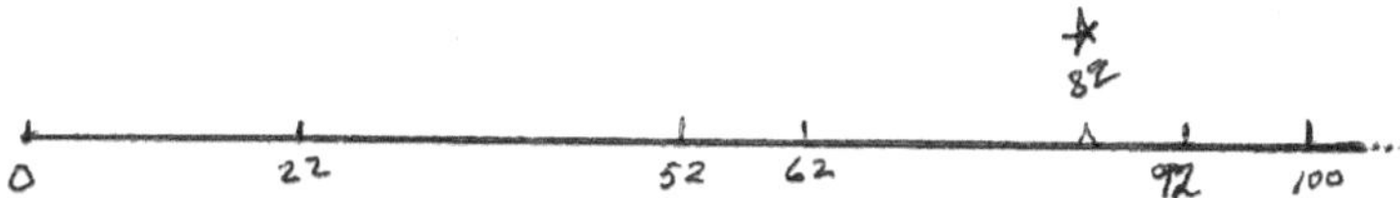

Why are we doing this? When workshop participants do this for the first time, they report a sense of unreality because we seldom think of time *to scale*. We usually shrink or amplify particular segments in our mind. The biggest surprise is what a large percentage of our expected lifespan "the retirement years" represent. For now, it is just a pencil line on a piece of paper, those twenty to forty years. I encourage you to post this drawing somewhere visible—the refrigerator door or above your home-office desk. We'll call this concept line our "longevity." It takes a while to sink in.

This simple drawing is designed to help you grasp just how inappropriate our grandparents' retirement expectations are for us today. And, more critically, I hope it illustrates the importance of making well-considered, intentional choices about how you will live this long life ahead of you.

We must begin to recognize just how much of this second half of our lives needs re-examination and rewriting. We require a whole new narrative for this thing we have called "retirement."

Changing Assumptions about the Eternal Vacation

Our culture erects a major obstacle in our path as we try to get beyond the confusion, frustration, and even fear over our dissatisfaction with retirement. The obstacle is the myth that retirement should be an eternal vacation. I call it a myth, but it is also an unconscious assumption about how we should live our lives. It has mythological proportions because it is backed by the most powerful consumer society the world has ever seen. The main premise—and this is preached to people of all ages, not just retirees—is that buying objects and buying experiences will bring us happiness. You already know about this, but many of us fail to notice its corollary:

Buying things and entertaining experiences is the whole point of retirement.

We are sold the idea that this is our whole purpose for being at this stage of life.

I met with a book club recently. They call themselves, with tongue in cheek, "the philosophers." They wanted to hear what I was writing about. Below is an abbreviated version of what we discussed about this myth and how it dominates our sense of purpose.

I started by explaining the basics—that our culture is built on buying stuff, as if buying is our life purpose. We are flooded with messages about *buying* happiness. Do we really think buying a more upscale purse, just the right car, miracle skin cream, or even visiting a certain famous resort will make for a satisfying life?

The group chuckled at the absurdity—and the truth—of my example. I had encouraged dialogue, not a lecture, and someone jumped in.

"I'll grant you that less wrinkled skin and a flashy new car won't give me eternal bliss. But what's the problem here? Isn't this the American way?" Her tone was slightly sardonic, but I went with it.

"The problem," I said, "is that consumerism, materialism, has been sold to us as *the* thing you do when you retire. Think about it.

Name ten things that you have heard you are *supposed to do* when you retire."

People started tossing out ideas. Travel. Downsize to a condo that costs three times more per square foot than your house. Play golf. Collect art. Volunteer. Pamper your grandchildren. Play more golf. Buy a second home somewhere warmer. And take up new hobbies and new sports that require lots of new equipment or club memberships. Buy clothes when you get bored…wait—that last one has been here since high school.

Unfortunately for about 70 percent of the senior population, most of these retirement expectations require more money than they have. We could have spent a whole session just on the income disparity, and the hardship these expectations pose, but for the moment we stayed with our main point.

"The reason this is a problem for us is that we unconsciously assume that all these activities are our *purpose* for living, the reason we get out of bed in the morning," I said. "But we don't even get this philosophical about it—we just start doing these things, as if that's what life is all about for us at this stage. To keep ourselves entertained. When we get restless or anxious, we do more of the same to try to fix it. And then we're perplexed when life feels pointless and unsatisfying."

Another member said, "I think I'm starting to understand. My friend Marcy, who travels a lot, confessed to me that when she got back from her latest trip, once she had unpacked and restocked the refrigerator, she suddenly felt empty. She confessed to me she didn't really have a 'life' to come back to. Then the next day she was booking another trip! I think she might be running away from her meaningless life, and I think she half realizes it, but she doesn't know what else to do."

"An excellent example. The deeper problem here is that we have all been sold this lifestyle as the normal option, or even the only option, even though we could probably name all sorts of people who are exceptions. It's our unconscious acceptance of this model, this narrative, this assumption. It feels like it has us fenced in. And we've hardly noticed.

"To deepen the dilemma, the constant message is, 'If you're not happy, it's because you haven't yet bought—fill in the blank with whatever is in the next ad you see.'"

I let the silence allow this to all sink in. Then someone offered her stark realization: "There are billions of dollars at stake here, aren't there, doing all they can to keep us buying into this model?"

"Yes, there are. Massive industries. The point for us is, we have a choice, if it is not serving our true needs, not feeding our soul. But we have to get smart about it. Unpack the mythologies and assumptions that we all carry around."

I described briefly to them what it was like for me growing up in Berkeley. We would often see the bumper sticker "SUBVERT THE DOMINANT PARADIGM."

The woman who was hosting the group said, "Looks like that sentiment is still needed today, isn't it?"

I suggested we review history for a moment. "Right now it's like a drug. We've been convinced to buy things in order to try to feel good, feel better, solve our problems. But throughout human history, people have had to work simply to put bread on the table. Then the more privileged people began to work to put lots more than bread on the table. And then they invested what's left over in creating even more money. We call it capitalism.

"But the sleight of hand that's happening now with the boomer generation is that we automatically assume that the purpose of our lives—once we quit working at that career that bought the bread and the houses and the cars and the trips—is to keep on *buying* more stuff, more experiences, more happiness. We too rarely question that world view.

"To talk about this today is like asking the fish about the water. We call it the American way. And you quite reasonably ask, 'What is the alternative?' I don't see us abolishing capitalism in our lifetime, although you can read arguments for that being a healthy idea."

Freedom to Choose a New Narrative

The point is, we each have a choice about what we select as the *purpose* for our life. We don't have to live to spend. We don't have to get out of bed in the morning for the sole purpose of entertaining ourselves with what we can buy. We don't have to live only for ourselves.

Here is another historical thread worth noticing.

In 1935, in the middle of the Great Depression, President Franklin Roosevelt signed the Social Security Act. It was decided that at age sixty-five people would get small pensions from the government. This was great, even lifesaving for most seniors, but part of the rationale that was rarely mentioned was that this would also free up more jobs for the many younger people who desperately needed employment. At the time, life expectancy was much lower than it is today. So, to oversimplify just a bit, the narrative was, you work hard all your life, you retire, relax and sit on the porch for a few years, then you die. Some policymakers reasoned that they could afford to sideline the seniors because they wouldn't be around much longer anyway.

I hope you can see now how this loops back to our discussion about longevity.

This 1935 narrative no longer fits our reality, but it does dovetail nicely with the retire-to-keep-buying myth. If all you want to do when you retire is keep spending money for a few more years, there is no need to question the system. Our grandparents' retirement narrative helps preserve the commercial status quo.

One More Dominant Paradigm that Needs Subverting

Psychologist Ellen Langer at Harvard has shown many times that *what we believe* about aging has real, measurable consequences. Her studies suggest that many so-called declines are not inevitable—but learned. In possibly her most well-known study, older men were placed for a week in an environment designed to replicate their youth (same décor, same music, same conversations). Their strength, posture, memory and cognition measurably improved.[2] Mindset matters physically. Langer's work underlines with scientific data why we need to rethink retirement itself: when we stop seeing it as a slow decline and instead as a phase of reinvention, new life becomes possible. Literally.

Naming It at Last: Embracing Prime Time

In chapter 1, I pointed out that we dissatisfied retirees have a big problem, and part of that problem is that we don't even know how to talk about it. In 1963 Friedan called the problem she was describing *The Feminine Mystique*. Her decision to name the problem this way made sense at the time; I have no problem with that. But today I believe it is more important that we look forward, rather than critiquing our past. Visualizing a new future is the only way we will be able to create it, and where we focus our attention makes all the difference.

For over a year I ruminated about how to name the problem itself, along with potential names for this book. The Internet offered an avalanche of advice for how to choose a "bestselling" book title. They advised, "describe the process you are offering," "use an alliteration," "look at current bestsellers and imitate what they do." On and on, and of course I considered Friedan's strategy of naming the problem itself.

But ultimately, I decided that naming what has gone wrong would be a mistake. Too much attention in the wrong direction. Instead, I wanted to capture a vision for where we want to go.

After sifting, examining, plowing through options, exploring, and weighing about sixty-eight images and synonyms, *Prime Time* leaped off the page as the most accurate metaphor for the life we want to create after sixty.

I believe it works on several levels.

Prime Time gives us a name for where we want to go and how we want to feel. It also offers a powerful analogy for what this phase of life can be. Instead of seeing our later years as a winding-down period, we are reclaiming them as a peak opportunity for finding and following our calling. It means new ways of belonging, marking achievements, and making a contribution. This is indeed our Prime Time—our chance to step into the most vital, purposeful, and impactful chapter of our lives.

To initially gauge reactions to Prime Time as the book's title, I met for coffee one Tuesday morning in Santa Fe with two "retirement specialists." By this, I simply mean that they have been doing it for a while. Fred, seventy-one, is a retired physicist and an ardent hiker around the southern Rocky Mountains. Marta, at sixty-eight, served most recently as a lobbyist for higher education in Washington, DC, before moving to Santa Fe three years ago.

Marta got right to the point. "So, Prime Time. That has a certain ring, but what does it really mean? Are we just trying to put a positive spin on getting older?"

"Good question, Marta," I said. "Prime Time is more than a slogan. What is your first association? Television?"

She nodded.

"Think of it this way," I continued. "Prime Time, in the tradition our generation grew up with, is when the most important, valuable programming airs. I know the image is a bit dated, but our peers know exactly what it stands for in that realm. Follow the metaphor. It's when the network pulls out all the stops to capture attention and make an impact. This phase of our lives—our sixties, seventies, and beyond—can be just that valuable. It's when we have the time, the experience, and the freedom to focus on what truly matters to us.

But it's also a choice point. We can either settle for reruns—or step into the spotlight with something new and meaningful to offer."

Fred jumped in. "OK, but how does that help with the restlessness I've been feeling? I'm retired, but I don't feel like I'm actually *doing* anything that is, well, 'prime.' Some days it's more like rerun episodes in a long-running series." He scrunched up his face, feigning agony.

I caught his eye and grinned. "If we can carry the comparison a little further, the eternal vacation model can be all filler and little substance. Reruns at best. Prime Time challenges that idea by shifting the focus. It's not about just sitting back and consuming life—it's about creating, contributing, and connecting. It's about recognizing that this isn't a postscript to our lives—it's our chance to produce our best work yet."

Marta chimed in. "I think I get it. Prime Time isn't about what we've stopped doing. The old word 'retirement' did that. Instead, it's about figuring out what we're starting."

Fred leaned forward. "Exactly! I see now what you are getting at. My life isn't about recreation for its own sake, to keep myself entertained. So if it isn't about reruns of what we've done before, I need to be writing a whole new show."

Marta piled on. "It's not an afterthought phase of our life, it's the richest, most important drama yet. This reminds me of all the years I spent skiing. Early on I learned to lean forward into where I was going."

She thought for a minute. "And tennis too. I started late with that—took my first lessons in my fifties. The pro taught me to stay forward on my toes. If I played back on my heels, I wouldn't get to the ball soon enough. I learned to apply that attitude in my work, but it never occurred to me to shape my retirement—oops—I mean my *Prime Time* that way too."

Fred pushed back his chair, letting out a deep sigh. "The significance of what you are saying, Marie, is beginning to sink in.

Frankly, it suddenly feels like a big job, that much reorientation. That much reinventing what I do."

I told him I appreciated his honesty, not only with me, but honesty with himself. Then I asked him if he knew the work of Brian Arthur.

"Yes, of course, he was one of the earliest members of the Santa Fe Institute. An economist, as I recall. Why do you ask?"

"Do you remember anything about his breakthrough work?" I asked.

"Yes. Increasing returns. A lot of people call them virtuous circles now."

"Hold on," Marta broke in. "I majored in political science a million years ago. Can you fill me in here before I feel like I'm on the wrong planet?"

I obliged and also invited Fred to fill in wherever he wanted. "I'll explain the theory in terms of what it means for Prime Time. It used to be that everyone assumed the world, if left to its own devices, would wind down. Entropy. Gradual decline."

"Second law of thermodynamics," Fred chimed in.

"Oh, that's helpful," Marta said, rolling her eyes at Fred.

I pressed on. "This applies directly to our old assumptions about retirement. It says we quit our professional job, and then we slowly wind down until we die."

"Yikes! OK, I see what you mean," Marta said.

"But Brian Arthur's contribution gives us great hope!" Fred almost shouted. He was catching on fast. "Brian Arthur pointed out to the world that sometimes *a small new action* can take the feedback loop in a positive direction, instead of decline."

"Yes," I said. "In the old model, the 'vicious circle,' you retire, step back, relax, and avoid challenge. Without challenge and purpose, your mental and physical engagement level can decline. The loop continues. With less engagement, you lose curiosity. Maybe you move toward social isolation, and your world shrinks.

This less-engaged life leads to declining energy, which confirms your false belief that retirement must be about slowing down. You can see how the results feed on themselves, leading to stagnation, a sense of irrelevance, and even depression."

"And finally, death," Fred added brightly.

I could see he was enjoying this.

"But in the *virtuous* circle," I said, "the positive loop takes 'retirement' into Prime Time. If you start with the belief that this is the moment to redefine our contribution and create a whole new life, you can take just one small first action. For example, take on one meaningful challenge. Volunteer somewhere where you are excited about their mission. Or start a project on something you are curious about. Learn something new."

"Or write a book," Marta added slyly.

I grinned. "The initial benefit of that action is a sense of purpose, and the engagement creates new energy and excitement. The loop reinforces itself—that new energy leads to more opportunities. You meet new people; you have new creative ideas. Your brain neurons actually change for the better. The spiral continues upward as you take on the attitude of lifelong learning, making a contribution in other ways, and seeing expanding possibilities."

Fred stood up and started pacing around our table in his excitement. Fortunately, the coffee shop was not crowded as he explained, as much to himself as to us, "I can see now that it's not either/or. I don't have to give up my hiking. I could look into how I could help a little with trail maintenance while staffing in our parks is low. And ask around to see who else is working to change that problem. I have also had vague thoughts about how I might 'adopt' one or two promising physics students at Capitol High, see if I might help them widen their interest in the field. Maybe tutoring, or maybe more like the Big Brothers program."

I underlined the importance of the mindset shift at the outset. "Because you reversed your assumption about your own decline, and instead you dared to picture a different, positive, and growing future, you can then begin to create that future. That is where the 'increasing returns' start to grow. And then taking that first small action puts other factors in play."

The Circle Widens

As if on cue, at that moment a slight, white-haired woman at a nearby table who had seemingly been buried in her laptop spoke to us.

"I couldn't help but overhear. Can I add a comment?"

(One of the things I love about Santa Fe is that the coffee shops sometimes take on the role of a small, informal community center. One assumes, for example, that if you are sitting in Downtown Subscription—which isn't even downtown—you must be neighbors.)

I smiled and encouraged her to join in.

She said, "I happen to be a relatively new student of neuroscience. It's sort of my new hobby at seventy-eight. What you have just said—" she gestured to Fred "—also has positive effects on your brain. When you feel gratitude for your beloved mountains or for the opportunity to help the young physics student, your brain produces dopamine, which feels great. And doing the physical labor on the trail, in addition to the hiking itself, stimulates endorphins. You probably already know that part, as a hiker. I could go on about natural oxytocin and serotonin that also boost your mood, making you more likely to branch out to even more fun and rewarding activities."

She stopped and caught her breath. "Sorry, I got carried away."

"No, it's fine," I said. "Thank you for filling in those gaps."

Not finished yet, she added, "And if you want to remember all those brain chemicals, the acronym is DOSE. I learned that on Instagram last week!"

We laughed with her contagious enthusiasm.

"That's serotonin, your laughing, you know," she couldn't resist adding.

As Fred and Marta each introduced themselves to her, I could see that new acquaintances had already sprouted out of our informal meeting over a book title. I could feel my dopamine—or was it my serotonin—shooting through me.

Later that evening I received a call from another informal group that was sprouting. I could never have guessed what was about to unfold.

Highlights

It's easier to solve the problem we are experiencing when we recognize, define, and name the problem. We can start that process in the following ways:

- **Question our hidden assumptions.** Our perceptions are shaped by our beliefs, but new information can cause us to notice and then rethink our fundamental assumptions—particularly those that no longer fit our current reality.

- **Consider the parallels to 1960s feminism.** Our "retirement problem" is a problem with no name, and nobody is talking about it. Materialism isn't the answer to more happiness. The media portrays retirement as affluent and relaxing. Retired people are being denied the opportunity/ expectation of meaningful work. Biology is destiny—or so they tell us—that because of age, we must set aside our skills, interests, and work relationships.

- **Update our understanding of longevity.** We need to take into account the scientific fact that, as baby boomers, we will live longer than any other generation has before.

- **Critique the "eternal vacation" model.** The old way of looking at retirement was that you work hard all your life, then you retire, relax and sit on the porch for a few years, then you die. That old expectation has not disappeared even though the reality has changed. We are also being sold the idea that buying things and entertaining experiences will now be our whole purpose for being at this stage of life, whether that brings us fulfillment or not.

- **Embrace Prime Time as the new narrative.** Prime Time challenges the old ideas by shifting the focus. It's not about just sitting back and consuming life—it's about creating, contributing, and connecting. It's about recognizing that this isn't a postscript to our lives—it's our chance to produce our best work yet.

Exercises: Personalizing the Concepts

1. **Journal Reflection: Learning from history.** What personal experiences have you had from the women's movement that might now inform how you think about retirement and Prime Time? Have you noticed any parallels of your own that are significant or informative? Do these insights spark any action you might take? Or a person you might talk with?

2. **Journal Reflection: Longevity.** If you have not already done so, draw your timeline as suggested above in the longevity section. Basically, draw the decades of your life on a line, to scale, marking with a small star your current age. Then capture in writing your feelings and impressions about how you have viewed the years ahead of you. What old assumptions have you held? What new assumptions might you develop, based on what you have learned so far? (Note: See the <u>Sourcebook for Chapter 2</u> for a list of new freedoms.)

3. **Journal Reflection: Purpose and eternal vacation.** Spell out in your journal what your assumptions have been about the purpose of life in retirement. How do you feel about advertisements that ask you to buy happiness or peace of

mind? This is not always black and white. You may have conflicting thoughts and feelings. That's OK. Write them out. If you are in a study group, talk about them, taking care not to be judgmental when others offer differing viewpoints. What is important is to start to sketch out how *you* want to proceed on this topic. How do *you* want to think about and reshape your own future, given what you are discovering?

4. **Journal Reflection: Prime Time.** At this point in time, what does the phrase "Prime Time" mean to your own personal journey? What aspects of the phrase and its implications are most meaningful to you? Are there aspects of the metaphor that are troublesome? Write out your thoughts so you can refer back to them later, as you travel through the chapters ahead.

5. **Action Step: Increasing returns and virtuous circles.** This exercise will help you understand how to apply the transformational potential of a virtuous circle to your own life. In the <u>Sourcebook for Chapter 2</u>, you will find a summary that describes how *virtuous* circles work differently from *vicious* circles. Read this summary carefully. You will see that the following page, titled "Fill in the Blanks," is designed for your repeated use. You can make multiple copies for future use, writing in different circumstances as they occur.

   For example, think of a circumstance from your life where things seemed to "go downhill." Under the Old Model section, fill in specifics for your Expectation, the Reality, the Outcome, what acted as Reinforcement, and Result. Then choose a circumstance where you would like to move forward. Fill in specifics for your New Belief, First Action, Initial Benefit, Reinforcement, and Upward Spiral.

   Using this worksheet can help you identify such questions as, "What initial assumption or mindset change would you like to start with?" "What small action might you experiment with?" and "What results might you anticipate, following this model?" Take new, small action steps and see what develops.

Prime Time Milestones

Take a breath. Pause. What are you noticing at this point in your journey? As you reflect, write your thoughts in your journal.

Insight. I see something new…

Sample response: *The cultural story I've been handed isn't the only one. I could choose to rewrite it.*

Shift. I feel something changing…

Sample response: *Skeptical, but also intrigued. I want more than leisure—I want something that lights me up.*

Step. I'm ready to try…

Sample response: *I'll look for moments this week when I feel most alive—or most drained—and jot them down.*

CHAPTER 3

The Six Guides Who Will Walk With Us

*Ever since college I've always wanted to make a difference,
but what happened this year…the cliff crumbled, and
the path I had always trusted was gone into the sea.*

—SHIRLEY'S JOURNAL ENTRY

Shirley closed her journal and reached for the Kleenex box. It had been six months, and she still felt off-center from her sudden dismissal. Her mind circled again around the question, "How could they do that to us?" Her mind wanted to argue with the circumstances, but she was learning to catch the loop. "Ruminating isn't going to solve my future," she reminded herself.

Her phone rang. At eight in the evening, she wasn't expecting to hear from anyone. She picked up with a tentative hello.

"Hi, Shirley? This is Himari. I know we said we would have lunch again soon, but I really need to talk to someone sooner than that. Is this a good time?"

Shirley was a bit surprised to hear from her. She had really hit it off with this new friend she'd met at an art class. "Sure," Shirley said. "I was just reading. I'm all ears."

"Great. I'll just jump into what's bothering me. I've enjoyed getting to know you since I moved to Santa Fe, and I was thinking you might be a good person to ask my question because you've lived here for a while. Since I retired from the medical center in San Francisco—oh, by the way, Jerry is loving his new position at the Institute—I've been having trouble figuring out what I want to do next.

"People keep suggesting that I volunteer at the animal shelter or become a museum docent. But it's not sparking for me. One person even sounded me out for the Hospital Foundation Board, but that's the last thing I want to think about right now. Frankly, I'm starting to get depressed… " She paused. "I'm kind of embarrassed to admit that."

"I'm really sorry to hear this is so depressing for you. There are plenty of interesting ways to stay busy in Santa Fe, but—I'm just guessing here—I have a hunch you're not talking about staying busy. You're talking about something deeper, am I right? Something beyond keeping yourself occupied or entertained?"

"Your hunch is right on," Himari answered. "I don't even know what 'something deeper' means for me, but that feels right."

"Himari, I have actually been wrestling with some similar questions, so I'd love to talk about this with you. Maybe if we kick the ideas around, it might help us both."

"Really? You too? But you seem so together. You have your art…"

"Yes, I experiment with art, but I only occasionally wake up in the morning excited to do it. I'm looking for something, but I have no idea what it is or how to find it."

Himari was surprised. "Since we met at that O'Keeffe Museum class, we've really only talked about art. What were you doing professionally before you retired?"

"Well, I'm not technically retired. I'm sixty-four and I got laid off. I was managing a team of graphic and web designers for a major corporation."

"I'm sorry to hear that," Himari said.

Shirley paused, then decided there was no point trying to sound "professional" any longer. "I'm struggling to figure it all out. We came to work one morning to find an email in our inboxes. It said the division was ceasing operations in New Mexico and our jobs ended at three that day. I was a contractor, and we had a year to go on the project."

"An email?!" Himari almost shouted her disbelief into the phone.

"Yes. I know. Unreal. Inhuman. But why do we ever expect corporations to act like humans? The shock went deeper for me because I had been planning to retire anyway, but not right then. I felt ambushed."

Shirley took a breath and continued. "I think I've been in a mourning period. It's disorienting, because I've always been proactive. Working out on the edge, driving change. Helping people understand the changes I've pushed for. Now I sit home way too much. I signed up for that art class just to get out of the house. But I have no idea what to do next."

The conversation hung in a comfortable silence. Then Shirley said, "Tell me more about what you think *you* might be looking for."

"I really need something in my life that I can get my teeth into— but not anything that feels like it's a continuation of my job. I want more free time, and I want to be more challenged creatively, but without all the heavy responsibility I had as a medical director."

"I get that. Go on," Shirley said.

"I've wanted to serve others since I decided to apply for medical school. The seduction now is, do I just fall into societal expectations and start going on cruises or buy a villa in Italy? Surely it can't be an either-or choice: volunteer for Doctors Without Borders versus raise money for the opera. I have no clue how to come up with good options. I don't want to just pick something to stay busy."

"I don't have any answers either," Shirley said, "but I'm aware my default response is to think I have to figure this out all by myself. But here we are. I would love it if we could work on this problem together. I feel like I'm taking a big risk even asking, but too much is at stake for me to be shy any longer."

"Thank you for taking the risk, Shirley, because I just came to the same conclusion. Shall we meet tomorrow in person and talk some more?"

"Yes." Shirley chuckled. "I just happen to have a spot open on my calendar."

They both laughed.

Himari said, "Come over here to my house at two, and I'll have some tea ready."

After they hung up the phone, Himari noticed she was feeling starved for the deep friendships she'd left in San Francisco. There she had often lost track of older colleagues after they'd retired, so she was now realizing her challenge wasn't just moving to a new city. She realized she would have felt this loss even if she had stayed in the Bay Area after retirement.

She found herself saying out loud, "I have absolutely no idea how to go about this!"

The next day when they were settled with tea at Himari's house, the women looked at each other, took a deep breath, then laughed.

"Where in the world do we start?" they said, almost in unison.

Shirley suggested, "Why don't we start with a little more family history."

They did so eagerly, telling stories, laughing, and musing about how such influences might impact the way their futures would unfold.

"On a different subject," Himari said, "we should see if we can find more people to join us."

Shirley chuckled. "If two heads are better than one, five or six could be brilliant!"

"Do you have someone in mind?" Himari asked.

"Yes. I just thought of my friend Martina."

"What do you know about her situation?" Himari asked.

"She grew up here and has been back in Santa Fe for a couple of years. When I ran into her downtown this week, she mentioned something vague about what she was up to, in an 'it will do' sort of voice."

"Do you want to call her and explain what we are up to—as if we know," she said, "and see if she's interested?"

"Sure, I'd feel comfortable doing that."

Himari drummed her nails on her teacup. "I just met someone at a lecture who might be interested. I should call him. His name is Samuel. We stayed for a long time afterward discussing the talk. He seemed to be wanting to shift gears. He's a PhD philosopher, very deep."

Shirley said, "That would make four of us."

"Let's just do it!" Himari said.

"Swoosh!" added Shirley, laughing. "Text me as soon as we know something so we can schedule a time to meet."

Shirley met with Martina to explain what she and Himari were brewing. As expected, she was enthusiastic.

Within two days, they had added not only Martina and Samuel to the group, but they had come up with two more interested people, Alicia and Paul. Alicia offered to host the first gathering at her house.

The Group: Finding a Path to the Path

The group of near strangers convened at Alicia's house the following Tuesday. Alicia insisted they arrive in time for a buffet lunch so they could take a little more time to get to know each other informally before they began their meeting.

Shirley arrived a few minutes early in case Alicia needed any last-minute help. The front door was slightly ajar, so she poked her head in and called, "Hi, Alicia! It's Shirley."

A voice called back, "Come on through to the kitchen."

She followed Alicia's voice and saw a generous dining table that could easily accommodate eight. Beyond that a large white granite island set off the kitchen, with a cheerful skylight illuminating the island. Bowls and platters of food were set out on the island.

"Here's a pitcher of ice water and another of iced tea, if you would please put them on the table. We're almost ready," Alicia said.

Shirley noticed Alicia's willingness to put her guest right to work. She thought to herself that this attitude would set a great tone for helping the group relax.

The doorbell sounded, and the others began to stream in. Everyone introduced themselves to each other because no one person knew everyone.

After lunch Himari said in a loud voice, "Who called this meeting?"

Everyone laughed, then Paul said, "Why don't we rotate an informal convener for the first few meetings? Himari, you got me into this, so I am nominating you to take the first turn."

Himari, having chaired seemingly thousands of meetings of physicians and finance people, easily agreed. She invited them to leave the table as it was, bring their water or tea glasses, and move to the more comfortable couches and chairs in the living room. When everyone was settled, she began.

"You realize, of course, that no one in this meeting has any idea what we are doing here. But if you are OK with that, I'll wade in."

The room responded with "Yes!" and "Go for it!" and "Our leader!"

"I noticed as we were eating that some of you told a bit of your backstories to whomever was next to you. At the risk of a little repetition, why don't we go around and each give a brief bio?" She suggested each bio include the following:

- Where they were born, or where they grew up.
- A word about their family.

- What kind of culture shaped their early years, if that is significant to who they are today.
- A brief sketch of their professional life.
- Tell the group how long they have been retired and
- If they can, a sentence about what they thought, just *before* they retired, that retirement would be like.

"And I'll start, to give you time to think about your answer."

Himari's Story: Roots in Community

"A decade before I was born, when my older brother was a baby, my parents and he were taken as prisoners from their home in Los Angeles to Manzanar, on the eastern edge of California. It was one of the camps hastily established when World War II started, where the government locked up all the West Coast Japanese people. After the war the three of them returned to LA to try to rebuild their lives, and I came along later, sort of a 'second family' for my parents. I grew up hearing very few tidbits of stories of life in the camp, but I watched as my parents banded together with their friends to help everyone find jobs, buy homes again, and restore a sense of community. Everyone really depended on one another.

"As I said, I was born after they resettled back in Torrance. I went to college and medical school in California, and most recently helped run a medical center in San Francisco. My husband was asked recently to come affiliate with the Santa Fe Institute. That's what brought us to settle here. It's quite a culture change from San Francisco…and from working nonstop for so many years.

"I suppose that's one reason that having a community, networks of people who depend on one another, matters to me. I've been feeling a little desperate. But I also feel a strong determination to rebuild my life, and my life with my husband, here in New Mexico. And I can see now that having a clear purpose, not just looking for 'things to do,' is at the heart of this journey."

She added that although she had known she would be retiring on a certain date and had given the administration plenty of time to appoint her replacement, she really had very few specific ideas about what retirement would be like. Then, when her husband was offered the position in Santa Fe, the tasks of selling a house, buying a house, and all the details of moving took her full attention. When they were settled, it hit her as a shock just how little she knew about what she wanted to do and how far away her former community was, with nothing to put in its place.

Himari took a sip of her tea. "One more thing. My husband's appointment at the Santa Fe Institute has given him the gift of an instant community. And I am delighted for him that he has that. But it is not automatically my community, though I'm already being included in a few gatherings. His situation just underlines for me how important my own search is at this moment in my life. The feeling is one of apprehension mixed with overflowing abundance and possibility, even though I have no idea where I am going."

Shirley: Working at the Edges

Shirley went next. "I too feel grateful for being here. I'm sixty-four. I've been in Santa Fe for about ten years. I grew up in Connecticut as the only child of a single mother. My father was a success in business, so Mom and I had money in those days, though eventually she blew through it all. We spent one summer during high school in Hawaii where I learned to surf and scuba dive. When it was time to choose a college, I chose California and I chose biology because I wanted to scuba dive as often as I could. But after a faculty-harassment situation on a field trip, I changed my major to art. That was the building the farthest across campus from the life sciences building.

"I got into web design early, but I have always managed to stay an independent contractor. That's how I ended up with a contract that disappeared in a hail of digital impressions—a sudden shock when our whole division was let go recently with absolutely no notice. I had planned to retire next year, so I thought I had a year to plan. I am still reeling.

"Perhaps because I was raised by a single mom and she was at work a lot of the time, I've always felt like I was on my own to figure things out. I work well with teams when I'm in charge, but learning to trust peer relationships is still a challenge for me. Part of me likes to stay near the edge so I can make a quick getaway if I need to."

She let the silence hang to underline her words, then continued. "I mention this to tell you how grateful I am that we are embarking on this journey *together.*" She smiled. "Now, whose turn is it?"

Martina: Longing for Structure Again

Martina spoke up. "I'll go next, since Shirley invited me here. I grew up in Northern New Mexico in the midst of a huge extended family who have lived here for many generations. I'm sixty-six. I went out of state, to the Midwest, for college. I studied political science, but I think I actually majored in living a long way from home. My first job was in government, as a college intern, and eventually I headed a state department as an elected official. It wasn't as glamorous as it may sound. I was Secretary of State, which no one ever knows anything about except at election time.

"When I took retirement, I decided to move back here to be nearer to family, though sometimes I second-guess my motives. I grew up Roman Catholic, but I'd describe myself as pretty lax, much to the consternation of my aunts. Right now I have no idea what to do with my life, which has the *tias* even more worried, since they have plenty of ideas for what *they* think I should be doing. I need to do something heartfelt, not a 'should' that I inherit.

"This group is what I've been praying for, only I didn't even know it! In state government that was my whole world. Everyone knew each other. Coworkers made up most of our after-work friends. The job also created nearly all of the structure in my life. It had a lot of routine that I never even noticed until it was gone. The slower pace now still feels strange, unfamiliar, even though at one level I like being able to sleep in when I feel like it. But the big thing is, at work we always had a purpose.

"When I headed an agency, we knew exactly what we were there to accomplish. Or if the mission blurred under stress, it was my job to help everyone see more precisely why we were there, who we were serving. Since I've been back in Santa Fe, everyone who knows my family is trying to recruit me to help with whatever they are involved in. But so far, nothing feels like 'me.' The offers all feel like I would be trying to live someone else's dream."

Martina turned to Paul. "Your turn."

Paul: In Transition from Intensity

"Thanks for inviting me here. My wife and I are spending six months in Santa Fe as a kind of decompression sabbatical."

He looked around the circle and saw several understanding nods. He continued.

"I grew up in Boston, then went to college in New York. Unsure what to even major in, I somehow ended up petitioning a monk at a retreat center to let me spend a year learning silence and contemplative prayer. When I look back, doing that as a nineteen-year-old astounds me. Later, when I earned an RN degree and went into emergency medicine, that ability to hold a quiet center was a profound gift. I suppose it still is.

"As I mentioned to a couple of you at the table, I am now trying to decompress from a twenty-four-seven intensity that I sustained, miraculously, for decades. I didn't see much of my kids as they grew up, so my young grandchildren are an amazing blessing. But I know better than to try to actually major *in them* for the next fifteen years. This group is a just-in-time gift, much like the retreat center was years ago, to help me discern where life is leading me."

He paused to gather his thoughts. "I'm going to need something new to commit myself to, but definitely not at the same pace. You'll discover I have an active mind hovering under this deceptively calm exterior, and I look forward to helping us all pursue our path."

Samuel: Unnamed Hopes

Samuel picked up the conversation. "I was intrigued when Himari called me. It sounded perfect. I can see you all will be posing questions I didn't even know I wanted to ask. Hi, I'm Samuel, and I'm a transplant too."

"Hi, Samuel," the room echoed in unison.

"I grew up in New York City, and I'm seventy-five. I was raised Jewish, but, Martina, I also carry a 'lapsed' card. My PhD is in philosophy, and I taught that subject at the college level my entire career. We retired to Santa Fe over a decade ago on my wife's dream for adventure. She wanted to move as far from New York as possible, and I concurred. I think we succeeded in geography, but also culture and weather, and I love all of that. But I still haven't adjusted to no longer thinking deep thoughts with a lively group every day. I was ready to leave formal teaching behind, but I still haven't found a groove here that is really *me*. I do love learning, though, and I love exploring new viewpoints even more, so I'm excited about this group. I am honored to be a part of this…whatever this is."

Alicia: Unmoored but Eager

Alicia looked around the circle. "It must be my turn. I seem to have earned the 'youth award'— I'm sixty-one. As some of you know, my wife, Helen, and I had just retired here when she was quite unexpectedly overtaken by a very fast cancer. Her pain ended mercifully just a few months ago."

The group offered murmurs of support.

"Thank you. This group was just what the doctor ordered. I am so happy to share this space with you. I can just feel the history in these old adobe walls, and I hope it nourishes your spirits as well.

"I grew up in South Central L.A., though growing up in the Black community was probably pretty different from what Himari knew just a few miles away. I loved to run, so I somehow got a track scholarship to UCLA, then went on to get an MBA there. I figured out fairly early that I wanted to create a different life for myself, so I worked really hard in school. After finishing graduate school, I landed a job in the athletic shoe and apparel world and stayed there my entire career. I left after an exhilarating but challenging time being VP of a lot of people and a lot of projects. Martina, I really appreciate your inviting me into this circle. I'm going through a lot of transitions, as they say, and it's good to be in a circle with such thoughtful, curious, and, I can see, supportive people.

"I should add, my mother wasn't much of a cook, but she did teach me to make pies, and I have to say, this group came together like piecrust. You know, when you get the moisture exactly right and you can just press all those lumps of shortening and flour together, and very quickly you have a tight ball of dough that you can roll right out into a tasty dessert. I have a hunch that the very formation of this amazing group will have something directly to do with what I end up doing next. I don't even know what that means. It's just a feeling."

Himari looked from face to face around the circle. "I am very hopeful and expectant. We are embarking on something that will gather momentum, and eventually we will find answers. I know this even though we haven't even really done anything yet."

Shirley smiled as she looked out through the bare trees at the vivid blue winter sky, savoring the moment. "I feel as though I am on a fast-moving train, excited, but with nothing yet written on my ticket stub."

"Amen!" said Samuel. "I had no idea how we would plunge in, but I can feel a new energy that I haven't felt for years."

"Let's take a ten-minute break," Himari said. "Refresh your glasses, and we can come back to discuss specific expectations for what we want to do together."

Expectations for the Process

"I am here to do something else besides what I see my peers doing, which is a lot of trial and error," Shirley said as the group sat down to resume the conversation. "I watch them doing mostly error. We have to find a better way."

"Thanks, Shirley," said Himari, "for identifying your expectation for where we are going. That certainly makes sense."

Samuel nodded his head enthusiastically, miming, "Me too!"

Himari continued. "Here's one of mine. I know I have some blind spots. They might be unconscious assumptions—they might be mental habits that I've had too long to notice. They are undoubtedly more obvious to you than they are to me. I'll need your help in spotting them. I am operating from the Einstein quote that we have to do something different if we want a different outcome. My blind spots need to be outed so they don't keep getting in my way."

Alicia spoke up. "We need some way to curate the ideas that come up. I don't just want a list of all the existing volunteer positions in the city. I hope we can be creative, but then I'll need some criteria for narrowing down, for focusing."

Himari said, "Alicia, I want to build on your point about curating. I'd like to see one outcome be a personally tailored plan *for me*. If I have a new calling out there, it needs to be my own personal calling, not some generic statement that I found on the page of a self-help book."

Martina said, "Building on your mention of creativity, I'd like to expand my ability to imagine things that don't exist yet. If my path were in sight, I'd be there already."

"I need some intentional time for self-reflection," Paul said. "I've been on the run for too many decades. In a good way, I'd like what we do here to be like therapy, but not in a clinical-fix way. I'd like to do some self-examination. Ask disciplined questions of myself. Not all of you may want this, but I know I'll find a more balanced outcome if I take this path. It certainly fits Himari's Einstein-quote test."

Samuel cleared his throat. Eyes turned to him. "I am wondering if there are some experts that have been down some of these paths already. This is a group of smart people, but none of us majored in what we are trying to do here. We are intentionally pushing our edges, but I don't think we need to necessarily try to reinvent the wheel. Is there recommended reading we can do? Tried-and-true methodologies out there that would apply to what we are attempting? I know you are thinking, 'That's the professor speaking,' but I hope you see the wisdom in my point."

"I have an idea!" Alicia blurted out. "It didn't occur to me before because until just now I hadn't seen the bigger picture of the dilemma. I have been so focused on one-day-at-a-time."

Samuel gestured to her as if to say, "Out with it."

"I just heard about someone here in Santa Fe who is writing a book about what we are discussing. I wonder if she would be willing to help us with how to proceed."

"I'd be willing to call her and ask," Samuel said eagerly.

Himari looked around the room. "Agreed? A subject expert or a facilitator would certainly accelerate our progress." She saw only enthusiastic nodding.

Highlights

Character-Based Reflections – All of us come to this discussion with different but often overlapping circumstances, motivations, and desires that propel us toward Prime Time in place of traditional retirement. These common themes are embodied in the stories of our six characters:

- Wanting to ask the elephant-in-the-room questions – Shirley and Himari

  Shirley risked her usual independence to ask aloud what many hesitate to voice: "Is this all there is?" Himari echoed the question, rejecting shallow volunteerism and probing for deeper meaning. Their honesty opened the space for the group to form.

- Feeling the need to reach out – Himari

Though new to Santa Fe, Himari took a leap and called Shirley, revealing her uncertainty and need for connection. That one call became the seed for a gathering that would reshape all their lives.

- Looking to build a new community – Himari

Remembering the collective spirit her parents nurtured after the internment camps, Himari felt an instinctive call to recreate belonging. In co-forming the group, she was both honoring her roots and building a future.

- Feeling isolated from working at the edges – Shirley

A lifetime of self-reliance and edge-dwelling left Shirley deeply unmoored when her contract ended abruptly. In naming her vulnerability, she began to move from isolation toward trust.

- Missing the structure a career provided – Martina

Martina, once surrounded by the rhythm and purpose of government service, now finds herself disoriented by too much freedom. The group offers her a scaffolding of shared inquiry and intentional growth.

- Wanting to transition out of intensity – Paul

After years in emergency medicine, Paul seeks a gentler rhythm for his life. He brings a contemplative presence to the group and a longing to reconnect with his own center.

- Wanting to rediscover and reinvent intellectual stimulation – Samuel

Having left academia behind, Samuel yearns for spirited conversation and ideas that matter. In this circle, he sees a chance to stretch his mind while shaping something real.

- Mourning and needing to reframe life after loss – Alicia and Shirley

  Alicia, newly widowed, feels unmoored but hopeful. Shirley mourns not a person, but the sudden collapse of her professional identity. Both women seek a future that honors their pasts without being bound by them.

These shared yearnings are what give the group its shape, its spark, and its possibility. As each person dares to show up with honesty, they begin to co-create something none of them could have built alone.

Exercise: Personal Check-In

1. **Journal Reflection:** Note in your journal any questions the characters raised for you.

   - What parts of yourself did you notice in any of the stories? If so, note what resonated.

   - What issues had not occurred to you before?

   - What concerns would you like to follow up on?

   - If an aspect of a character's story affected you more deeply than the others, do you have any hunches about why this might be significant?

   - What else sparks your curiosity to explore?

2. **Action Step: Find or Form a Group.** The group that met at Alicia's house is already starting to experience the benefits of working together as a group rather than in isolation on their own. Here are just a few of the advantages of finding and working with a group for the journey:

   1. The group **multiplies our networks** and connections. For six people, for example, that means six times the networks, six times the opportunities for each individual.

2. It provides **honest feedback** and a more accurate picture of ourselves, underscoring strengths and revealing blind spots.

3. It offers **accountability** to encourage us to do what we said we would do. It keeps us moving forward instead of procrastinating.

4. It **expands our vision** and our ability to see possibilities and opportunities. We are able to see more options through others' eyes.

5. It creates **energy and momentum**—even synergy. Encouragement from others makes taking action easier.

6. It is **fertile soil** for synchronicities to happen. This may be a summary of all the above.

At this point you still might be imagining reasons you do not feel ready to find or start a group. In the <u>Sourcebook for Chapter 3</u> you will find a list of *objections* to taking action. If you feel hesitant, read these objections over now, as a gift to yourself, to nudge you out of your reservations and into a learning edge that just might make the difference to help you discover the new life you seek.

Prime Time Milestones

Take a breath. Pause. What are you noticing at this point in your journey? As you reflect, write your thoughts in your journal.

Insight. I see something new…

Sample response: *Maybe I'm not the only one asking these questions. It feels oddly comforting to hear others wrestling with the same things I haven't dared to name.*

Shift. I feel something changing...

Sample response: *A quiet sense of belonging. Like there's room here for my doubts, my dreams, and my not-knowing.*

Step. I'm ready to try...

Sample response: *I'll speak one true thing to someone I trust—even if it's just, "I don't know what's next."*

PHASE II

What to Do and How to Do It:
Two Essential Tools

Chapter 4

Meet the (Inner) Cast: Understanding the Voices that Shape Us

When a system is far from equilibrium, small islands
of coherence in a sea of chaos have the capacity
to elevate the entire system to a higher order.

—Ilya Prigogine, Nobel laureate chemist

Samuel called me at 7:15 p.m. He introduced himself and briefly explained the nature of the ad hoc group he and five other people had put together. Then he haltingly asked if I might be interested in helping them get started. Perhaps I might be able to point them in the right direction, maybe suggest some book titles or research to review?

I commended him for asking for help rather than just struggling along. I asked more about the individuals involved and about their goals, or at least their hopes for the process. I asked if he could assess how motivated they were. As he spoke, I took some notes. I was impressed with how they were taking initiative. When he finished, I made a counterproposal.

I explained that I was always in research mode, and their quest intrigued me. I told him I would be willing to provide ongoing facilitation, along with teaching specific skills and methods that would help achieve the results they were looking for.

He asked how much I would charge. I quoted my regular fee, then explained that if they proved to be truly motivated to make changes in their lives, I would waive that fee in exchange for using their stories—with identities altered—in the book I was working on. He seemed surprised but promised to check back with the others and then contact me about the next meeting date and time.

Note: Glance through the exercises now at the end of this chapter so you can be prepared to make the best of this chapter as it unfolds.

How to Shape a Group

At Alicia's house the following week, I introduced myself with an abbreviated life story, then I offered a quote from Nobel laureate Ilya Prigogine: "When a system is far from equilibrium, small islands of coherence in a sea of chaos have the capacity to elevate the entire system to a higher order."

I added with a grin that if churches in general these days didn't have such a bad rap, I would be tempted to found one called "An Island of Coherence."

"An island of coherence is what I hope this group will be for you," I explained. "It's a place to distill the coherence within you, at your soul level, but also a place to set up new frames and filters for the tsunamis of information that bombard us all."

Samuel had already reviewed for me their list of expectations voiced at the previous meeting, so I asked them to briefly tell their own biographies for me to hear, but also for them to hear themselves once again. Since they had already heard each other's accounts, I suggested they also each add their own specific answer to the question, "How will you know when you have succeeded at the task we are undertaking?"

In order to ensure psychological safety, I then explained it was advisable to establish together a short list of group norms and behaviors. The group could generate their own list from scratch or adopt and modify the list I had used with other groups. (This list is in the <u>Sourcebook for Chapter 4</u>.)

"The most crucial items," I said, "are confidentiality, not giving advice, and not interrupting. A fourth would be to listen to yourself to assure that respect is fully showing up. The list is based on the Golden Rule. Said another way, 'Be the change you want to see in the world.'"

A Gift of Daily Practice: The Journal

"Before I get into specific content for today," I said, "I have brought you each a gift." I pulled out a shopping bag from behind my chair.

"Here is a leather-bound blank book journal for each of you. Wherever this journey takes you, your daily recordings of insights and experiences will, I promise you, greatly enhance your discoveries. Nearly everyone has a mind with holes like a colander, but more important, when you first hear something, it means one thing. But when you review it later, it can mean something quite different. Your journal will help you bridge and then build on those gaps in understanding."

It felt like Christmas morning to me as I handed out the soft suede volumes.

"You have each found your way here today because you sense something is missing in your life. You have retired from a professional career, but you haven't found that sweet spot for what you want to do or be next. You may have tried some of the obvious alternatives—travel, volunteering, hobbies, just hanging out and being spontaneous. But I'm guessing you wouldn't be here unless you had a hunch—or perhaps a hope—that there is something more, or different, in your future. When Samuel briefed me, he mentioned that a couple of you think you might have a 'calling,' but I understand that you may not even really know what that means.

Sometimes it's a restlessness or a sense that you still have something to give. So consider this room today as a safe 'container' for a search, the beginning of a journey."

The Need for Intentional Time and Space

"To strengthen this container," I continued, "I hope after today you will commit to regular meetings for at least two to three months, longer if you wish. Here is why a framework like this can be so valuable. There is a secret sauce here—you may already have sensed it—specific reasons why meeting in a group to discern your future is far more effective than if you were to each pursue your search on your own."

I explained that this whole period in their lives can be what Irish and Celtic peoples like to call a *liminal space*, the Latin word *limen* meaning "threshold." The term points to the space in between here and there or between the visible world and the world that is not visible. It can be a geographical space, such as Stonehenge or Sedona. It can be a time of year. Religious holidays used to have that feel before they were commercialized.

I continued, "The word is also used for that time in the morning where you are just a little awake, but maybe still dreaming, yet aware it is morning. Sometimes that is when your most profound ahas come to you—*if* you don't reach for your phone."

I explained that in that scenario, we have left one place—sleep— but aren't quite into the next place—being fully awake. It is also, if we are paying attention, a time when we can break a habit and try a new way of doing something. After a good night's sleep, we may wake up five minutes ahead of the alarm and decide to take a walk instead of heading straight for the shower or the coffee pot.

"This is one of the gifts of not *having* to go to work every day. At a soul level," I said, "a major alteration of your life as usual can put you into liminal space."

I listed some examples of such alterations. Graduating without a job was one. Having a baby when you don't really know yet what one actually *does* with a baby. Moving to a new city, especially when you are not the one who's dropped immediately into the new job. And of course involuntary job loss…and even planned retirement. It is an invitation—sometimes disguised as a crisis—to become a new person.

"Liminal space can often feel like being less in control. We feel vulnerable for that reason. But as I hope you are already beginning to realize, it is a time of grace and gifts. An opportunity. And, as you here have already demonstrated by forming this group, it can be a time of being particularly more teachable."

I underlined for them the importance of keeping an open mind, never taking this vulnerability and grace for granted. "Think of this state of liminal space as truly a gift."

It is a natural human instinct to avoid liminal space if we have a choice. There is discomfort there. That is normal. Well-designed retreats are based on this dynamic, understanding that the work of authentic spirituality and human development is to help participants into liminal space and then keep them there long enough for the transformation they seek to actually occur.

In addition to a personal, private liminal space, I explained that forming this group can mean a decision to intentionally create a liminal space to hold this tension long enough to find the new path.

"Having a group where you learn to deeply trust one another makes it possible to embrace your fears and your letting go. It will also be a place to celebrate successes and cheer your triumphs."

I gestured to the room we sat in. "This generous 'container' of Alicia's home is where you can explore these life changes. You will learn from others what you could not have figured out for yourself. And the others will affirm you, cheer you on, because, I promise you, they will see your potential before you can see it yourself. You will be emboldened by their faith in you and see why you are here on this planet at this specific time. I look on this as holy ground."

I looked deliberately into each person's eyes. "You are entering a process that can literally rewrite your life story, rescript your destiny. You have a valuable chance to consciously affirm your choice of this group as your first milepost along the journey." I held their eyes to allow all of this to settle in.

A First Inventory

To shift the energy, I invited the group to take a fifteen-minute *silent* break, refill their tea, and take a walk out into the courtyard or the garden, journal in hand, for the following assignment.

"To launch our first topic, please make a brief list—five or six— of some of the many polarities—think contradictions or opposing voices—that you notice within you." I listed some examples.

- Keeping a neat desk vs. letting it get messy
- Desire to move with caution vs. desire to chase dreams
- Wanting to make spontaneous decisions vs. a tendency to overthink
- Jumping to conclusions vs. the patience to inquire further
- Immediately feeling attacked and then lashing out vs. realizing what is not actually an attack and giving the person the benefit of the doubt or letting it go like water off a duck's back

When the group returned I explained the background for our work that day. Every one of us has different voices in our heads that chatter to us throughout the day, often below our conscious awareness. Highlighting a few of these voices that present themselves as polarities is a simple and efficient way to learn how to have more constructive conversations with them.

> Note: In the <u>Sourcebook for Chapter 4</u>, you will find an example of Shirley's list of polarities and the names she gave to these voices as they popped up. This step of giving names is optional.

Another thing I told them to keep in mind is that it's difficult to discern a new path while the old ways we've always done things color our thinking. Consider the metaphor of blinders. They keep us from seeing paths that are lurking off to the side of the main route. An example: For the first four decades of my life, I assumed I had to impress people so they would put me in the best reader group (first grade), hire me (at age twenty-two), give me raises, accept me into a graduate program, allow me to pass courses. It wasn't until age thirty-nine, as I approached the final interview at my church denomination committee to see if they would approve my ordination, that I suddenly saw this need-to-impress assumption for what it was. I realized my best strategy was to just be myself, my humanity exposed, along with the seminary transcripts, recommendation letters, etc. When one committee examiner asked me what I considered my greatest shortcoming, I recognized that only a truthful answer would allow me to "pass the course," and so that's what I gave them. This need to impress was a set of blinders that I had carried unconsciously, probably since I was three. Notice that this isn't about *doing* your best, it is about the unconscious filter or tyranny of the voice that says, "Only *show* your best." After the interview (they approved my ordination), I became daringly candid, and I was undoubtedly a better leader for allowing a more authentic person—my true self—to be seen.

Removing Blinders with Inner Character Work

I said to the group, "Our method today that will help you lift the blinders so you can see farther and wider is called inner character work. You've heard of multiple personality disorder? This is exactly the opposite. We could call it multiple personality *order*."

I explained to the group how this method was based on two assumptions:

First, the voices we hear in our heads, these inner characters, are largely based on the past. They have developed from our history.

They usually have the best intentions to keep us safe, but as adults, what seemed like an essential safety move at age six rarely applies at sixty-five.

Second, we all have multiple voices within us. Each one sees the world slightly differently, or in some cases hugely differently, and these voices hold differing opinions about how we should handle the circumstances we encounter. By giving voice to these opinions, or world views, by literally *speaking* them out loud in the room, we can start to sort out the inherent conflicts between them, weigh their value to us, and begin to see how we want to go forward.

"You will see," I said, "as the exercise unfolds, that we move back and forth between three different chairs placed in the center of the room. We use separate chairs because it helps us feel how we embody each of the characters differently as we work with them. You will notice your whole posture may change, your sense of who you are may seem to shift. And when you are in what we will call the Liminal Space chair, you experience in your body the inner wisdom, the balance, the integrity of that most centered place in your own life. It can be quite remarkable."

As the group took in this introduction, I said, "I want to pause and give deepest thanks and offer tribute to my mentor Charles M. Johnston, MD, a Seattle psychiatrist and futurist who died rather suddenly in 2023. He developed this method in the 1990s, when I trained with him. Much of his work as a futurist has been well documented by his many books and by the Institute for Creative Development, managed posthumously by his followers in Seattle. But today we will be experiencing his less well-known insights about inner characters. My hope is that our work here together will help others access this valuable methodology.[3]

> [*A **cautionary note to the reader**: These exercises are intended for self-reflection only, not as a substitute for therapy. If you feel distress or unsafe while trying them, pause and seek professional support.*]

"Dr. Johnston's guidelines are simple. We will each identify one inner polarity—that means two inner voices—that are well known to us. To illustrate, let's start with a simple example, our neat-desk self and our messy-desk self. For some of you these two inner characters may be continuously at war, while others of you may experience a 90 percent to 10 percent power balance.

"These two characters will each take a chair in the room. I'll ask Paul and Martina to bring three dining chairs into the circle and form a triangle. The third chair belongs to our liminal space position, the key to our coherent living.

"The primary rule is that Neat Desk and Messy Desk *may not talk to each other.* They may only converse directly with Liminal Space. You already have plenty of practice with the first two inner characters arguing with each other, so there is no value in revisiting that dynamic.

"Liminal Space will interview one, then the other, and the one not being interviewed will have the benefit of hearing—but not directly responding to—what the other has to say. Liminal Space acts as a sort of moderator, at this point, making sure each one fully has their say. Each character can only speak when you, the person doing the work, are physically sitting in their chair. To illustrate, Shirley cannot answer for one character when she is sitting in a different character's chair.

"Let's get into a real example, and I'll point out what happens after that as we move along. You'll see that this is a very efficient but also a compassionate way of coming to a new place where you've not been before.

"Shirley, would you be willing to go first?"

"Of course." Shirley gulped. Then she reminded herself out loud that volunteering as guinea pig was always the best chance to learn.

"Which polarity from your list would you like to work with?"

She chose Work Alone vs. Trust the Group. I reassured her that I would help her through the preliminaries to model the process for the group.

Shirley's Lone Ranger

I asked Shirley to picture one of her two inner characters in the polarity she chose, as if it were in a play. What do we, in the audience, see? What is their age? Stature? Is gender important? Or not? What are they wearing? Can you give them a name?

She started out haltingly, not sure what to say. This was perfectly normal.

"Her name is the Lone Ranger. She is a cowboy. She is ten years old. She has a cowboy hat and black boots. She can do anything. She has a big silver horse that can gallop faster than any horse around."

"Excellent image for us to see," I said. "Now, go sit in the Lone Ranger chair. Feel your way into the part."

Shirley swaggered over to the first chair. You could almost see her in her big black boots. She plopped down in the chair, feet spread wide apart, hands on her knees. She then sat up very straight. You could almost sense her big silver horse waiting nearby.

"Good. Now come sit in the third chair, the Liminal Space chair, and describe who is in the other empty chair."

Shirley took the Liminal Space chair and looked to the empty chair. She said she had to think for a bit.

I told her to take all the time she needed. After nearly a minute she began again.

"She's kind of blurry. As if there is a dense fog around her. She's tall and thin, maybe five ten. She is in her early forties, and you can tell that she has been athletic, or maybe a classical ballet dancer. She has the look of being very intellectual. Maybe she's a professor. It's hard to say because of the fog. In spite of her clear looks, I can see that it is going to be hard to figure her out." Another long pause, then she continued.

"I can tell that she thinks things through very carefully, very thoroughly. She has an important project that she wants to accomplish. It is quite experimental. It will require some steps that she hasn't tried before. In her bright brain, she knows there is more to the project than she knows how to do. She could learn those new aspects, she says to herself, but that wouldn't be very efficient. Maybe there wouldn't be time to learn it all, if there's a timeline for getting the thing done.

"She is realizing that she'll probably have to find a team to pull it off. But that's not something she has a lot of comfort in doing. She feels her own ambivalence."

I asked her, "If she was at a party, what would her just-for-fun name tag say?"

"Team Player…well, actually it's Professor-of-Team-Player."

The group laughed softly, appreciating the nuance.

I said, "Ask her to describe what she is wearing but go sit in her chair so she can answer out loud."

Shirley changed seats to Professor-of-Team-Player's chair.

"Oh, this is my classic business attire—a black skirt and a red blazer. Black stockings and high heels. I also brought along the book I'm currently reading."

"Thank you, Shirley. Now return to your Liminal Space chair. Can you sense who would like to speak first?"

There was a long moment of silence before she said, "Yes, it's Lone Ranger."

"Go ahead and ask her what she has to say for herself. She will speak directly to you, in Liminal Space."

Shirley sat there, a little confused.

I prompted her. "Shirley, go over and sit in the Lone Ranger chair. Take a moment to get into character. Feel your way into your real Lone Ranger inner character. Then tell Liminal Space whatever you want to say, speaking to the chair where Liminal Space sits."

She moved to the Lone Ranger chair and automatically took up the posture from before.

"I'm not really just ten. I'm also sixty. I've been the Lone Ranger my whole life. I grew up alone in the house while my mother was off at work. I came home after school and had a room full of toys and projects. I had three Lincoln Log sets, so I could build whole compounds all over my room at once. I had little figures of cowboys and Indians and their horses, and we had adventures, attacks on the forts, horses racing around. Then I would go across the street to where the twins, who were my age, lived. Their mom was always home and I was allowed to go over there anytime before my mom got home from work. The twins and I climbed trees, built treehouses, swung through the bamboo forest in the backyard, played Tarzan. But anytime I got tired of the twins, I could just go home. Read a Nancy Drew book until dinnertime. I was on my own, and I loved it.

"After college I had to support myself. I worked independently and was attached temporarily to many organizations over the years. But I always felt a bit removed. I learned how to supervise a team, but I never really felt I belonged.

"I would work with a client, learn what they needed, develop a program, and deliver it over the course of weeks or months. I would find peers, other consultants, and we'd get together to compare notes, figure out the best way to handle different situations. We even formed an informal think tank. And I sought out a lot of advanced training myself. But I always felt like a one-person company, even as a consultant inside an organization. It never really occurred to me to do it any differently.

"The irony was, I taught team building many times over the years. I guess I understood the theory pretty well because people told me I'd helped them a lot. My head has always been way ahead of my doing. Underlying it all, being on my own feels much more secure. I know I can always count on…me…to get it done. I get it right because I always think it through in advance."

I coached Shirley to return to her Liminal Space chair and then thank Lone Ranger for sharing, which she did.

"Now, Shirley, from Liminal Space chair ask Team Player if she would like to speak. If she agrees, go take that chair and speak directly to Liminal Space chair."

Shirley sat in the Team Player chair. You could tell looking at her feet that she was wearing high heels. Her knees and ankles were held tightly together. She smoothed her skirt and looked around the room.

She said, "Some of you may be wondering who I am. I'm not sure I know myself exactly. I know it's foggy in here. That's because I'm still figuring out exactly who I am. Up until now, I've been a figment of Shirley's imagination, or so it seems. But I am real too. Because, as you can tell from my outfit, I am all good sense.

"I am well aware, intellectually, that some endeavors are bigger than one person can manage. Look at the Golden Gate Bridge. It could only have been built by a bunch of people who were well coordinated. Look at Times Square. It's not even square. Obviously built by a lot of uncoordinated people, but still a bunch of people. Most of civilization has been built by groups of people coming together to accomplish something bigger than themselves. Yet for myself, I'm still taking shape out of this fog. Maybe the fog of fear."

Her eyes turned to the Lone Ranger chair.

I prompted Shirley to come back over to Liminal Space chair and ask Lone Ranger if she would like to respond to what she's just heard. I added, "Remember to speak to Liminal Space, not to Team Player."

Shirley did this, speaking as Lone Ranger. "Ouch. Yes, there is some fear over here, if I am really honest. I've just never been sure I can count on others, even though it *seems* logical that they'd come through most of the time. Employees, sure, but not peers. Maybe it's because I grew up alone. I'm out of practice. Actually, I never really had to practice, except when the teachers set up temporary projects or told us to put on a skit or something. I hated team sports. Didn't understand the point. Run around some bases. I liked tennis better. Or hiking in the forest. Lots of big rocks and trees to collaborate with." She chuckled.

I prompted Shirley to change chairs so Liminal Space could ask Lone Ranger if she would mind if Team Player got to try out some new moves in order to learn how to practice. She did so. Moving back to that chair, Lone Ranger answered Liminal Space's question.

"Sure, I guess she…we…could try that. I don't even know what that looks like. When I was in junior high, a bunch of girls would gather after school at Janice's house. I'd go, but I never really knew what to do. So I would just listen to the other girls. If Team Player tries that, I'll just watch and listen. Seems safe enough. All you nice people here, nice grownups, nice comfortable welcoming house. But ask me again later, if the stakes go up, and we'll see."

I prompted Shirley to change chairs again so Liminal Space could acknowledge that tentative willingness. She did so, and then she (as Liminal Space) asked Team Player where she was right now, with what was going on.

Shirley took Team Player's chair.

"I understand the opportunity is to try out some collaborating that will be a stretch for me. Or maybe the stretch is actually for Lone Ranger. That's not for me to say, or be concerned about. I'd like to become a fuller, clearer character, not be a blurred image in the fog. I'd like to take my full place in Shirley's life, moving forward." Then she hesitated.

"But there's one thing I'd like to ask for help with. I still have some tender spots from times when I've tried to get friends to join in a project and they would just look at me deadpan, as if they had no idea what I was even proposing. At those times, I suppose I gave up pretty quickly when I got that kind of feedback. I'll need some encouragement to stick with it, or pivot ten degrees and try again. Or something. I guess I'm asking for coaching from some of you who have more experience with this."

The others in the room nodded, acknowledging support.

Then I asked Shirley to return to Liminal Space chair one more time.

Anchoring

"Shirley, I invite you to sit as Liminal Space with your strongest but still relaxed posture, whatever that feels like, but let it be tall. The top of your head reaching toward the ceiling, toward the sky. And let your feet be firmly on the floor, feeling the connection deeply into the center of the earth. Are you feeling really grounded? Balanced?"

Shirley nodded and adjusted her posture accordingly, settling into it.

"Shirley, this Liminal Space position is the character that is most deeply and authentically you. It is the place from which you listen to all your other inner characters. It is the place from which you draw out each one's concerns, their fears, their worldview. And this is the place from which you make the best choices because you can see life most clearly from here." I paused, in case she had any questions, then continued.

"You can go to this place at any time, particularly when you feel like some other character is trying to commandeer the bus, trying to seize the steering wheel. You are the only driver of the bus.

"I want to help you anchor the *physical feeling* of being in this state. We call this an *anchoring gesture*. Take a deep breath, then think of a simple gesture that you can do anytime, any place, without drawing attention to it. It could be twisting your ring, gently grabbing one ear lobe, or moving a hand in some way. Take a moment to choose what that motion will be."

Shirley paused, then put her thumb under her chin as her index finger went up near her temple, the remaining fingers relaxed and slightly curled downward on her jaw. She looked relaxed but pensive.

I instructed Shirley to put both hands in her lap, close her eyes, and feel the top of her head reaching to the sky, feet grounded on the earth, and her whole body strong, relaxed, aligned.

"When you have that feeling solidly, bring your hand up to your face as you had it a moment ago. This is called *anchoring*. It's from NLP—neuro-linguistic programming. Relax, hands at your sides.

Now head up, feet grounded, feel the balance, and anchor it with your hand to your face. Relax. Then do it one more time. Good."

Anytime you are in a meeting, I explained to the group, riding in an Uber car, on a subway or an airplane, about to make a speech, if you need to feel centered and at your best, just visualize your head up, your feet grounded, and touch your face in this same way. It will bring back the full-body feeling of yourself at its most balanced, at its strongest.

"Shirley, good job. You've got this!" I said.

The group suddenly applauded. Shirley grinned.

I looked slowly around the room, into each person's eyes, as if to ground the whole experience in each one's own body and soul because I knew each person had been with Shirley, while at the same time being with their own inner voices, and with their own strongest, balanced self.

Shirley had returned to her seat on the couch, but she leaned forward and with her hand gestured "one more thing."

I nodded and she said, "It's not really the *Lone* Ranger, you know. Never was. The TV series referred to a solo Texas Ranger, but the character always had Tonto, played by Mohawk Jay Silverheels, at his side. In fact, Tonto had to rescue his partner from numerous dangerous situations. Fortunately, we white folk see through different eyes today than we did in 1949, when the series was launched. The metaphor of lifesaving comrades is not lost on me."

"Your point is well taken," Alicia said.

I suggested a break. "When we come back, we'll give another person a turn."

When the group reconvened, Himari raised her hand.

"I'd like to go next unless someone else is eager to do so. I had some pretty significant polarities come up for me while Shirley was working. I'd like to see where they lead."

I asked her to briefly tell the group about her list of inner characters.

Himari's Polarities: Work or Flow

"My first character probably won't surprise anyone. It's my study-hard-and-excel voice. It's my parents' voices inside me. It's been there for as long as I can remember. It got me through medical school." She rolled her eyes and laughed.

"The polarity is, now that I'm retired, I feel like I should be learning how to relax, go with the flow, be impulsive, and learn to do inconsequential things. Isn't that what retirement is about? My question is, can I learn to relax without betraying everything my family has lived for? Everything that has made me successful as an adult?

"My second polarity is similar. I've always wanted to serve. Choosing medicine. Working at a university hospital. But in retirement it seems like I should just kick back and relax. I've heard talk of finding a third way, but I cannot see how that would work. I could really use some help with this one.

"But my polarity that feels most urgent is finding friends or colleagues, a new network, here in Santa Fe, now that I don't have my work to rely on to provide that."

I asked her some questions so we could hear more. "Are there feelings tugging in different directions? Can you identify what the polarity is, whether there is tension there?"

"Well, it feels awkward to just go out and ask people to be my friend because I'm new in town and I don't have work friends anymore. It even feels a little scary. And I wouldn't know who to ask anyway. So I guess coming at it by hard work and trying to excel at it feels exactly wrong. But just relaxing and going with the flow feels like nothing at all would happen. And where would I go to do all that relaxing and flowing?"

Everyone laughed and smiled.

I asked Himari if she could see in her mind's eye two characters taking part in this debate and to try to describe them for us.

"Absolutely. The first is called 'Get to Work.' She is saying, 'Go find some friends. What are you waiting for?' She actually kind of looks like my father, in his suit. His shoes are polished, and he has a new haircut.

"The other character is telling me to go with the flow. Ha ha. She looks kind of like a hippy. I think I'll call her 'Trust the Universe.'"

I prompted her to take the Liminal Space chair and acknowledge these two characters. "Take a moment and see each one in their chair. Then ask if one of them would like to speak. Go and sit in whichever chair wants to go first."

Himari did so, taking her time to feel each character's experience. Then, moving to one of the other chairs, she finally spoke in an authoritative voice.

"Hi, I'm Get to Work. I don't know what the debate is here. Himari just needs to get out there and start meeting people. Go to a lecture. Join a club. Volunteer somewhere. She is sure to meet some people. She's outgoing enough. She'll do fine."

We could see that Himari was remembering the process from watching Shirley. She moved back to Liminal Space chair and thanked Get to Work for enlightening us, though her tone was not at all sarcastic—it was respectful. Then she took Trust the Universe's chair.

"Hi, all. I heard that. I'm not quite a hippy, but compared to Get to Work, maybe I look like it. I don't wear gauzy dresses or go barefoot, but you might find me in jeans and an oversized chambray shirt. OK, and, yes, sandals."

Trust the Universe sat with one leg draped over the arm of her chair. There was no question she was relaxed.

"But you've probably noticed that I look a little foggy, like Shirley's character did. I don't get out much because Himari and I spend so little time together. Sometimes I sound to her like some sort of *should* character. What retirement 'should' be like. But Himari and I could have a lot of fun if she would lighten up."

Himari returned to the Liminal Space chair and looked at me questioningly.

I said, "Thank you to both of you for your honest sharing. Trust the Universe, do you know why you are in Himari's life right now? Do I sense a bit of pushback against Get to Work?"

Himari changed chairs and Trust the Universe said, "Well, there was a time, back in high school, when I really wanted to push back against all the strict rules about finishing homework before I could go out with friends. But by medical school I could see the value of this discipline. Today, I just want Himari to have a more balanced life, a more *fun* life. I think she could learn to love some things in life that have—of necessity—been neglected before."

Himari returned to her Liminal Space chair, then asked Get to Work a question: "Would you be willing to give Himari some sort of vacation from your oversight? Maybe a few months, as an experiment?"

Himari changed chairs, in order to speak as Get to Work.

"Well, I suppose, with me on sabbatical in Bali and her no longer having the daily responsibilities of her job, maybe we could negotiate something. I actually would not mind seeing her find more simple joys in her life."

Switching chairs, Liminal Space asked Trust the Universe, "Would you be willing to do some of the 'work' while you are in this six-month experiment?"

Trust the Universe said, "Of course I would. Wait. What do you mean by work? I'm not opposed to getting things done, but I prefer to allow more space for serendipities. It doesn't all have to be *hard* work, does it?"

I asked Liminal Space how she was feeling.

"I feel surprisingly balanced, as though I really do have a taste of Trust the Universe's spirit pumping through my veins right now. It's exciting, but in a reassuring way. And I can really feel Get to Work backing off for a while. Giving me some space. I feel strong. As if maybe I can pull this off.

"But I have one question. I don't know if it's from me, my Liminal Space grounded self, or if this is from some unnamed other inner character. I'm wondering if I need to find a project, and then the friends will come along naturally with that, or should I find other ways to make friends, and from those associations a new project will come up that I would never have thought of on my own?"

I responded to Himari that this sounded like a balanced and reasonable question, although there could be overtones of a taste of stalling to avoid the new steps. But, I suggested we not overthink it.

"For now," I told her, "hold your question on a handy shelf, where you can come back to it when it calls to you again. As our conversations here evolve," I looked at the whole group, "I suspect that you'll each have some insights that will help you answer such questions for yourself. And you'll answer them in ways you could not have predicted yesterday."

I prompted Himari to take one more step. "Stay in Liminal Space chair. Take a deep breath and recenter yourself. Breathe again and feel your feet grounded in the earth and the top of your head drawn to beyond the sun."

When I could see her body shift into a centered state, I told her to think of a simple gesture that she could adopt to *anchor* this feeling, her *anchoring gesture.*

She held her left hand out a bit from her waist, palm up, and rubbed her wedding ring slowly with her thumb.

"Good, now let's go through the centering and anchoring three times, as we did with Shirley. Take as long as you need to each time you repeat, to deeply absorb the full feeling in your body, then do the motion again."

When she finished, Himari slowly got up and returned silently to her seat on the couch.

After a stretch break and walks around the grounds, Martina offered to go next.

Martina's Concern: Creating New Structure in Her Life

"My first deep experience with a polarity," Martina explained to the group, "was deciding to go out of state to college. It was something about wanting to make my own path."

She briefly interjected some background that she had since learned. "Sharon Parks, PhD, who spent her career at Harvard, called it 'pushing away from the dock,' and she explained that it is a normal, even necessary developmental stage. At the time, all I knew was that I felt completely submerged in my extended family, and I needed to breathe.

"But then after college I started working in state government in the upper Midwest and eventually ran for office for a state administrative role. Looking back now, I realize I had acquired another extended family, another place where everyone knew me. It was another complex structure that formed my life.

"Retirement for me has been both real and a metaphor: I walk into a crowded room now and no one knows me. But the most unsettling part for me is a sense of not knowing who I am, without the official role.

"I still occasionally wake up in the morning and my first thought is that who I am—as Secretary of State—will determine what I do that day. Then when I realize that is no longer the reality, I wonder, 'Well, then, who am I?' Do any of you have that experience?"

Several in the circle nodded.

I prompted Martina for more by asking, "Where is the tension? Is there an alternative or differing interior voice?"

"That's easy. Unlike Himari, I have a pretty strong lazy-self inside. It's just that I've kept her in line for all these years. I sometimes feel like she is going to rise up now and take over, and I'll become a hermit with lots of cats, someone who is still in my bathrobe at two p.m."

The group laughed at the image.

I motioned Martina toward the Liminal Space chair. "Can you describe either of your characters, or name them?"

"That chair is… let's see…. I'll just call her Secretary of State. That's a shorthand for all my years working in an elaborate bureaucracy, working my way up. Responding to a thousand needs, following the demands of the structure, the system itself. She's wearing a dark business suit and high heels. Her hair is perfect."

Martina described the second inner character as she pointed to the other chair. "OK, she can stay in her bathrobe." She grinned. "I might as well fill out the fantasy. But she only has two cats. And her hair is a tangled mess."

"Her name?" I asked.

"Bathrobe."

After moving to the Secretary of State chair and sitting properly, Martina elaborated on how much the system had defined her every waking moment, defined her very identity. And how alarming it was now, in retirement, to have none of that when she woke up.

Liminal Space thanked her for being willing to share her vulnerability, then asked Bathrobe to speak.

I was pleased they were picking up the rhythm of the encounters.

"I have no incentive to get out of bed in the morning. Friends invite me to things, but I am indifferent. Going through the motions of something that doesn't give me juice just makes me feel worse. Staying in bed and reading a book until noon is my default position. My friends from so many years ago don't see this, of course. I'm not about to let on that I am struggling. After all, they assume that having it all together is the real Martina."

I prompted Liminal Space to ask the characters if either of them could see a connection between the sense of having no identity and the feeling of loss of structure. It was more of a leading question than I usually asked, but I wanted the group to begin to make more nuanced observations.

Liminal Space asked the question, and Secretary of State responded.

"I don't see myself at all as one who can actually produce structure. My world has always provided that for me, just delivered it at my door the second I wake up. My identity, then, is a *not*-structure-producer."

Bathrobe heard this and wanted to respond, so Martina changed chairs.

"And I certainly can't create structure to my day. I have no idea how. I'm clueless. And terrified because I am so inept at it. No will. No desire. *No purpose.* 'What is the point?' is all I can say to my day. My identity, if you can call it that, is a *non*-structure-producer."

I gestured Martina to return to the Liminal Space chair, and I took a moment to offer a commentary to the group.

"You can see what's developing here. Both characters are starting to feel a helplessness. This is good because they are naming the problem out loud. But we don't want Martina to stay there, much less become overwhelmed by this. So I will engage Liminal Space, who is always the one with the most potential to have an insight, so that she can move the characters forward.

"Liminal Space Martina, can you imagine a scenario where these two characters might collaborate on a new plan moving forward? Take all the time you need."

Martina took a couple of minutes to think about this. I reminded her to do so in a posture of tall strength while feeling firmly connected to the earth.

"First of all, I want to give the bathrobe character a different name. It will be You Can Do This, Kid. Now, I want to invite her into a new place. YCDTK, would you be willing to go with us on an adventure to try a radically new third way of living?"

Martina moved to the YCDTK chair, and then pondered the invitation with eyes closed for a long minute.

"Yes, I'm willing to try almost anything. I hate how helpless I feel not knowing what to do, not feeling like doing much of anything. I hate it."

Martina resumed the Liminal Space chair and addressed Secretary of State. "Would you be willing to suspend some assumptions, say for ninety days, and try this experiment with me in Liminal Space and with YCDTK?"

From the Secretary of State chair, Martina paused, then said, "I suppose so. I don't know what can come of it. There is either structure or there isn't. And right now, Martina doesn't have any. If she did have two cats, she would probably forget to feed them. She doesn't have a purpose to her life. But I don't want to be the one to block her finding a solution because I know she's miserable right now."

Martina came back to Liminal Space Chair. "Thank you, both of you, for your willingness."

After a moment she turned to me. "I'm stuck. Now what?"

Leaping into New Territory

I described to the group what I was seeing. "Martina, you and your inner characters are standing high at one side of a very narrow canyon. At the top, it is narrow enough to leap across to the other side. To try to climb down the canyon wall and see if there is a safe way to scramble up the other side is one possibility. But it would be a long climb, and there is no guarantee that rains won't come and wash out any trail, wash out rocks, and make the climb too treacherous. The other option is to leap across together and see what is on the other side. The leap itself is doable. It is a matter of commitment and determination to find a new path on the other side.

"The secret is *you*, in Liminal Space, must be willing to take on the identity of the best of both inner characters and more. Are you willing to try on the costume, as it were, of Martina who can create her own structure? It is clear that YCDTK doesn't feel up to it on her own. And S-of-S is skeptical because she only knows things as they have been before. But you, Martina, in your strong Liminal Space place, can take this on. You don't need all the answers ahead of the leap. They will begin to appear once you are on the other side. All you need is to make the commitment to leap, with the expectation that *something* will manifest when you need it."

Martina let all of this sink in. The group held the silence with supportive expectancy.

Martina then asked me, "Can you help me here? I don't even know what 'leaping' means."

"Let's try this. Alicia, Samuel, Shirley, grab those chairs and move them completely out of the circle so we have a clear space. Martina, as you embody Liminal Space, stand here near the center, and hold out your hands to each side, so you can grasp hands with YCDTK and Secretary of State, as if they are standing on each side of you. Now, see that line, the design on the rug? That is the chasm, the narrow canyon. When you are ready, say to the other two characters what you intend to do, right now, in this room, together."

Martina closed her eyes and took a deep breath, then spoke out loud, in a calm, strong voice. "You two, and probably some other inner characters that we have not named yet, we are going to take a huge step right now, here, together. We are going to step across this chasm into our unknown future. You have agreed to come along, and I appreciate what a challenge that is for you. It feels like a huge challenge for me too, as leader. When we get to the other side, we will be making it up as we go along, and I will appreciate your counsel, but we will be in new territory. This is not about reliving the past. Are you clear on that?"

Martina looked to her left and right, paused, took another deep breath, and then took a long step across the rug. Her hands suddenly covered her face, and she started shaking with laughter, tears, and relief.

Shirley started to take a step toward her, as if to comfort her, but I motioned her to stay still and signaled silence to the others.

After a long minute I asked Martina how she was feeling.

"I am in a new place that I have never been before. I just crossed over into my new life. Nothing has changed, but everything has changed. I feel chills and excitement."

"I invite you to *anchor* this moment. Close your eyes, then think of a motion, your *anchoring gesture*, that is simple and natural for you. When you are ready, keep your eyes closed, feel fully the step you have just taken, and then do the gesture."

We watched as Martina spread her feet apart and put her hands on her hips, stretching tall.

"Excellent, now relax for a moment, shake out, then repeat this anchoring gesture twice more."

Each time it seemed as if she was standing another inch taller.

I explained to Martina, but also to the others, "You are anchoring the bodily sensation of this shift. Whenever things feel uncertain, and I promise you they will, you can take this stance and regain your power and your connection with your higher self. You can reopen your liminal channel. You can connect with Source.

"You cannot see yet today how exactly you will build new structure into your life, but having your *inner state* shifted as you just did is the essential first step. If you had moved ahead without this, any structure building would just be head-tripping. It wouldn't hold the deeper meaning you seek."

Martina kept her strong hands-on-hips posture a moment longer, then relaxed, opened her eyes, and looked around the circle. The others glanced at me, and I nodded. Instantly they were on their feet, encircling Martina in a hug.

"Thank you" was all she could say to them. Then she turned to me where I was standing to the side. She brought her palms together, touched her forehead and bowed her head ever so slightly, mouthing, "Thank you." I could feel us all standing on holy ground.

Individual Leap—Collective Insights

As everyone returned to their seats, I asked if anyone had any questions.

Himari spoke up. "You used the phrase just now with Martina 'connecting with Source.' You didn't say it that way when it was my turn, but as you spoke it just now I had a flashback to my work here, and I felt that too. I just didn't have words for it. Thank you."

Shirley sat up straighter and took a deep breath. "When I asked, from my Liminal Space, if you all would help me learn to collaborate, I think I felt that too. Something greater than the sum of the parts of this group. I want to meditate in my journal tonight about what that means to me."

I addressed the circle. "You can see now how the group going through this process together is far richer, and works in a different sort of way, than if you each were only coming to see me one-on-one to learn this inner-character method. I appreciate you being so willing to bring your hard questions into the circle."

Everyone nodded and smiled, and a few exchanged hugs.

"Now," I said, "who would like to go next after we take a break?"

Paul raised a hand. "I'm happy to give it a try."

Paul Meets Three Inner Characters

I asked Paul which issue from his polarities list he would like to start with. He reminded the group of his long career of unending dedication to emergency medicine, as well as the toll that had taken on his body, his family, and even his spirit. He described it as a long marathon run. At one end of some internal spectrum, he said, was the temptation to find another worthy cause or project that would be as absorbing again. He loved the feeling that he was being of significant service to others. And he loved seeing tangible results.

At the other end of his spectrum was an image of simply playing with grandchildren, hanging out with his wife, getting his body back in shape, advancing his cooking skills, and learning to paint. He thought of this character as All-Play. The tension, Paul said, was that at some point he wanted to make some kind of contribution again to the larger world. But he feared he simply did not know how to strike a balance in his life.

I suggested he select a chair for his Liminal Space and take time to see who might be in the other two chairs.

After several minutes, he said, "On my right, not in the dining chair but over there, in that big easy chair, is All-Play."

I asked if he, as Paul in Liminal Space, knew yet who was in the other chair. Paul wasn't sure. I suggested he go ahead and hear what All-Play had to say.

Paul walked over to the easy chair, sprawled comfortably, and spoke. "I am called All-Play because I make Jack a good boy." He chuckled, glancing shyly at the ground. "We all know Paul needs some serious recovery time. I'm here to remind him not to be *too* serious about it. We just want to kick back and make up for years of lost time. I'm not downgrading the contribution he made, but enough is enough. Paul needs to hang out with me until play is his default position, and I can make sure he has fun doing it."

Paul fell silent. I motioned him back to his Liminal Space chair. Then I let the silence hang, wanting to let Paul consider what might come next.

Finally he said, "There is a guy pacing around over by the windows. He is muttering."

I suggested Paul ask him if he might like to speak.

Paul did this from his Liminal Space chair, and then stood and walked over to the windows that overlooked the garden. He paced back and forth for a minute, then spoke. "Paul is going to get bored. I know he is. Eventually. He can't make lasagna forever, no matter how elegant the accompanying wine is. When that happens, he is likely to start getting depressed, and not know why…"

He trailed off, then stood there, silent.

I motioned Paul back to his Liminal Space chair. I asked if this character had a name.

Paul studied the windows for over a minute. "He's called Invitation." Then he was silent. Finally he spoke toward the windows. "Would you like to explain your name?"

Paul rose and resumed the position standing by the windows. "I am here to help Paul see the invitation that awaits him. He thinks that because he is worried and uncertain about how to balance play with a new calling, he should just hang out with All-Play. He thinks that will prevent him from getting addicted to a new endeavor. But he is bigger than that."

Paul returned to Liminal Space, looking troubled. "I wasn't expecting that! What he said scares me a little."

"OK," I said slowly. I paused to let him process what was going on. "Can you ask him when he first showed up in your life?"

There was another long silence before he spoke again. "Actually, I think he had another name long before it was Invitation. If I'm honest, I'm afraid I have to admit his name was Being Golden Boy. You see, ever since my teens I used to get a lot of attention, a lot of recognition, for being a quick study and being willing to take on responsibility way beyond my years. Being Golden Boy was in charge of my life for years. I can see now that Invitation being here in this room today is a bit of a Trojan Horse. He wants me to get back in the game and find some more glory. I don't begrudge him all the lives he helped me save, but dashing right back on the field just keeps me trapped in the same old polarity. And All-Play doesn't have a chance."

I asked him if there was another character in the room experiencing fear.

Paul glanced around the room, then back and forth between the empty chairs. "Yes. He's sitting right there." He gestured to the empty chair on his left. "His name is Frankly Worried."

After a pause, Paul moved into the empty chair, took a deep breath, then began. "Yes, I *am* Frankly Worried. Paul spent decades throwing himself into important positions that had impressive results. Saved many lives. Changed the system in the process. Now he is unwinding, which I cannot argue with at all. But asking him to *balance* those two opposite lifestyles. That's asking a lot. I'm afraid it's asking too much. I don't think he can pull it off."

Paul moved back to Liminal Space. I prompted him to take a few deep breaths and center himself. I reminded him that from this position, he is driving the bus, and he has access to the infinite wisdom that he has been in touch with since he was nineteen.

Paul adjusted his posture, took another deep breath, let it out slowly, then shook out his hands and placed them on his thighs. He spoke to Frankly Worried in the chair at his left. "I know you only want the best for me. I know you think you are looking out for me. I know you, just like all my inner characters, want to keep me safe. But I am going to talk again with Invitation, and I don't want you to be nervous about that."

Paul instinctively moved into the chair at his left, looked back at the Liminal Space chair, and nodded in the affirmative. Then Paul moved back over to the windows.

"Thank you, Paul, for giving me a chance to speak further. I am in your life right now because you are at a crossroads. Frankly Worried is unable to realize this from his normal defense position, but you are capable of more, going forward. I want to emphasize to you that you have Superpowers that are still needed in the world, and I urge you not to let fear keep you from that."

Paul leaned against the wall next to the windows for a long moment, then returned to the Liminal Space chair. He sat for several minutes, head down, leaning forward, hands on his knees. Then he looked over to me for guidance on what might come next.

"Paul, you are in your Liminal Space right now. Your most wise place, with access to great wisdom. What are you feeling right now?"

Paul sat up straight. "Message received. I hear Invitation loud and clear. And I also can see that I don't have to take orders from Invitation/Golden Boy as a knee-jerk reaction. In addition, having

Frankly Worried over in that wooden chair, rather than buzzing around inside my head, is really helping me see that he is just a voice, not my full self. I know that today is not the day where I can see how it will all work out, but I am willing to take on the challenge. I want to build a balanced life, with plenty of time for family, and for my artistic side, and also do whatever I can to discern my next calling."

Paul started to slump down, exhausted.

I reached over and touched him on the arm and spoke clearly. "Paul, before you return to the couch, let's *anchor* this whole experience. Stretch into your tallest, most balanced posture, recapture that felt sensation of being connected to Source as you listened to Golden Boy/Invitation, Frankly Worried, and All-Play. Now, choose your *anchoring gesture* to lock in this feeling of being centered and connected to Source."

He did so, moving his hand in a certain way.

"Again," I prompted. "Do it again. OK, once more."

Then he sat for a silent moment with his eyes closed, opened them, and slowly scanned the group, his eyes meeting with each person. "Thank you," he finally said, and rose to move to the couch.

As Paul sat down, I suggested a silent break, but asked first if someone would like to be next when we returned. Alicia gave a tentative wave.

When everyone returned, Alicia said, "I wasn't sure about all this when we started, but I think I'm getting the hang of it. I have a couple of polarities I jotted down. Should I explain them?"

I answered yes, to please give us a quick rundown.

Alicia Names Her Conflicts about Achievement

Alicia started by saying, "One polarity was my drive to get out of here—meaning my neighborhood—at any cost, which was my predominant mindset all the time I was growing up. This inner resolution got me into UCLA and then an MBA there. This is in tension now with a desire just to be myself, and not have to be so constantly trying to impress people, to get ahead.

"Another polarity is more vague. It's a fear of losing control, as in, if I'm not paying attention all the time, something will slip. I know I learned this very early. My mother was an alcoholic, and as the oldest child, I pretty much had to manage a lot of things raising my younger brother and sisters. The polarity with that is, now that I know I'm not in charge of all those kids, I'd like to just relax. In the corporate world this served me well because I did have to keep a lot of projects moving. And sometimes manage the 'kids,' who were my own age, my staff. But now I seem to have an *on-alert* button that is hard to turn off.

"The third polarity has to do specifically with retiring. In my career I used to be able to get a lot done on the momentum of my reputation of being a superstar in my industry. In Santa Fe, no one has heard of me. I feel a vacuum, or a black hole, where if I try to get involved in something, I'm not sure how I could get anything done, especially if it's far from my areas of expertise."

She stopped there and took a deep breath before glancing around the circle.

"Thank you, Alicia," I said. "We appreciate your being willing to share those stories." I asked her if one of these polarities had the most juice for her in that moment.

"I'm not sure. They all seem to be connected."

With the three chairs back in the triangle, I invited her to come sit in her Liminal Space chair, breathe, then close her eyes. I prompted her to take as long as she needed to just see if someone showed up in one of the other chairs.

Alicia stood up, adjusted one of the chairs slightly, then sat down in it. She closed her eyes again. After a couple of minutes, she opened her eyes suddenly and spoke. "Here I am! On Alert is here. I am fifteen. I am tough, organized, and bossy. I keep my sisters and my little brother in line and the house in order. I also make time to study and practice my sprints at the track.

"I run to live. But my job, for as long as I can remember, is to keep the chaos at bay. I'm very good at it. My sisters pretty much do what I tell them. They all have chores. My baby brother does OK, but it's going to be touchy when he gets to gang age. Later, when I moved into corporate, it wasn't that different. A lot of people running around in circles. The first time I heard the phrase 'herding cats,' I laughed out loud. That's exactly what I do. Looking back on all my promotions, I seem to be pretty good at it. Now this retirement thing, I just don't know…"

Alicia moved back to her Liminal Space chair.

She said, "Thank you, On Alert, for being willing to talk with us here. What are you most worried about today?"

After a moment, Alicia changed chairs back to On Alert. "I really don't know what to do with myself in this big, beautiful quiet house in this big, beautiful, quiet city. And especially now with Helen gone. It's a different world than I've ever known."

She moved back.

Liminal Space said, "I appreciate your honesty, On Alert. Now we'd like to take a few quiet moments to see who else is here." Remaining in the Liminal Space chair, Alicia closed her eyes again.

I found myself appreciating how she was going with the flow of the conversation.

"Free to Be Me is here." Alicia pointed to the other chair. "She is ready to speak." She moved to that chair.

"Yes, here I am. Free to Be Me is definitely my name. I have been a long time coming. I feel like a butterfly just struggling free from my fifty-year chrysalis. As a caterpillar I was too small to be seen, although the Alicia who ran track was me, in a way. That was a long time ago. When Alicia and Helen decided to retire and move to Santa Fe, I saw some hope for me. But it's going to be a struggle. On Alert plays the heavy in this movie."

Alicia immediately got up and returned to Liminal Space.

"Free, it is wonderful to have you here! I know you feel lots of energy about becoming more a part of our life. We will work on that. And don't trouble yourself about On Alert. It's my job to make sure you have the time and airspace you need."

Alicia turned toward me then spoke to the group. "Whew! Can you feel the energy crackling in the room? This is going to get very interesting."

I prompted Alicia further. "Can you ask each character if she is willing to trust you as Liminal Space as you all go forward?"

"OK. On Alert, do you trust me as our centered self, connected with our Source, to be the one in charge of our journey going forward?"

She changed chairs, to speak as On Alert.

"Let me think about that a bit. You know, I've been pretty much in charge since we were little. Maybe the question is, do you no longer trust me to be driving the bus? I've done a pretty good job of getting you this far."

Alicia returned to Liminal Space chair.

"On Alert, I have a massive amount of respect for what a great job you have done. It is not a lack of confidence here. We need to make some changes because the situation no longer demands of us what it did for all those years. Let me make you this promise. I will always take under advisement any alert you want to make me aware of. You will always be my senior advisor. But I am asking you not to expect to drive anymore. I will be doing the driving as we move forward."

Alicia paused and turned to me and said, "This is a lot of running back and forth between chairs."

"Agreed," I said. "But it is vital for you to keep clear on who is running your life and who is lobbying you to make your choices as you make these important changes."

Alicia nodded and took the On Alert chair again.

"I see your point about who is driving. I agree that conditions are not the chaos of our growing-up years, nor do we have a corporate environment to manage. I am willing to trust this experiment, as long as I feel like you are at least listening to me."

Alicia returned to Liminal Space.

"Free, how are you feeling about all these changes?"

She changed chairs.

"I am excited about the prospect that On Alert will become an advisor only. I need room to stretch and grow. As long as On Alert is not always leaning on me, pressuring me to back off, I'm good."

Alicia returned to Liminal Space.

I let her sit with the whole conversation for a minute, then I said, "Alicia, take a moment to get fully centered in your body and in your mind. It is time to anchor this experience and this new place to stand. As we've done with the others, I'd like you to choose a gesture that you can use to anchor and re-center yourself whenever you need it."

Alicia adjusted her position in her chair, then stood up. She stretched her arms above her head and shouted, "Yes!"

I said, "Again. Two more times."

"Yes! Yes!"

She took her seat back in the circle.

I surveyed the smiles around the room. It was clear Alicia's energy was contagious.

I said, "This device of anchoring can serve you in many ways. For Alicia, obviously she may not want to literally stand up and shout in the middle of a meeting when she wants to re-center herself. But just as mentally practicing shooting free throws actually improves real-world scores, she can mentally picture herself standing and doing her anchor gesture, and it can still have the desired effect of re-centering her and helping her feel connected to Source. Her whole body will feel her visualizing the move."

I suggested a half-hour break and encouraged them to go in silence, to walk around the neighborhood, explore, and mull over what they had learned.

> *Note: Jot down any personal applications or questions that reading about the characters doing their work has raised for you while it is fresh in your mind.*

Your Turn 

Samuel returned from the half-hour walking break excited about what he had stumbled on. The group was grabbing tea and more snacks as he spoke.

"I didn't realize the Santa Fe River is just two blocks down the street! For someone who grew up overlooking the Hudson River, calling this one a river seems, well, ironic at best." He grinned. "It's only a few feet across, but I guess for the high desert, that's doing well. I realized, as I leaned over the bridge railing to watch the clear water making its way around the rocks and plants, it still tells the same relentless story that the Hudson does. People and beaver build dams, but the river pushes on despite obstacles. It *must* make its way downhill.

"I was hypnotized, feeling its force. It is not at all deterred by its rocks or its own small size. I took it as an omen for our little group. We came together rather quickly and effortlessly, and I can already feel our momentum, a kind of spiritual gravity pulling us along on our search."

I asked if he would like to go next. Everyone laughed because Samuel was the last one.

Samuel Discovers Sacred Ground

Samuel went from describing the auspiciousness of the river to jumping into his polarities. "The first polarity I identified is between my lifelong commitment to *tikkun olam*—to repair the world— versus the hunger I feel to delve into deep and complex subjects. Working as a philosophy professor provided plenty of the latter. With *tikkun*, I have always taken that as a calling to do very practical things in the world. Not everyone interprets it this way, but that is what I grew up with. Volunteering at the Santa Fe Food Depot is my current example. I don't know if that is the *right* way to interpret it. I do know some people are involved directly in fighting for justice issues, but this is the means I have chosen.

"A second polarity has more bite for me, more of a growing edge. It is my desire to find a deeper purpose for my life from today forward. It pushes against a seemingly unconscious fear of going deeper into the Mystery. I can feel the inherent tension. I am an apprehensive explorer.

"The backstory for me comes from the twelfth-century Kabbalah, Jewish mysticism. It counsels that a personal guide is needed to avoid the dangers inherent in mystical experiences. You may be more familiar with the shaman appointed to guide a person on a vision quest. So, my fears are not unique to me personally, or even to my tradition.

"I still carry a vivid image in my mind. A group of us toured through Mexico a few years ago. We went into a small village where they had pieces of contemporary sculpture on display. Some workers at a co-op were replicating the designs that some Benedictine monks had made. I saw on a wood panel a semi-abstract representation of a burning bush, and down at the bottom of the panel was a little pair of brass sandals, placed carefully to one side. The reference, of course, was to Moses, as told in Exodus, facing the burning bush, being instructed, 'Take off your shoes, for you stand on holy ground.'"

He paused in the silence.

Then Shirley half whispered, "We never know, do we, when we are standing on holy ground? We are *so* not attuned to that."

Alicia said, "We are all profoundly rooted in Spirit, if only we could recognize it."

I found myself feeling bemused that the others were engaging Samuel during his introduction of his characters. Normally interruptions can break the flow and I don't encourage them, but I decided to let this potential diversion continue, trusting the energy in the moment.

"Whenever we do inner character work," I said, "if we are touching deeply and authentically into our inner characters and our Liminal Space, and if we are fully attuned to the process, we do tread on holy ground. Liminal Space is the place where we draw nearest to touching into Source. This is our avenue not simply into finding creative alternatives with our polarized selves, but truly breaking through to *a third way*, engaging discovery, truly doing creation work."

I let the silence soak in, then asked Samuel if there was a polarity he would like to work with.

"I think I am willing, but I am not sure how to do it. My fear of the Mystery seems even foggier than a couple of the other foggy inner characters we have met here today."

I offered encouragement. "We can begin, and we can always stop if you wish."

"OK. I'll trust you to help me tiptoe in."

I set the stage. "Let's start by you choosing which chair is your Liminal Space. Go and sit there. Then tell us about the character who is wishing to find a deeper purpose for your life. Tell us what you see."

He shifted tentatively in his chair. "Her name is Bella. She wears a big hat. She is committed to making a difference in the world. And she is very outspoken. Much more even than I am. She has a clear sense of justice, and she is relentless. Maybe she was the one transfixed by the river just now."

I motioned for him to take Bella's chair. I wondered to myself if this was a personification of Bella Abzug, but I said nothing. Not mine to need to know.

"Hi. Thanks for inviting me here today. I am honored to be part of such a spirited circle of people. Samuel alluded to what I am about. I need, *we* need, to make more of a mark on the world before my—sorry—*our* days are done. Not a mark, really, it's just that I know I have some skills, some gifts, and I don't want those to go to waste. I do not want to die before they have all been shared. We have been in Santa Fe for over a decade, and I've come to terms with the reality that my formal teaching years as a philosophy professor needed to come to an end. But I know there is more. And I am clueless, as they say, about why it is so hard for me to see what's next."

Samuel returned to his Liminal Space chair. "Thank you, Bella, for sharing your dream for social justice with us. We are going to see whether someone in the other chair might shed some light on our search."

Samuel turned to face the other empty chair, then moved into it. "Finally" he said, "I have a chance to speak. My name is Sarah. The first Sarah dared to laugh when God, Elohim, promised her a son in her old age. The Sarah I am here today has some sort of deep understanding of the Mystery, while at the same time I am nervous about stepping closer. I sit in a tent, so far into the deep shade you cannot see what I am wearing. It could be ancient, it could be modern. I do know that I speak with confidence. I seem to be defending a boundary."

Samuel then suddenly pulled a pillow off a couch, moved the chair aside, and sat on the pillow on the floor. "Samuel thinks that I am confident. But actually that's not quite accurate. But I do indeed feel the need to defend a boundary. Bella seems to think that she should point the way to Samuel's new purpose for his life. But it's not that simple. When you ask the Holy One for direction, you need to be prepared to follow the word that comes. My ancient namesake Sarah's spontaneous response was to laugh when she heard that her new purpose, in her nineties, was to give birth to a son who would found a nation.

"I hear Bella's earnest desire to find a new purpose for Samuel's remaining years, and find that in social justice. And I am sure the Mystery honors that desire but..." Sarah trailed off.

After a minute of silence I gestured for Samuel to return to Liminal Space. "Samuel, take your strong and centered posture, feel deeply your connection not only to Bella and to Sarah, but also your connection to the Holy One as you know it."

Samuel did so and took several minutes in silence, his eyes closed, hands clasped at his heart. Then he reached down and slipped off his shoes and placed them carefully next to his chair. He stood, eyes still closed.

Then he took three cautious steps across the rug. He slowly opened his eyes. He was under a skylight. He raised his arms to the sky and said, "Here I am. I have no idea how to think about this. I sense there may be a third way beyond Bella's and Sarah's instincts, but I cannot see it. I am willing to take the first step into the unknown."

He returned to his Liminal Space chair and waited in the deep silence.

I waited a bit too. Normally at this point I would lead him through the anchoring gesture sequence, but I sensed that lifting his arms to the sky and addressing the Mystery *was* his gesture, and it would not need three repetitions. His body already "got it." I would mention this to him privately, just to confirm at a cognitive level.

I suggested a ten-minute break in silence. Samuel picked up his journal and headed outside.

The group drifted back and took their seats in the circle in silence. When everyone was settled, I said softly, "No words of mine can add anything to what we have experienced today. You each have been touched in a different way, both by your own work and by the others'. Some of what you have learned won't even come to your consciousness for several days, or perhaps longer. It won't be hurried.

"I encourage you to take some extra time with your journals tonight. Write slowly so that new awarenesses have a chance to surface. If any questions come up about your inner character work, or about how the process itself works, make a note in the margins and we can talk about them at a future meeting.

Two Homework Gifts – A Practice and a Book

I said to the group, "Now I would like to give you two homework assignments. I know this isn't graduate school, but I offer what might seem like extra work with complete confidence that you will grow significantly from taking this seriously. There are no tests or grades, just your precious life to shape.

"The first assignment is what I call simply a daily morning practice. Every spiritual tradition has some form of retreat and focusing. You know how the world clamors for your attention, and this is a way of coming back to what matters most to you. Every single day. At first it may seem onerous, but I promise you will soon notice a vacuum, or a hunger, when you miss a day. I suggest you make a photocopy of the following text and tape it into the front of your journal. I'm including it here with permission from Otto Scharmer as featured in his book *Theory U*.[4] You will find it most helpful at the outset to begin your practice with your liminal space anchoring gesture, the one you created and learned today." [See also Sourcebook for Chapter 4 for additional reflections by Kelly Wendorf of *Equus*.]

Note: Copy and attach in your journal

Your Turn

Daily Morning Practice by Otto Scharmer
(10–30 minutes)

- Rise early (before others), go to a place of silence that works for you (a place in nature is great, but you also may find other places that work for you), and allow your inner knowing to emerge. [Keep liminal space alive by not opening your phone.]

- Use a ritual that connects you with your Source: this can be a meditation, prayer, or simply an intentional silence that you enter into with an open heart and open mind.

- Remember what it is that has brought you to the place in life where you are right now: Who is your Self? What is your Work? What are you here for?

- Make a commitment to what it is that you want to be in service of. Focus on the outcome that you want to serve (the larger whole).

- Focus on what you want to accomplish (or be in service of) on this day that you are beginning right now.

- Feel the appreciation that you are given the opportunity to live the life that you have right now. Empathize with all of those who have never had all of the opportunities that led you to the place you are now. Feel the responsibility that comes with those opportunities, the responsibility that you have to others, to all other beings, to all of nature—even to the universe.

- Ask for help so that you don't lose your way or get sidetracked. Your way forward is a journey that only you can discover. The essence of that journey is a gift that can come into the world only through you, your presence, your best future self. But you can't do it alone. That's why you ask for help.

For the second assignment I recommended that the group try a book club format. I had taken the liberty of ordering each person a copy of *The Essentials of Theory U* by Otto Scharmer.[5] I distributed copies to the group.

> *Note: I suggest that for fast delivery, you order this book from Amazon—or seek out your favorite source. Reading it concurrently with chapter 5 will deepen your understanding.*

Your Turn

I explained where we were going with this next subject. "We have learned to listen more clearly to our past through inner characters. Next, Otto will teach us a method to listen to our future and what it may be whispering or calling us to.

"When we meet again, we can discuss each of these essential actions that Otto teaches: open mind, open heart, open will. We will also be introduced to connecting with Source, coming from a slightly different perspective. Keep your journal handy as you read and notice both what sounds most promising for you and what aspects seem most challenging."

Shirley said, "Listening to the future. I'm intrigued. I notice that Otto's book is only about a hundred and fifty pages, but shall we give ourselves two weeks before our next meeting, so we have time to digest it?"

"Agreed," someone said, and several "ayes" echoed.

Highlights

Best Practices – There are positive steps to take as you begin this journey that will help you throughout and beyond:

- **Establish Norms for a Group** – It's a good idea to establish together a short list of group norms and behaviors, such as the following:
  - Confidentiality is sacred.
  - Give no advice.
  - Never interrupt.
  - Listen to yourself too.

- **Use a Journal** – A journal is an invaluable companion for this work. Wherever this journey takes you, your daily recordings of insights and experiences will greatly enhance your discoveries. When you first hear something, it means one thing. But when you review it later, it can mean something quite different. Your journal will help you bridge and then build on those gaps in understanding.

- **Embrace Liminal Space** – This term refers to a state of being between different worlds, a threshold. It's an uncomfortable space we tend to avoid. A major alteration of your life as usual can put you into liminal space, where you feel in between and uncertain. While it may be disguised as a crisis, liminal space is an invitation to become a new person. It's a gift, a time when we can break a habit and try a new way of doing and being. Liminal space is also the secret sauce of listening. From within, our own state of liminal space can serve as a moderator between the voices in our head pulling us in different directions. It can help us see things from an authentic place and make choices.

- **Create an Anchoring Gesture** – An anchoring gesture is a physical gesture, such as a hand motion or stance, you create that helps you connect to the state of liminal space.

Here you can feel your most balanced and strongest self to make decisions and feel centered and connected to Source.

- **Make Daily Morning Practice a Habit** – This format suggested for your journal brings you back, every single day, to where you are focusing your attention. Doing it first thing allows you to reset priorities before the world starts shouting its distractions and demands.

Polarity Issues That Shape the Journey – Our six characters exhibited a range of forces/personalities/voices in their heads that pull them in sometimes opposing directions, making it difficult for the characters to make choices and plans that reflect their true selves and calling. The whole point of our inner character work here is *not* to choose between the polarities, nor to "compromise." **The genius of Liminal Space is that this wisest inner voice allows us to create a *third way*.** Examples the characters uncovered include the following:

- **Independence vs. Collaboration (Shirley)**
  Should she keep operating like the Lone Ranger—self-reliant and solo—or learn to share purpose and effort with others, offering help and receiving it in return? What will be her third way?
- Work Identity vs. Creative Flow (Himari)
  Should she continue to lead with her identity as a medical professional, or loosen her grip and allow space for play, artistry, and rest? What will be her third way?
- Collapse/**Sloth** vs. Rebuilding Rhythm and **New Structure** (Martina)
  Should she surrender to exhaustion and disengagement, or gently begin to shape a new daily structure—one that honors both her need for rest and her desire for contribution? What will be her third way?
- Striving vs. Joyful Ease (Paul)

Should he stay focused on achieving meaningful impact, or give himself permission to play, laugh, and let life unfold without an outcome in mind? What will be his third way?

- **Achievement**/Control through Achievement vs. Discovery through Meaning (Alicia)

  Should she try to manage uncertainty through high performance, or begin to trust a slower, more personal process of finding what matters now? What will be her third way?

- Conviction vs. Open Will (Samuel)

  Should he continue to pursue his twin passions—justice and spiritual insight—with conviction, or allow himself to surrender into the unknown, trusting what wants to emerge next. What will be his third way?

Exercises: Making It Real and Specific

- **Action Step:** If you're working within a group, then as a group, generate a list of group norms or consult the <u>Sourcebook for Chapter 4</u> at the back of this book and adapt the recommended list of norms for your own use. Additionally, a "Prime Time Facilitator's Guide" provides a weekly plan for your use (see <u>Sourcebook for Chapter 4</u>).

- **Action Step:** Make a copy of the Daily Morning Practice and add it into your journal. For those readers who have delayed starting a journal, now is the time!

- **Journal Reflection:** At the end of each character's segment of working on their polarity issues, jot down any issues their work has raised for you. What questions are you curious to pursue? Did what the characters uncover stimulate your own memories or questions? Take notes so these glimmers are not lost before you read on to see what happens next.

- **Action Step:** Do your own inner character work. The method illustrated in this chapter with the chairs is a challenging exercise to do at home on your own. It can be done successfully, but it may take several tries to catch on and find your rhythm. The Sourcebook for Chapter 4 (see "DIY Inner Character Work") includes detailed instructions to supplement the text of this chapter. After you have read the account of our six characters as they go through the process, I encourage you to set aside at least an hour where you will not be interrupted. Follow the prompts in the Sourcebook and I promise you will learn about yourself at a whole different level than reading about the experience of others can ever accomplish.

Prime Time Milestones

Take a breath. Pause. What are you noticing at this point in your journey? As you reflect, write your thoughts in your journal.

Insight. I see something new…

Sample response: *I carry many parts of myself—some helpful, some outdated. I can listen to them without letting them run the show.*

Shift. I feel something changing…

Sample response: *I feel more compassionate toward myself. Less critical. Curious about what else might be in me.*

Step. I'm ready to try…

Sample response: *I'll name one "inner voice" that tends to take over, and practice asking it kindly to step aside.*

CHAPTER 5

A Quest to Hear the Future

What sets us apart as human beings is that we can connect to the emerging future. That is who we are. I was lighter and free… part [of myself] drew me into the future— into a world waiting for me to bring it into reality.[6]

—OTTO SCHARMER

Pausing to Take Stock

We studied our inner characters in chapter 4 so we could grow more aware of our various internal voices and begin to integrate unhelpful conflicts. In short, the practice of inner character work helps us get out of our own way. Now we turn to ask, "What's next?" for our lives. If we think about chapter 4 as looking inside and looking back, chapter 5 looks forward into our future.

This chapter offers us an alternative to being guided by our past. It gives us a framework and a series of practices for listening to our own emerging future. With the world changing faster than ever— and disruptions and breakdowns accelerating—looking forward is the key to living adaptive, creative lives. If you are reading this book, you have probably already chosen action over tuning out and checking out. Chapters 4 through 9 give you specific methodologies for stepping creatively and adaptively into the future you choose to create.

You will find common threads running through chapters 4 and 5. Liminal space and your capacity to connect with Source lie at the heart of both inner character work and the framework we spell out in this chapter. You can enhance your ability to consult your deeper wisdom and connect with something larger both by having conversations with your inner characters from the Liminal Space chair and also by adopting the practices we will discuss in this chapter. These practices include open mind, open heart, open will, and what we call *presencing*. These will all help you learn to listen to your own emerging future. As we join the group at Alicia's house, the meaning of these at first rather abstract terms will become apparent.

The Challenge of Attention

I told the group as we began, "The single most important thing I want you to grasp in this coming session is that *where our attention originates* makes *all* the difference. Where our attention lies is a vital determiner of our path, and yet hardly anyone is aware of the power of this awareness. I know this sounds abstract, so a metaphor may help.

"In the book I suggested to you by Otto Scharmer from MIT, *The Essentials of Theory U*, he offers the analogy of the artist's blank canvas. Typically, we as observers pay attention to *what* the artist creates—the painting. Or we may focus on *how* the art is made—the process, such as Van Gogh's brushwork. But what is going on with the artist while the canvas is still blank? If we ask *where* the artist's actions are *coming from*, we often cannot really say. The artist cannot always say. What holds that artist's attention regarding the future of her canvas? Research into creativity certainly describes part of the story, but what is the overall state of mind of the artist?"

Shirley chimed in. "I would ask the question as, 'Where is her attention focused before she moves the brush or her palette knife?'"

"Exactly," I said. "What *sources* does she draw on? What is the quality of her attention? What sort of person does she bring into her studio on a certain day? Or, you could ask, what sort of person—i.e., quality of attention—did Van Gogh bring to the canvas on a given day. Or Camille Pissarro? Winslow Homer? We cannot know the minds of these historical figures, but I hope this shines a light on how their quality of attention can change the course of their action, moment by moment. We are speaking of the artist, but keep your interest also focused on what *you yourself* do moment by moment."

"It's all so invisible, so abstract," Martina said, groaning.

"Yes, it seems that way because we just haven't paid enough attention to how this works," I said. "But we can get sharper on this. It is a learnable skill. Stay with me."

I went on to explain that Scharmer distinguishes two different sources of our learning. First—the one we take for granted—is learning from the past and learning about the past.

"The second source," I said, "came to me as a surprise the first time I heard it. I'm grateful to Scharmer for bringing it to our attention. It's *learning from the future*. Specifically, 'learning by sensing and actualizing emerging future possibilities' is how he puts it.[7] For the artist, it means consciously—and unconsciously—sensing the emerging future possibilities for the painting."

Alicia asked, "Do you mean listen for the *painting's* own future? Instead of thinking, will people like this painting when it's done, or will I have this ready in time for the show, or what if the public isn't buying saturated colors these days, yada yada, the brain chatters on?"

I nodded. "We have the opportunity, and, I suggest, *the responsibility*, to learn and to practice this new skill of listening for our own emerging future every day."

"So," Alicia asked, "are you suggesting—am I hearing you correctly—that we sit in our Liminal Space chair when we contemplate where our life is going, or could be going?"

"Precisely, Alicia. That's the thread we're following. And it's not just contemplating *about* our future, it's actually learning how to listen directly for what the future possibilities want us to bring into the daily reality of our lives."

"Wait a minute," said Paul. "That last distinction is a little subtle, even for me. You're suggesting we actually listen to *the voice* of the future?"

"In a way, yes. Remember when you each were doing your liminal space work, and you had a thought—a resolution to a dilemma, an insight—that just sort of came to you?"

"Yes!" said Alicia. "It was loud and clear."

"You see, you have already experienced a taste of what I am talking about. We're just giving it some new labels and metaphors, giving it a larger frame of reference."

Martina frowned. "You're quoting Otto Scharmer. The book says he is at MIT! But this all sounds a little woo-woo to me."

"Otto and his colleagues have investigated the work of some of the world's leading cognitive scientists, as well as esteemed followers of meditation practices from ancient civilizations. They found those tracks actually cross and overlap. If you think about it, that's not too surprising. Some very smart people have been saying for a long time that the mind is capable of a lot more than we realize. I am confident this is one of those instances. I encourage your healthy skepticism, and let's keep going so you can experience it for yourself."

Samuel Reflects on Disruptions—and Opportunity

Samuel said, "The importance of this skill, or this practice, is slowly dawning on me. Never before in human history has there been a thirty-year window of opportunity to live productively beyond the point where we let go of the constraints of our professional careers. This much is clear: The future will not equal the past. It makes sense to me that we should base the design of our new life on the emerging future, rather than on a past where our assumptions may no longer apply. This is not an either/or polarity, it is a matter of emphasis, but above all, I can see that an open mind—Otto's term—toward future possibilities is required of us."

"And paying attention," Himari said. "Paying attention to our attention!" She did a sweep of her arms and brought her fingertips together.

Alicia attempted to summarize what she was hearing so far: "It is better to be shapers of our own future rather than unconscious victims of our past."

Martina added, "Most of us wouldn't drive a gas-guzzling 1950s car today, so why would we live in a 1950s-designed retirement? Marie, are there other metaphors that will help us understand?"

"Yes. Otto says that one reason this question of how we attend to our attention isn't well understood is that there simply hasn't been a detailed enough map of the territory. On our phones, when we search the map for directions, if it comes up showing both 'here' and 'there' on the same screen, we reflexively know to pinch the screen to come in closer, so we can see the corners where we are to turn. Today we can zoom in closer and examine the working parts of how we source our attention. Shall we zoom in?"

Open Mind

I began in familiar territory. I suggested to the group that they had probably all had the experience where they are listening to a conversation and they become aware that they are actually formulating their own response, rather than really listening. We do this because we think we already know what the other person is going to say. Otto uses the term *downloading* to characterize this. We download our assumptions about what the person is talking about, and on top of that, we frequently download our own response, one that we've given many times before in similar discussions. The net result is that no one really learns anything new. We just exchange downloaded information and opinions.

"This is what makes most cocktail parties *so* boring," quipped Alicia.

"This sounds like the first kind of learning," Martina suggested. "At best, it is learning from the past."

"So what we need to do instead," I continued, "is to practice coming to each conversation with an open mind. And slowly break our habit of downloading. This is tricky because our minds, our whole selves, prefer the comfort zone of things we already know, things that don't upset our certainty. It's normal to have a don't-rock-the-boat reaction to new information. It's been a survival skill. But it doesn't always serve us as well when the world is changing as rapidly as it is now."

I added some wider context and explained how at a societal level, none of us want schools that prevent our children from learning the life skills they will need for the future, and we don't want healthcare systems that treat just symptoms, not causes. Ultimately, we don't want industrial systems that are at odds with the planetary systems that life depends on. But we still struggle with ways to change all this.

Shirley said, "This fits perfectly with what Samuel just said. We really *cannot afford* to design our retirement lives only drawing on what we already know. I for one do not want to end up living the past for the next thirty years."

I gave a thumbs up. "Cultivating your open mind means learning to see with fresh eyes, and to intentionally suspend your assumptions and mental habits. Doing this gives us the possibility of not reenacting old patterns that no longer serve us."

"Is this like critical thinking?" Samuel asked.

"Yes and no. It is like critical thinking in that you are looking for alternatives, not just taking what you hear as the only way. But it is unlike it in that with critical thinking, we often bring an already-known alternative to the table. With open mind, you hold everything more lightly, holding your mind open to possibilities that you cannot even imagine in that moment. In critical thinking, we sometimes rely on our *voice of judgment*. That is Otto's term for the major enemy of open mind. If voice of judgment were an inner character, it would wear a frown and it would try to convince us that it knows better than we do. It's the person at the cocktail party where, after they speak, the conversation just stops, and people turn to slip away and refill their glasses. Our goal is to minimize the ways that voice of judgment *limits* what we can explore."

I offered an illustration. "Peter Senge, a mentor of mine since 1990, is also from MIT. He introduced the image of watching yourself from the balcony. It takes practice to be both fully engaged in a conversation and, at the same time, watching from the balcony in your mind to notice how you are thinking, acting, reacting. You might say that this is what our Liminal Space chair does for us—it observes both what our other inner characters are saying, thinking, and feeling, and Liminal Space also notices how it itself is processing the whole interaction."

I watched for nodding around the circle to make sure they were beginning to understand, then I suggested we move on to the second skill and personal practice, open heart.

Open Heart

"Let's step back for a moment," I began. "*Resistance* is a name for what keeps us in the same-old, same-old. Resistance is voice of judgment in action. Resistance is kind of an inner character of its own, and it also operates through many of our other inner characters. Its self-appointed job is to keep us safe. But it often has an overly protective sense of what keeping us safe actually requires. In times of change, when we need to be highly adaptive, resistance can be a formidable enemy of our true best interests. Think back to your own inner character conversations. Resistance was working hard to guard you from your beckoning future."

"Amen!" Paul boomed.

"The form resistance takes with open heart is what we call the *voice of cynicism*. In an attempt to protect us from our natural vulnerability, it does its best to distance us from the reality in front of us. 'To feel less is to not be hurt,' it tells us. That is how resistance sums it up."

"Guilty as charged," Samuel murmured.

"But, Samuel, we don't actually need to *feel* guilty when we catch ourselves here. It's just a human, self-protective reaction."

I continued. "If we want to learn from the future, one vital feature of doing so is to cultivate the ability to truly see how things seem from another person's perspective. This is empathy. This is open heart. If you will allow me to overgeneralize for a moment, we already know that women are lots better at empathy than men tend to be, so I won't prolong this point. If we do notice cynicism creeping into our thoughts or feelings, the invitation is to pause and ask where we might be feeling threatened and what we are trying to ward off. We can spot some inner characters having this conversation. Frequently the danger isn't all that resistance would like us to believe."

Alicia said, "In the corporate world there's usually someone in the circle who plays the cynic. Looking back, I think I intuitively knew they were acting or speaking out of self-protection, so I tried to ignore it. But I also sometimes got defensive and felt like I needed to prove that I was not naïve or soft. I never liked feeling like I had to play their game. I'm grateful, now that I am retired, that I can let all that go. I'm sure I'll still run into cynics, but now I don't have to try to impress them or get along. I can determine my own path through the noise."

"Tell us about open will," Martina said. "What is that about? It's not as apparent to me as the first two."

Open Will

I took Martina's invitation to move on. "Open will, indeed," I said. "It will be easiest to start with its primary enemy, which is fear itself. Going forward into the unknown—which is inevitable in Prime Time—it's only natural that the whole process would make us nervous. At some point, though, opportunity always comes sooner than we feel we are ready, and we must take a leap of faith. I know you understand this already, conceptually, but at the raw experience level, it seems to keep coming back to bite us.

"I read recently about a woman who, in her seventies, went to Africa for the first time. She was volunteering at a wildlife center in Namibia. As you can imagine —even though she was fulfilling a childhood dream—the night before the flight and when the plane landed at her destination, she was thinking, 'What am I *doing?*' Open will includes the conscious decision, again and again, to enter the state of letting go. It's feeling the fear and letting go to move ahead anyway.

"So far this is nothing you haven't heard. You experienced this in your inner character scenarios. Open will goes deeper. As you learn to sit in your Liminal Space chair more and more frequently, and connect to Source more deeply, there is the possibility of a more enveloping *letting go* that you allow when you tune into that greater wisdom. You lean forward to try to hear the future. We have touched on the mystical flavor this sometimes has, and that is where open will is even more important. Think back to Samuel's work in our circle, how it would have felt for Moses to hear, at the burning bush, 'Take off your sandals.' Our instinct is to flee back to what we fully understand. Open will says, 'I am willing, in the face of potentially terrifying unknowns.'

"But it goes even deeper than that. So far, what we've established could be describing steep downhill skiing on a mountain you've never been on before. Open will asks us to do it with a brand-new untried style of skis, without having seen a map of the ski runs. It is what you need when you decide to leave your old self and squeeze through the eye of a needle—without baggage—to the larger self that you are invited to become."

"This feels like leaping across a chasm far wider than Alicia's rug," Martina said softly.

"Well put," I said. "It adds a whole new dimension to 'faith leap,' but I have found that, oddly, it seems to add a certain reassurance at the same time. Here's how."

I explained that the "Self with a capital S," as Otto uses the term, is you when you are connecting with Source, engaging with the greater wisdom of your unknown future. It is this Self who is invited into a new work, a new calling, a new way of being in the world that you have never known before. This is a calling worthy of the next twenty or thirty years of your life.

"We experience this Self as having an ongoing connection with our highest future possibility, and this is the Self that is equipped to live in the most life-giving way in an emerging world. I know this still sounds abstract, but stay with me.

"Hand in hand with letting go, we find the opportunity for *letting come*. We could spend a whole day on this, but put simply, letting come is a new level of faith in our emerging future that wants to manifest through us. It may feel like a huge step, but it is also quite simple. Now, how are you all taking this in?"

Martina said, "I think I am following you, but it does still seem pretty abstract."

"Martina, can you recall, at the gut level, how it felt when you decided to leap across the chasm of Alicia's rug?" I waited for her to get in touch with that recent memory.

"Yes, and I think I see what you mean now. I knew it was just a rug, of course, but I really felt at a deep level that something I trusted in was asking me to take a huge leap into my own future, and that future, on the other side of the chasm, would be a whole lot different from anything I had experienced so far. I felt both confident in my choice and felt some trepidation, both in the same moment."

"Yes," I said, "and we could feel some of that as we witnessed you. Can you say now how this relates to open will?"

"I would say—now that you've given us the framework to think about it—that I consciously and confidently threw myself into my future. I opened my will to the future, and I trusted in something I could not explain. That's my explanation of open will."

She laughed. Her delight was apparent.

Some Implications for Open Will

Shirley said, "I see all sorts of implications spinning in my head. Letting go, I suspect, means being willing to let go of my identities: competent professional manager, consultant, even artist. Intellectually, I can imagine that a new identity will emerge down the new path, but letting go of the old, familiar, reassuring identities is…well, yes…it is triggering some fear. Fear of the unknown, I guess. A little voice says, 'What if I don't find a new identity?' Or worse: 'What if it's one I don't like?'" She glanced around the room and saw several reassuring nods.

She continued. "It took me years to get used to thinking of myself as an individual contributor even while I was officially a manager at an organization. Now I have to go through that again? On the other hand, what are my alternatives? I'm not satisfied with making art. It's fun. It's OK. But it's not tapping into a lot that I have to offer. So what would hanging on to it as an identity actually gain me? I suppose that embracing the unknown—this open will—could be oddly reassuring."

Samuel chimed in. "It has taken me a decade to let go of *professor*. As I've opened my hands and released what that meant to me, it is bewildering, and it makes me nervous to wonder, 'Who will I be now?' Trusting in that possibility seems to be part of this open will."

"It's the daily encounters that sometimes bother me the most," Himari added. "You meet someone, and they want to know what you do. Even if they guess you are retired, they want to hear about an engaging hobby or an exciting recent trip. It's the way people seem to need to make conversation. I'm guilty of it too. I'm not quite ready to ask, at that first encounter, 'What are the most compelling emerging futures that you are considering these days?' Yet I find it really lame to answer them, 'Oh I used to practice medicine,' or 'I used to help run a hospital.' It invites them to tell their favorite doctor story, and that's not what I want to talk about."

Martina said, "I'm with you. I can assure you that saying I was in state government is even more boring and predictable than doctor stories. I can see that letting go into a new identity will be a necessary step for me, in order to have something that I'm excited to get up for in the morning. I am also really challenged by the discipline of open mind. My work has always been, well, predictable, even though I had to deal with unpredictable problems every day. There were always—dare I say—*bureaucratic* ways to deal with them. I'm going to need all your help in learning to reawaken my curiosity and suspend my voice of judgment."

"It will be an ongoing challenge for all of us, I expect," Alicia said. "For what it's worth, you are not alone, Martina."

I said to the group, "Let's now consider a common term and a mental model we take for granted."

What Is "The Future"?

"We need to revisit this concept of *future*," I said. "We assume we know what that means, but Otto Scharmer says we have a special relationship with the future. He reminds us that we usually imagine the future to be about a different place than now, where *different people than us* do whatever it is that they do, sometime a long time from now. But, instead of that usual image, *our emerging future is personal.*

"A future possibility looks to me, me personally, because it depends on me in order for it to come into reality. Otto recounts that innovators, entrepreneurs, and social entrepreneurs think like this, but they seldom talk about it. It is time for many more of us to start talking about it.

"We must acknowledge our intimate relationship with these possibilities. They are not abstract. They are subtle, but they are concrete. Otto refers to a body of resonance that we can connect with specifically at the heart level. Some think of this as intuition. Some people call it attuning to a vibration. Our heads grope with words, but the experience itself can be palpable.

"Please keep this up-close-and-personal definition of the future in mind while we delve into one more significant concept."

Presencing

"I would like to introduce the concept of presencing for you to ponder," I said to the group. "I know it can seem quite abstract at first, so let me start with two approaches. First, some definitions, and then I will offer a metaphor.

"*Presencing* is 'meeting the emerging future in the present moment.' It is the 'innate human ability to *sense and actualize* our highest future potential.'[8] Presencing is what can happen when you have moved through embodying the three 'steps'—open mind, open heart, and open will. It is a word for when you 'connect with the Source of the highest future possibility to bring it into the now.' It's the movement where 'we approach our Self from the emerging future.' And 'perception begins to happen from a future possibility that depends on us to bring it into reality.' The beauty of it is 'we step into our real being, who we really are, our authentic self.'"[9]

"You're right, Marie," said Samuel, "that's pretty abstract, even for me. You're quoting Otto Scharmer, and it seems to me he is trying really hard not to use theological language because that can be such a trigger for people these days. Am I right?"

"I can't speak for his motivations, but that appears to me to be what is happening. However that doesn't make the experiences he is pointing to any less valid. Is that fair to say?"

"Yes, I suppose so," Samuel said. "I think I'll just paraphrase your definition's language for my own use. I hear you saying that *presencing is when you hear Source trying to coax you into your own best future.*"

"Well put! Thanks for that, Samuel," Martina said immediately.

Himari chimed in. "It's pretty mystical, but so is a person who recovers from advanced cancer when there is no known medical reason for that to occur. Both say to me that there is a lot we don't understand yet, but it is still real. I like the idea of a Greater Wisdom helping me to steer toward my highest calling. Especially now that I am no longer practicing medicine and have no idea what to do next."

"I appreciate your willingness to tolerate so much ambiguity and work with it, Himari. Whenever we are during a major transition, it's particularly helpful to give voice among friends to this kind of stretch. Verbalizing subjects like what Source or Greater Wisdom might mean to us helps us all find our new ground to stand on."

"Now," I said, "let's try the second approach: a metaphor. The more I have studied what Otto and his insightful colleagues have written, the more I have realized it is like riding a bicycle. Let me explain.

"Can you remember when you first learned to ride a bike? A nearby grownup could explain, or they could guide you. But no amount of words could prepare you for that magical moment when, instead of your lurching as they ran alongside or you were wobbling on training wheels, suddenly you were balancing. Your body found that special secret combination where everything coordinated to keep you upright and you sailed down the street. And, as they say, once learned, it always comes back to you.

"Presencing," I continued, "cannot be adequately explained verbally ahead of your experiencing it. The value of reading others' accounts of it is that, once your 'bicycle' balances you in your own experience of presencing, you recognize it from the descriptions you have read."

A Personal Example of Presencing

"Let me offer a personal example, if I may," I said, "to give you a better sense of this."

"Please do," Paul said with a smile and a groan. "I need something concrete."

"When the idea to write this book came to me, I had been preparing the soil, so to speak, though I did not think of it that way at the time. Because I knew the principles that we have discussed in this chapter, I was working at keeping an open mind as I agonized over what to do with my life (at the age of eighty, with a decade or two to go, or so I hoped). I started noticing how much empathy I felt for my peers who were also asking these 'What now?' questions. Call this open heart. Then at some point I let go into whatever might be in store for me, with absolutely no idea what that could be.

"This letting go is not a rare experience, when you think about it. Alcoholics Anonymous holds this as a core principle. Several traditions teach, 'Let go and let God.' 'Leap of faith' is a common phrase in our vocabulary. And creativity studies suggest that after agonizing over a problem, when we go for a long walk we forget about the problem in order for the answer to finally make its appearance.

"*Presencing*, however, makes a useful distinction, and this became apparent when I glimpsed the possibility of my book. In presencing, we experience 'a *deeply personal sense* of a future potential.' Remember how we redefined 'future'? Our focus is on what seems about to unfold from the very moment at hand, what is present for us in the here and now. It's not some rumination about 'someday.' It's not daydreaming. At that point we can ignore the impulse, or we can act on it. If we act, we begin to feel a deepening sense that this is what we are here to do. And 'once established, this sense does not go away.' Our Self—the highest form of who we uniquely are—is *connected to* this future potential.[10]

"With the idea for this book, I could suddenly see, that afternoon gazing at the purple light on the Sangre de Cristo Mountains, how all the major pieces would fit together. How both my training in the 1990s in inner character work and in presencing in the early 2000s, my decades of leading small groups in leadership development, and many additional pieces, all could come together for the purpose of helping my peers find their new calling after their professional careers ended. *All of this* seemed to be saying to me, 'We can make this real, we can make it happen, and we must, somehow, do so.'

"Notice there is also a very tangible and specific skill or practice at work here. At the end of our work on inner characters in chapter 4, I introduced you to a daily practice. It *pays attention* each day to that connection with our higher Self—this is what enables us to eventually tune in to our calling. You might characterize it as going to a 'hearing gym' every day to teach and train ourselves how to listen more deeply. Daily practice 'helps us to sense resonances that are critical for navigating our path forward into uncharted territory.'"[11]

Shirley leaned forward. "Can I attempt a summary? Are you saying that presencing is regularly staying attuned to Source and to Self for the specific purpose of listening for our calling?"

"Yes," I said, "and with the purpose of listening for how our own immediate future is beckoning for us to create that particular future."

An Abundance of Resources

I suggested to the group a wealth of readily available information for learning more about presencing. (They are also listed in "Additional Reading.") Most recently, Otto Scharmer and co-author Katrin Kaufer published *Presencing: 7 Practices for Transforming Self,*

Society, and Business. Earlier, Otto and his colleagues Peter Senge, Joseph Jaworski, and Betty Sue Flowers broke ground with their fascinating book called *Presence: Human Purpose and the Field of the Future.* It recounts stories of their interviews with a collection of profoundly insightful people. You can also read chapters on presencing in Otto's foundational work *Theory U.*

"Let me leave you with the vision, possibility, and promise, that as you move repeatedly through open mind, open heart, and open will, you will go 'through the eye of the needle,' where none of your baggage will fit through, and you will start to experience presencing as you contemplate your possible future."

Alicia quipped, "Got it! So, to paraphrase a famous Supreme Court justice, 'We'll know it when we see it.'"

"Thank you, each of you, for your succinct paraphrasing. I know you will be fine with this as you ease into it with hope and intention."

A New Spiritual Practice

"Now," I said, "we come around full circle to where we began this conversation. We talked about where we place our attention, then we touched on the possibility of listening to our immediate emerging future. Now that we have been introduced to the disciplines we call open mind, open heart, and open will, and looked at presencing as a practice, I would like to take it a step further into action. I propose a challenge: *make a spiritual practice out of listening to your emerging future.*

"Let me lay out the foundational pieces, then we can discuss what this might look like in our daily lives." Then I proceeded to go through the steps of such a practice.

- Start in liminal space: Activate your physical anchor gesture and enter deep silence.
- Suspend judgment: Let go of preconceived ideas (open mind) about what should happen or how things should be.

- Direct your attention: Shift focus from reactive patterns (our past noise) toward signals of what wants to become.
- Notice if inner characters resist: Acknowledge them, note them briefly in a journal, and offer them a sabbatical or day off.
- Cultivate open will: Surrender control and trust the unfolding itself, allowing intuition and inner knowing—Source itself—to guide you.
- Listen: The opening of *The Rule of St. Benedict* (from 530 CE) says, "Listen with the ear of your heart."
- Keep a journal at hand: Record thoughts, impulses, and insights. Revisit these at a later time to gain new perspective.

I gave the group time to absorb the pattern, knowing it was a review but that they may hear it in a new way this time around.

After thinking about it, Martina said, "I'm struggling with this. I've been doing something like this with my morning practice, and I notice an inner character keeps showing up. I call her Captain Strategic Planning. I actually used to teach my staff quite a bit of strategic thinking, trying to make our bureaucracy run more effectively. So this whole conversation, Marie, has me feeling pulled in two directions."

Himari spoke up. "It's no surprise you would feel that way. I do too. We both ran large organizations where our decisions affected a lot of lives. The beauty for us of studying this material *now*, in our 'golden years,'" she laughed, "is that we have nearly infinite freedom to experiment. What's the worst thing that can happen?"

"Wow!" Martina gasped. "I hadn't even noticed how different it is now. I mean, I know I'm not still working there, but my psyche apparently hasn't quite caught up. I am still as on guard as ever, thinking I must discern the right answer at every turn."

Paul spoke up. "This invitation to us at this point in life, this frontier that all of us, as retired professionals, as boomers, holds so much potential, it takes my breath away if I let myself think about it.

I am beginning to see that a daily practice of listening to my future whispering to me is huge! I wish I were a writer or a poet so I could say it as big as I mean."

Martina was gesturing with her hands, trying to find words. She finally managed to blurt it out: "It just came together for me! Letting go and letting come. I *see* what it means. When I sit in the silence, I can let go of all the old *musts* that I carried for so long, and then I am free, like…what…like an empty soup kettle, to let come whatever new future I am being invited into. This is a dumb example, but my tennis coach used to try to teach me a rhythm: bounce/hit/bounce/hit. Let go/let come. Let go/let come. It's all one dance."

Samuel turned to Martina. "I can see that the tension I'd never noticed in your face has just relaxed."

"And your whole body," Alicia added. "It looks more…more fluid. I'd say your body is catching up with your arrival in Prime Time. Congratulations."

Samuel said, "As I have tried my own feeble attempts at morning practice, I also notice that as I let go of small assumptions, those 'musts' as you called them, it seems to be freeing space in my head to notice new things. This seems trivial, but I am beginning to notice the sound of the birds outside my window. Usually, I am just so in my head with an idea, I hardly hear such things. But I am also more aware of—it's just a felt sense—that there really is an actual path opening up for me. A path where I can share my years of knowledge in some new way. Is that what you mean, Marie, when you call it discerning our future?"

"Yes, it is," I confirmed. "What you are sensing is one of the clues. One of the hints. More will come as you make time for the intentional silence. More will become clear as you take action steps as well, as we will discuss in a couple of weeks. I'd like to share a story. It will serve as a metaphor about the path you just mentioned."

The Metaphor of the Cross-Country Wilderness Hike

"The summer before my senior year of high school," I said, "two friends and I went backpacking in the Sierra Nevada in California. If you start on the east side, near Nevada, the slope of the range is quite steep, and you can get above timberline in one good day of hiking. I love it up there because you can see forever. It is nothing like walking along through a thick forest.

"On our third morning we decided to leave our backpacks in camp after breakfast and scale a nearby peak. Well, it was more like an exaggerated hill above the trail, as it turned out, but it felt like a peak. When you are seventeen, as you probably recall. anything is possible. We put our topo maps into our daypacks, grabbed water and snacks, and started up across the short grass, crossing vast flattened white granite boulders, making our way up, with no trail and no precise idea of where we were going. Just heading up toward the high rise to the south. An hour later we crested what we thought was the peak we had been aiming for. We stopped for a sip of water and looked back down. The trail and our small tent were no longer visible. Then we turned back around and saw there was another peak above us. The rise we were standing on at that moment had masked the fact that there was a higher peak behind it.

"We consulted our topo map and realized that our current destination was merely a shoulder to the unnamed peak we thought we had aimed for. We huddled and decided on two actions. First, my companion wanted to name the unmarked peak after her boyfriend. OK, we agreed, that's easy. That night we'd find a pen in our gear and write it on the map. Gene Mountain. The thrills of high school. Second, we agreed that we still wanted to break camp after lunch and continue along the marked trail toward a lake that was our final destination. It was time to turn around and return to camp.

"As we took a few steps down, one of us asked, 'Where exactly are we aiming? We can't see our tent from here.'

"We pulled the map out again and carefully positioned it, with the aid of our compass—we were skilled Girl Scouts, after all. We lined up the map with a major peak to the north and another to the southwest. We had camped at an elbow in the trail, so we could place that on the map as well. Our consensus was quick. 'We're going that way,' we said as we pointed north-northwest down the slope. We stopped every ten minutes to check that we were on course, and eventually our tent came into view just where we expected it. Back at the tent for lunch, we celebrated our adventure with a chocolate bar.

"Samuel, here are the parallels I want to draw to the trek we are each on today. First, we are walking in unmarked territory. We have chosen to leave the marked trail of consumer society's 'retirement.'

"Second, we are above timberline, so we can see farther than we could when we had a forest of career restrictions crowding us. And we can walk in nearly any direction, thanks to the acknowledged good fortune of our savings, pensions, and free time. This represents an enormous freedom, as several of you have noted.

"Third, we are trained to read the signs around us. Generally, we know up from down, so there's little chance of walking in exactly the wrong direction. We have core values and a sense of right and wrong that guide us, usually unconsciously. But we are also learning to read the subtle signs, with our open mind, open heart skills. This is presencing, triangulating off distant peaks such as our Superpowers, which we will discuss next.

"Finally, our daily practice represents that stopping every ten minutes to consult the map. Our journal and our weekly discussions here also inform our cross-country journey. Before long, we will break camp and head for a 'lake' we have selected as the first tangible project in our journey."

"Marie, I started noticing something," Alicia said, "as you told that story. I used to think that action was everything. I lived in a Just Do It culture, after all. But now I see the value of the pause, the stillness. That's where I can find a truth that is a different truth than the one that action has taught me. But here in this room just now I also felt something else. I can feel that each of us in our own way is already feeling the call to climb the peak that is off the trail. That is why we are here together on this search. Something larger is whispering to us."

The hush in the room was palpable, and I let it hang as each person gazed out the window or at the floor, letting Alicia's truth sink in.

At just the right moment, it seemed, Himari stood and spoke. "I have been watching us wrestling to integrate what is tangible in our lives with these fascinating, intangible, and even spiritual concerns. I have also been thinking a lot about the idea of purpose in our lives. I have been musing about how to go about *thinking* about the subject, while these decades of life ahead are staring down on me. If this is a good time, I would like to share what I've found, and if you are interested, we could discuss the questions a bit more. I did a little research—no surprise—and came up with some data that surprised me."

Hearing Himari, I was delighted to see members of the group starting to take ownership of the process, so I gestured for her to go for it and took a seat at the edge of the circle.

A Question of Purpose

"As we ponder listening to our emerging future," Himari said, "it seems to be intimately related to questions about our life purpose. I have noticed, in my reading and in the media, at least two recent schools of thought, or really two worldviews regarding finding a purpose for our life at our stage in life.

"The first is what I'll call a secular or scientific view. Social scientists have studied how people go about this search for purpose and what they come up with. I confess I am editorializing a bit here, but I'll call this the 'go to the deli and choose' method. The scientific method assumes that there is no Higher Power or Greater

Intelligence, no spiritual category for the search for purpose. A social scientist would say you just have to pick something and run with it. You might go through a values clarification exercise or consider your history or other useful methodologies, then you pick."

Alicia interjected, "I'll have half a pound of the pastrami, thin sliced."

"Yes, something like that," Himari responded with a grin, handing her a virtual stack of meat.

"The second school of thought or worldview must be spiritual," Samuel said.

"Yes," Himari confirmed. "It makes all the difference to the person doing the searching, though to the research investigation it's just an academic question."

Shirley looked around the circle. "I would be interested to hear from each of us," she said, "if we know at this point, which camp we think we are in. It might make a difference on how we want to steer our conversation and our inquiries. Himari, since you started this, is it safe to assume from what you just said about ham and cheese that you're in the Greater Wisdom camp?"

Himari laughed. "So you picked up my oh-so-subtle bias, did you? Yes, of course I can't define what's out there in the Mystery, but my experiences over my lifetime tell me it's there. And I personally want to proceed on the assumption that I want to *discern* what my next purpose will be, not just pick something. To be fair, it probably takes just as much work to thoughtfully pick something as it does to discern. But yes, you guessed correctly." She paused for a moment.

"By the way, I should add that I don't see these as polarities or mutually exclusive categories—there are probably overlaps, and nuances, and it may even change for a certain individual from day to day as they explore."

Samuel volunteered his response to Shirley's suggestion. "I think I mentioned earlier that I've always been interested in the Jewish mystical tradition. That kind of sums up where I am coming from. And I agree with Himari that we should take care not to go in with an either/or mindset. This is all about exploration and trying to learn where we actually know very little. We're all beginners."

Shirley said, "I definitely will be proceeding based on my encounters with the Greater Wisdom, which I experienced when we did the liminal space work, but also from my own history. Alicia, you're leaning forward as if you're eager to speak."

"Yes, I definitely am eager to wade in. I *want* there to be a Greater Wisdom. This all feels way too serious to just pick a purpose off the shelf, so to speak. Did I mention earlier that I grew up in the Black Gospel church? I have felt the power of collective faith, and I have been the recipient of a contagious resilience many times from those gatherings. I'll be leaning into that heritage as I move forward. Why would I not?"

Paul spoke up. "You know I have monastic contemplation in my history. What I learned years ago is still with me. This is core to my being."

Martina was the last to speak. "I definitely grew up under the influence of the church, in my case Roman Catholic. It's been an important part of the fabric of my family's life forever. But I have also grown more than disillusioned with the institution, and with the behavior of many of those who put themselves in charge. But that does not automatically cancel out my personal sense of mystery, *The* Mystery. I'd like to learn to tap into that, like we do with liminal space. To my delight, doing that doesn't evoke or require all the trappings that I grew up with, and the institution is thankfully nowhere to be seen. I am eager to explore this—whatever that means. Just no more incense, please."

Shirley looked slowly around the circle, acknowledging each person with her eyes. "Thank you for responding so willingly to my question. I suppose if someone in another circle on another day wanted to approach the question from a scientific view, that group could figure out how to shape that conversation."

Samuel said, "I cannot resist pointing out that these inclinations we each just voiced are, after all, assumptions. We cannot, as thinking beings, operate without them. So these particular assumptions *will* affect how we listen to our emerging future and what we hear."

"Inevitably," Shirley said. "And I'm OK with that." Then she turned to Himari. "Himari, what else did you learn from your impromptu research?"

The High Value of Having a Purpose

"I want to underscore the science here," Himari continued, "with all the respect it deserves. It turns out there has been quite a bit of research on the physiological and mental effects that having a life purpose can have on people. I was delighted but not surprised to learn what a big factor purpose plays in longevity.

"You *could* go read a bunch of studies—that's one way to dive deeper—but you can find a great summation of data in a delightfully readable form in Barbara Bradley Hagerty's book *Life Reimagined*. She spent nearly twenty years as an NPR reporter, so she is a master storyteller. I highly recommend the entire book. In her chapter 5, "It's the Thought That Counts," she describes the MIDUS project—*Midlife in the United States*—that began in 1995. It found six attitudes or mindsets that seem to predict health and well-being, including factors you would expect, such as positive personal relations, self-acceptance, personal growth, and autonomy. But the most important one on the list is having a purpose in life. This means a sense of direction in life, or a search for meaning, or even a zest for life.[12]

"The health benefits of purpose in life, as shown by this study, are impressive. For example, 'Older people who score high on purpose in life were twice as likely to be alive over a five-year period.'[13]

"In another study 'Men who had a tangible purpose in life were 22 percent less likely to suffer a stroke.'"[14]

Paul asked, "Himari, I've heard that purpose can help defer dementia. Did you find anything on that?"

"Yes, and the item that surprised me most is that a full one-third of 500 people whose autopsies indicated Alzheimer's had shown no cognitive decline. In other words, the brain seems to have the ability to do workarounds when Alzheimer's plaque develops, so you don't necessarily lose your memory. In one study, 'People with little purpose were *two and a half times* more likely to develop dementia than those with a mission.'[15]

"That's more than impressive," Paul said. "Sign me up!"

Himari continued. "Dr. David Bennett, director of Rush University's Alzheimer's Disease Center in Chicago, describes purpose in life as 'almost a magic bullet'—as Barbara Hagerty puts it. He says that people at eighty-eight or ninety-eight are happy and looking forward to the next day, when they have a purpose. 'Somehow,' he says, 'people with more purpose in life have brains that are more plastic... They are not just able to tolerate stuff because they are hardwired better; they're able to tolerate it better because they have other ways of dealing with pathology that people without purpose do not.'[16]

"Hagerty summarizes for us: 'More than education, more than a happy childhood or a lifetime of learning, more than physical activities or eating right, more than any other thing, this engaged attitude toward life is the secret to a sharp mind right to the last day.'"[17]

Paul pulled out his journal. "This would be a perfect time for me to share a quote I ran across this week. I spotted it on Simon Sinek's Instagram feed. He says, 'Your purpose is not the thing you do, it is the thing that happens in others when you do what you do.'"

Martina stood and walked to the window, staring out. She turned back to the group. "A small part of me has been thinking that this search we are on was going to be a lot of work. You just convinced me that it's going to be more than worth it. Count me in."

I thanked Himari for her encouraging contribution. That sparked an enthusiastic round of applause from the others.

I said, "In order to ground this theoretical conversation in your actual lives, as people who hope to embody these principles, I would like to give you an assignment beyond your journaling for the coming week. It picks up on Himari's helpful contribution. I promise you will find it inspiring."

Highlights

What's Next for Our Lives? We don't have to be guided by the past. Looking forward is the key to living adaptive, creative lives. In this chapter, we discussed practices that help us listen to our own emerging future:

- **Attend to where you place your attention.** Where your attention originates shapes what becomes possible. The future doesn't just arrive—it depends on how you listen for it.

- **Practice an open mind instead of downloading.** Let go of the voice of judgment and your habit of assuming you already know. Learning to suspend old assumptions opens a doorway to insights you never expected.

- **Embody the compassion of an open heart.** Empathy is the antidote to cynicism. Opening your heart allows you to feel what others are experiencing—and to feel more deeply what matters most to you.

- **Dare to have the courage of an open will.** Open will means letting go of control and stepping toward the unknown. It's about trusting what wants to emerge—even when it hasn't yet taken form.

- **Redefine "future" as your personal, immediate reality.** The future is not a distant land where other people live. It's a possibility that's calling to you specifically, waiting to be made real through your actions.

- **Allow presencing to emerge in your daily life.** When you bring open mind, open heart, and open will into alignment, you can experience presencing—a state of attunement with the Self who knows what comes next.

- **Consider listening as a spiritual practice.** Instead of striving to decide, try listening. Attentive silence can reveal what your next purpose is longing to become—if you let it come to you.

- **Dare to hike across open ground.** Like a cross-country trek above the timberline, you may not see the full trail ahead. But pausing to reorient regularly ensures you're headed toward what truly matters.

- **Think of purpose as the thing that happens to others when you act.** Your purpose may not be a title or a task—it may be the ripple effect your actions create in others when you show up fully as yourself.

- **Practice gratitude for the high value purpose brings to your Prime Time.** Research confirms what many of us already sense: having purpose supports health, vitality, and joy. Your calling may be the best medicine of all.

Exercises:

1. **Journal Reflection:** Track in your journal this week the times when you notice these concepts cropping up:

   - Open mind – Have you reconsidered an assumption after noticing yourself or others doing downloading?

   - Open heart – When might empathy help you see from another person's differing perspective?

   - Open will – Does a moment arise when resistance whispers or shouts? If you have a chat with inner characters about this, record the highlights and insights that emerge.

- Presencing – See if you can catch yourself stopping to listen for your immediate emerging future. What do you see or hear? It can be a tiny thing. Note: Reviewing in the <u>Sourcebook for Chapter 4</u> the essay by Kelly Wendorf on practicing silence, *kairos*, and space will give you additional insights for practicing presencing.

2. **Action Step: The Purpose Prize.** In 2005, Encore.org in San Francisco launched the Purpose Prize with the aim of highlighting and supporting social innovation by individuals sixty and above. Marc Freedman,[18] founder and CEO of Encore.org, was an early expert on the longevity revolution and the transformation of retirement. This week, take some time to go to https://PurposePrize.Encore.org and scroll down to two aspects of this website.

First, the short videos by founders and jurors are inspiring. Second, the profiles of the winners and their projects will illustrate for you what a sense of compelling purpose can generate. Although many of these individuals were not retired when they started their projects, you will find the sheer variety and creativity to be excellent stimulation for your own exploration and discovery process. There is more here than you will have time to read, so browse randomly or use the search functions to explore areas that interest you.

The administration of the Purpose Prize was later taken over by AARP, and the threshold age was changed to fifty. You can also explore more recent winners at https://www.aarp.org/about-aarp/purpose-prize/. You will find some incredible stories. The descriptions of the winners will warm your hearts, and more important, they illustrate what can be possible. I know you will enjoy the tour.

Additionally, I encourage you to be persistent with your daily morning practice. Connecting to Source and returning to liminal space are your greatest assets for this journey.

Prime Time Milestones

Take a breath. Pause. What are you noticing at this point in your journey? As you reflect, write your thoughts in your journal.

Insight. I see something new…

Sample response: *I don't have to figure everything out with my head. There's another way of knowing—through listening.*

Shift. I feel something changing…

Sample response: *I feel less urgency. More spaciousness to be with the unknown.*

Step. I'm ready to try…

Sample response: *I'll take five minutes tomorrow to sit quietly and notice what arises—without needing to fix or solve.*

Phase III

Superpowers Unleashed

CHAPTER 6

The Three Essential Strategies that Fuel Our Calling

*I am neither especially clever nor especially
gifted. I am only very, very curious.*

—Albert Einstein

In March 2024, Cole Brauer, a thirty-year-old woman from Long Island, successfully completed an round-the-world solo sailing race, the first American woman ever to accomplish this feat.

Think about the first ships that left Europe and sailed west with their primitive guidance methods. The contrast is stunning, comparing those first ships to today's technology that guided Cole's path, helping her anticipate both weather problems and weather advantages, and even kept her on course while she slept.

When the group reconvened, I set the scene with Cole Brauer's story. "Each of you has started a voyage into the unknown. Each of you has a future seemingly almost as open-ended as the oceans Cole Brauer was crossing. Our generation has more years of life and freedom of time to design and plan for than any generation in history. And more promise of health and vitality for the journey than ever before.

"Cole Brauer crossed her oceans with the help of high-tech guidance systems. You too have a long-range guidance system wired not to instruments but to insight—into the future that is trying to reach out. So, metaphorically speaking, how do we select and utilize these guidance systems? We have looked at how our past has shaped our inner characters, and we have learned to speak with these characters from our most centered inner state, our liminal space. We have strengthened that listening muscle, so as to be more free, more *available* to apprehend and perceive new possibilities our future may offer. We have acquired the disciplines of open mind, open heart, and open will to help us position our receptors to what Source might convey to us from our future. We have also redefined "future" for our purposes to mean our own personal immediate future, the one that beckons to our highest self to bring that future into reality.

"This deeper form of listening, this intimate connection with our future possibility, is our long-range guidance system. It can guide us when exterior navigation and cultural guidance systems are unhelpful or even useless amid the continuously disruptive chaos of our world. To come full circle, it is our steps of open will and connecting with Source that allow us to navigate—to hear and sense and respond to this future possibility and its resonance with us.

"But there are three additional practices, call them complementary guidance systems, that we may be accustomed to thinking about in their most common form, but that we can specifically apply to our task at hand to assist us on our journey.

"Let's get specific: these three are *curiosity, passion, and self-efficacy.*

"I'll define that third one in a moment," I told the group, "but it's vital that you practice open mind to allow each of these topics to appear to you today as if you have just met them. These three concepts hold fresh possibilities. In other words, guard against 'already listening,' where you may be tempted to say to yourself, 'Yeah, yeah, I know about that already.' Instead, allow yourself to be surprised by a new insight or a new take on an old term. This is the perfect situation to practice open mind."

Curiosity: The Essence of an Open Mind

I slowly looked around the circle. The group watched me expectantly. I instructed them to start a new page in their journal. "Ask yourself how curious you perceive yourself to be. Jot down a number from 1 to 10, with 1 being just above the curiosity level of a snail and 10 the most curious person you can imagine. Now, double that number and write that number down, so 3 becomes 6, 9 becomes 18."

Your Turn

I looked around the circle again. "Did any of you start at three or below? You don't need to raise your hand, but if that's the case, I'm surprised you are still in the room. Surely you are curious about where this experience will lead you, no?" No one raised their hand.

"Now, take eight minutes and jot down as many things as you can think of that you are curious about, or things you just might possibly be interested in exploring someday. Quickly make a list— no essay answers required.

Your Turn

When they stopped writing, I continued. "What do you think your list would look like if your curiosity was at the level of the second number you wrote down? If you called yourself a four, what would you as an eight-level curious person be including on your list? Write whatever comes to mind. Be weird. Be frivolous. Take three more minutes."

Your Turn

I stood at the whiteboard Alicia had provided. "Call out to me some of the things on your lists." I wrote on the board as members of the group announced items from their lists:

1. Neuroscience—the impact of our thinking on health
2. Land preservation
3. Bison or elephant preservation
4. Solving the challenges of our times through the minds and work of retiring boomers
5. How can boomers age at home and easily get services they need
6. Interviewing and podcasting with interesting people
7. Working with a wind energy company to help birds avoid the rotors
8. New solutions for neuropathy
9. New solutions for osteoporosis
10. What could children's television look like today if I had an unlimited budget and a staff of highly imaginative people?
11. Breakthroughs in hormone replacement therapy in 70+ women
12. Coaching youth climate activists
13. Podcasting on food and cooking. What is a new angle?
14. Your29.com—Work with or perhaps for them on structure and expanding the mentor and scholarship side of their work
15. Training dogs, and training their people—what's a new angle?
16. Create a citizen science group for "newcomers" group in town
17. Create an annual travel/science/learning program for newcomers
18. Create an original, fun group activity for my friends—and friends of friends

19. Develop an Audubon Backyard Native Plants program where I live

20. Create marketing, online outreach, podcast for Scott Weidensaul's shorebirds and owl work

21. Create bird habitat programs for integration with land trusts (like a giant backyard bird program)

22. Bird habitat program for farmers and ranchers

23. What is Rachel Maddow's PhD in? From where? Where did she grow up? Is she really 5'11"?

24. Frontiers in neuroplasticity and things seniors can do to increase it

25. Teaching something unusual that I am good at to an interested 25-year old

26. Researching the latest architecture for homeless solutions

I gave them three more minutes to come up with more:

27. How do you get back up from a bungee jump?

28. Learning screenwriting, and how to apply it to what I am learning here. How much does it cost to make an indie movie?

29. Was Steven Spielberg really only 26 when he made *Jaws*? What could I do at 80 if I didn't know I was "too old"?

30. If the frequency of a cat purr helps speed broken-bone healing (a study I saw), would it help with osteoporosis? Do cat ladies know something we don't?

31. How could you make the Northern Lights into an art form? Performance art?

When the group had called out all they could, I asked, "In what ways do you think an active or even voracious curiosity might be important to you personally as we pursue this search for your new life?"

Alicia responded immediately. "Having had numerous glasses of wine with product-development people over the years, I can assure you all that the more options we come up with, the more chance that we'll come up with something really worthwhile. The first few ideas most of us think of are usually pretty predictable, or even stale. Nothing worth getting out of bed for."

Samuel added, "From a philosophical perspective I'll second that. And once you start collecting a list of new ideas, you can always 'cheat' by mix-and-matching—only it's not really cheating because more is better."

Shirley chimed in. "This is just a feeling, I don't have data, but I'm confident that our hopes and dreams actually harbor lots of things we are curious about. The demands of our careers have put many of them on the back burner, or they've even been long forgotten."

"When I think about medical research," Himari said, "I am aware that breakthrough ideas can frequently come from seemingly unrelated fields. Curiosity could lead to that unexpected mix and match."

Alicia quietly walked over to her laptop at the desk in the corner. Her printer whined briefly. She returned a moment later holding three pages of information. "This may be more detail than you want to hear, but let me pass around some examples of medical research inspired by ideas from other fields."

1. **Cochlear Implants from Electrical Engineering:** Cochlear implants, devices that provide a sense of sound to the deaf or severely hard of hearing, were developed by combining medical science with electrical engineering. Graeme Clark, an Australian ear specialist, applied his knowledge of electrical stimulation of the auditory nerve, drawing on electrical engineering principles he learned. He created the first prototype, inspired by his father's hearing problems. The results transformed the lives of many with profound hearing loss.

2. **Antibacterial Properties of Mold from Traditional Medicine:** While Alexander Fleming's discovery of

penicillin is well known, the antibacterial properties of mold were recognized in various forms of traditional medicine long before Fleming's time. Cultures around the world have used molds and other substances with antimicrobial properties to treat infections. Combining this traditional knowledge with scientific and keeping an open mind, research ultimately led to the development of modern antibiotics.

3. **Barbara McClintock and Genetic Transposition:** Barbara McClintock, an American cytogeneticist, discovered transposable elements or "jumping genes" in maize. She challenged the then current understanding of genetics. She was awarded the Nobel Prize in Physiology or Medicine in 1983 for her discovery of genetic transposition, becoming the first woman to receive an unshared Nobel Prize in that category.

4. **CRISPR Gene Editing from Bacteriology:** The revolutionary gene-editing technology, CRISPR-Cas9, was inspired by the way bacteria defend themselves against viruses. Scientists studying the immune systems of bacteria observed that they used CRISPR sequences to recognize and cut viral DNA. This understanding was then adapted to develop a tool that can precisely edit the DNA in the genomes of higher organisms, including humans, with implications for treating genetic disorders.

   Two of the most prominent figures in development of CRISPR gene editing are collaborators Jennifer Doudna and Emmanuelle Charpentier. They received the Nobel Prize in Chemistry in 2020 for their pivotal breakthrough work.

"By the way," Alicia added, "I'm still learning to use it, but ChatGPT is a friend for the curious. Anytime I find myself wondering about something, I just ask ChatGPT to quickly fill me in with background on my question. It's like having the Library of

Congress in my kitchen…with no commute. And one new idea always leads me to several more. You still need to double-check facts and sources, of course, but for generating ideas or opening up new subjects, it's invaluable."

"What I'm hearing here," Paul said, "is not that we should all go into scientific research but that we need to pay attention to following even random threads of thoughts that occur to us because they may lead to something we really love or could get committed to. I can see that I need to keep my journal closer at hand from here on. Hmmm. Another question just popped up for me. How many times a day do each of you turn to Google or Chat GPT?"

Shirley answered first. "Some days once or twice, but occasionally five or six times a day. During Netflix I'm always reaching for my phone to see where else I've seen a supporting actor…or how tall someone is, or how old. By the way, I gave myself an eight on the earlier quiz. It boggles my mind what a sixteen curious person might look like!"

Himari said, "I probably check Google for something at least once a day. ChatGPT was emerging just as I left working, so I'm a little rusty still on that. But this list we made has inspired me to start looking up things I'm curious about more frequently."

Alicia said, "I recently took a two-hour online course on how to get started on ChatGPT. There is a knack to writing effective prompts, but it certainly isn't rocket science for what we are doing here. I love using it. The speed of the responses is still breathtaking, but more important, once I got the hang of asking more specific and detailed questions, it felt like going to the library for a week but knowing exactly where to look—and only having to stay for five minutes. I know there are reasons to worry about how AI technology will be used, but for my own purposes, I am absolutely sold on it."

Martina added, "I probably get a low score on Google searches, and I haven't tried ChatGPT yet, but you've convinced me. I really need to get with the program, if I want my life to look differently in a couple of years. Let me read to you what I just wrote my journal while we've been talking:

> Curiosity: Wake mine up! Rehydrate it. Nourish it. Beef it up. (Find a vegetarian metaphor.) And look something up that strikes my curiosity at least once a day.

"Thanks, Martina," I said. "Great prompt. I want to underline our objective here. It is vital that we stretch our curiosity as much as we can because our calling may well lie outside of the sphere of reality that we have known so far. We also have a human tendency to unconsciously believe that if we haven't thought about it, it doesn't exist. Rationally, we know that is ridiculous, but regularly challenging ourselves to stretch our imagination will make a world of difference in where we end up. I can't emphasize this enough. Don't let your brain fall asleep!"

"Got it, Coach," Paul called out.

"We're all *curious* about what's coming next, Marie," Alicia announced.

"After our break, the next quiz will be to ask what you are passionate about."

> *There is no passion to be found playing small, in settling*
> *for a life that is less than the one you are capable of living.*
>
> —NELSON MANDELA

Passion: A Self-Assessment

Once the group settled back into our circle, I said, "To begin, jot down in your journal at least three things you are passionate about. They don't need to be earth-shaking. It's more important that you get in touch with a fire that is inside you, even if it is only a match-size flame. Take as long as you need because sometimes it takes a little while to get back in touch with something you haven't thought about for a long time. If others are still writing when you finish, feel free to jot down more details about the things you have identified."

Your Turn 

After a minute, Paul got up, went to the back of the room, and began pacing. That seemed to free Martina to slide off her chair and sit cross-legged on the floor.

Twenty minutes later, everyone had put down their pens. I told them, "I'm glad some of you felt free to stretch your bodies to loosen up your minds. How did that exploration work for each of you?"

"It was hard at first," said Alicia. "My life has been pretty here-and-now for the past year or two. But I was able to remember a few times, back at my company, when I caught myself gazing out the window and thinking about larger issues than the afternoon's stressful meeting. I'm not quite ready to share what I wrote out loud, but I did write a couple of pages."

"That's fine," I assured her. "As I've said before, no one needs to share out loud before they are ready. Anyone else?"

Samuel said, "I reaffirmed my excitement about helping people think through questions and issues that they are concerned about. I love this group because we are figuring things out in real time, pushing the envelope, as they say. I just can't see yet where I might do this with others. But I guess that's why we're here, to help figure that out."

Several in the circle nodded in support.

Shirley spoke up. "I'd like to suggest that we add the word 'longing' to the topic of passion. When I started our assignment just now, I recognized that somewhere in my gut there is almost an ache to do my purpose. It is passion I feel, yes, but 'longing' captures the flavor more accurately for me. Does anyone know what I am talking about?"

A comfortable silence settled over the room while people considered her question.

Finally, Himari cleared her throat. "I think I know what you are getting at, Shirley. My passion feels more like a longing too. It's still a foggy day in my visual brain, but I'm feeling like I want to do something humanitarian. It has a different feel than just going back to what I did professionally. We all know about Doctors Without Borders, and programs like that, and I applaud what they do. But what I am trying to find language for here is a longing to do something more informal…maybe small and local and not institutional. With medicine, it normally requires an enormous infrastructure, at least for Western medicine, but I'm pushing on that boundary with my longing-dream-wish."

"Maybe you should learn to be a shaman," said Alicia. Everyone laughed at the sudden image of Himari in that role.

"Actually," said Himari, "that's not such a wild and crazy idea. I don't mean I feel drawn right now to do that literally. Do you suppose the Navajo would take a Japanese woman into training? But this is exactly what we were talking about with open mind, and with pushing out our curiosity boundaries. So thank you, Alicia, for your impromptu comment."

Silence settled again, as each person returned to their own thoughts.

Martina finally said, "This process is really stretching my brain. It feels like I stretch a rubber band, and as soon as it gets longer than usual, it snaps back to all my familiar thoughts. I wonder if at some point you could all help me brainstorm my list, to trigger or activate my silent wild-and-crazy inner character?"

"Of course," said Shirley. "That's why we are here. To figure out how we can help and support each other. Before we leave today, let's take some time to help you with that. And thanks for asking for help! That encourages us all to remember to do that."

When Passion Feels Like Longing

I said to the group, "We've spoken about how the *process* is working for us right now. Does anyone want to offer more about the *content* of their passion or their longing, however small or blurry its surfacing may be for you right now?"

"I'm ready to do that," said Shirley. "My idea, my growing passion, my longing, has been simmering since almost the very beginning of this group. And the idea is still there every morning when I wake up. That's unusual for me, because I can be pretty ADD, off to some new thing that pops up. My dream is that I can help others do exactly what we are doing here in this circle. Maybe not this exact format because that will change and adapt. But I want to help people, probably all women at first—but that's a different subject— who are not satisfied with their lives in retirement. Specifically I want to assist people who want a more defined purpose for their life than keeping themselves entertained. You all could probably help me with this when the time is right by describing what exactly drew you to this group, or this process, in the first place."

"We'd be happy to do that," Alicia said, looking around the circle for confirmation.

Martina asked, "Shirley, do you have any vision yet for what that passion—or longing—might look like when it takes shape in the real world?" Then she chuckled. "Here I am asking for structure right away." The others laughed with her.

"Yes, actually I do," responded Shirley. "I am kind of surprising myself with this whole picture because I've worked in much larger organizations. I was daydreaming about it just last night. I am visualizing some sort of 'academy.' It's smaller and more informal than an institute. And it's more specific in intent than a college or a university. Since COVID-19, people are all pretty well trained in meeting on Zoom, so online is a good possibility, but I also really like coming face-to-face in a comfortable space like we are here at

Alicia's. Right now, as a working name in my head, I'm calling it the Santa Fe Academy for Purposeful Retirement. It could happen 'live' here in Santa Fe, but obviously we could have online groups for people anywhere. It's always fun to have someone from New Zealand or Montreal in a group."

"Is it OK if we chime in with other ideas when someone is sharing their passion idea?" Alicia asked.

"I don't mind, I'd love it," said Shirley. "But maybe each person could say, when they are taking their turn, whether they want input or not. That way we wouldn't overload someone whose flame is still really tiny. So, did you have an idea for me, Alicia?"

"Yes, I was remembering about all the stores all over the country, the world, actually, where our athletic wear is sold. You could train facilitators or coaches, or whatever it is Marie is doing here, to host in-person groups in whatever cities they spring up. Sort of like franchising, but not that rigid."

Shirley grinned. "I really appreciate your ideas and suggestions, and I'm excited that you can start to see it happening in your own imaginations. As we get closer to the how-to part, I'll ask you again for input."

Samuel chimed in. "Great idea. I can already see that these new leaders—or facilitators or teachers or whatever they are—would need to really *embody*, for example, open mind, and be deeply curious. And certainly they would have to have their own authentic experience with liminal space and connecting with Source. This is not a strictly academic exercise. That much is clear to me already." He paused. "Listen to me. 'Not strictly academic.'"

The group chuckled, but no one commented. Then Samuel burst back in, "These guides also need to be really passionate about baby boomers not sitting out this opportunity, this new era, when the world needs all the help it can get."

"Amen," said Alicia.

Principles Emerging from Passion

Alicia took a deep breath and said, "I am noticing that there are certain principles operating here. Or maybe they are just things worth noting out loud. *First,* we are talking about passions or dreams that do not necessarily have to earn a profit. We here in this room do not have to worry about making it support us going forward. That's a huge freedom. It opens up so many more options. I also realize that this is a privileged position to be in our society right now. There are millions of our peers who are discovering that surviving only on Social Security is nearly impossible. And if their savings is small, or they don't have much of a pension, it's really hard. I want to acknowledge this huge challenge."

"Helping to solve that might turn out to be a life purpose for some of us," added Martina. "I don't mean here in this room, necessarily, but for our peers who do have a pension and are looking for a purpose. But for us here in this circle, I think—am I speaking for all of us?—that we do appreciate our privilege, and that makes it all the more important that we find something worthwhile to do with our lives."

Alicia looked from one person to the next, around the circle, as each person nodded their agreement.

Shirley said, "Yes, I'd say that you are indeed speaking for all of us."

"A *second* principle that I am noticing," said Alicia, "is that a passion might fall in the category of a wrong that needs righting, or it could be simply a curiosity that is so strong that it will not shut up until we pursue it. Does that one resonate with anyone?"

Alicia paused for a moment, then when no one responded, she continued. "I think that might be true for me. There are plenty of righteous and vital causes still needing attention in the community I grew up in. And the whole question of the dominance of corporate America over our lives would be another obvious thing I could take up. But I have an inkling that my next step won't be that obvious. I don't have a glimmer yet, but I think pursuing my curiosities will be my key path to discernment."

I said to Alicia, "Your journal will be your best friend in the coming weeks and months. Tracking seemingly stray thoughts and ideas is essential. I have heard from many journal keepers that they are astonished to see ideas when they go back and read earlier entries that they didn't even remember thinking about. But in the rereading, something clicks with a more recent experience, and the dots seem to magically connect in ways they had never envisioned."

"Thank you," Alicia said. "We think we know so much, as we move through life, when really, our unconscious, and now I would add, Source, are working at a whole other level, attempting to nudge us along."

"A *third* principle I'd like to acknowledge," Alicia continued, "is that—wait, this isn't a principle at all, it's just my hunch! I wonder if we might have new inner characters that we haven't even spoken with yet. I can almost feel an athletic, maybe grade-school-aged girl inside me who will want to make an appearance someday soon."

She paused, a look of awe coming over her face. "I didn't even realize this until I heard myself say it. This is so cool. It's almost magical. I'm going to take her out for a walk after dinner tonight and see what she might want to say."

No one spoke. The group seemed to sense that something almost holy had just happened. A new voice whispering through the fog of unknowing that each of them was living in.

"Thank you," Alicia finally said. "Thank you for being attentive listeners while I figured out something I didn't even know I knew. I will keep you posted on what she says."

Is Curiosity More Adaptive, or More Resilient, than Passion?

After a break, I suggested we needed to put passions and curiosities in perspective. I noted that this was only my opinion, and I was open to other viewpoints, but I wanted to ask the question: *Might it be that curiosity is more sustainable or more adaptive or more resilient than passion?*

I elaborated on the thought. "I can remember plenty of days in the past ten years when I woke up not feeling passionate about anything, but I am almost always at least a little bit curious. Also, if you're feeling dull, you can choose to be curious, but I have never been able to turn on passion by deciding to do so. A simple example. You meet a friend at a café for coffee. You're feeling low, but you can look at the snacks under the serving glass and ask yourself, I wonder where the ingredients for that fruit tart came from? Who grew those raspberries? Where did the wheat grow? Did a local bakery make it and deliver it early this morning? What kind of person leaves for work at three a.m. every day? So if I can stir up curiosity just by paying attention to my surroundings but I have not yet figured out how to turn up the dial on passion, maybe one of you can figure it out. Are you curious about that? I'll check back.

"I experience passion as either it is there, or it isn't. The nearest I've come to stirring it up was the time someone asked me if I felt I was the object of some injustice. I've had my instances of being overlooked when a man is promoted, but I admit I've lived a fairly privileged life. Then I explained that I got pretty agitated, years ago, when I realized how my gay and lesbian friends were sometimes treated unfairly in the workplace. Still, I think it is a worthy question for us to ask: If you experience feeling agitated about injustice, is that a 'passion?' Your journal or your inner characters might have some opinions about this."

Paul suggested that each person assign themselves a specific journal question of their choice for the coming week, responding to my comments about curiosity and passion.

An example for myself might be, What was I curious about at age ten? And that question could lead to more:

- In high school, was I passionate about anything (besides dating)?

- Did I have any dreams or goals?
- Did I let a dream die by age twenty because I couldn't see how to go about it?
- Or did I just unconsciously set it aside?

Your Turn 

*Our number one challenge isn't biodiversity loss, climate change, polarization, countries falling apart, or AI. It is our widespread **illusion of insignificance**—the belief that there is nothing we can do about it.[19]*

—OTTO SCHARMER

Self-Efficacy: Built on Hope

On New Year's Eve 2024, Otto Scharmer contemplated the coming year. One crystal-clear realization had come to him, which he put quite eloquently: "Our number one challenge isn't biodiversity loss, climate change, polarization, countries falling apart, or AI. It is our widespread ***illusion of insignificance***—the belief that there's *nothing* we can *do* about it."

For retired professionals, our own *illusion of insignificance* tempts us to stay trapped in the roles of eternal vacation. One response, one way to reclaim some amount of agency over our own lives, lies in the imagery offered by Ilya Prigogine. We discussed his concept of islands of coherence in chapter 4 in the context of shaping a trusting environment, our group, our own island of coherence.

I read the Prigogine quote to the group again: "When a system is far from equilibrium, small islands of coherence in a sea of chaos have the capacity to elevate the entire system to a higher order."

There was a buzz of excitement within the circle.

"Wow!" Alicia said. "When I heard it the first time, I didn't even know what that meant, but right now, in the context of feeling insignificant, it sounds profoundly hopeful. I'm sure 'a system far from equilibrium' must mean something specific in chemistry or physics, but as a metaphor for the chaotic times we are living in, it's perfect. Does anyone know what an island of coherence even is? I love the imagery."

Himari picked up her phone. "I'm on it. It's just what it sounds like. Here is where one group has gone with the concept." She read from her screen: "a small stable space within a larger system that experiences clarity, alignment, and purposeful action, even when the surrounding environment is chaotic or uncertain."

I filled in more details. "The System Innovation Initiative (see systeminnovation.org) suggests there are three layers to the coherence that group—' island'—participants experience. The first level is when they *create a shared history*, where the participants experience it as a joint creation, not just something that arrived with a life of its own, as when a hierarchy assigns them. We can connect this back to Otto's observation of our illusion of insignificance. Participants are self-directed agents who take the initiative from the beginning.

"The second level occurs when they begin to make sense of the *current reality*. The participants' mutual desire and intention to create coherence and change helps make this possible. In short, they have to *want* coherence in the circle.

"Third, systems shifters—drawing on the contemplative practices we've been learning—can begin to discern *new pathways* together, different from what they might have found in isolation. This is where our trained ability to listen to our emerging future comes into play. These three levels together create a synergy that has more leverage than the innumerable 'committees' that we are all so familiar with."

Himari said, "So I am hearing the three parts as," she started counting on her fingers, "first, *taking initiative*—agency—to create a group or circle, then, number two, holding the conscious, spoken *intention* to create coherence in the circle. And finally, participants bring a set of *skills,* so their attention is more focused and their 'listening' is sharper than in past gatherings."

"That's it!" I said.

Then I offered to the group an impressively simple and effective set of instructions for conducting a one-hour process (which can be repeated indefinitely) for what the Presencing Institute at MIT calls *circles of coherence* (see the <u>Sourcebook for Chapter 6</u>, Circles of Coherence Guidelines).

"Great," Paul interjected. "From today forward, I am thinking of this group as my island of coherence. I want a safe space to grow and change, but I'd also like to help change the world…and do it coherently! Together with some kindred spirits."

"It's a worthy goal," Martina chimed in. "And I really like the idea of having the potential of shifting an entire system—whatever that might mean."

Samuel said, "We have the *capacity*, not just the potential."

I leaned forward. "Good catch, Samuel. And this is a perfect segue into delving deeper on our third essential tool."

The Psychology of Self-Efficacy

I started with the term itself. "Psychologist Albert Bandura popularized the term *self-efficacy* during his lifelong study of it at Stanford. He went to Stanford in 1953 at 28, and retired from there in 2010 *at age 85.* He defined the term self-efficacy as *our belief in our own ability to influence events and outcomes.* He called it the foundation of our motivation, performance, and emotional well-being.

"Meanwhile, across the continent, psychologist Ellen Langer (see chapter 2) was, in 1981, the first woman tenured in psychology at Harvard, and she continues there in 2025 at 78. Bandura offered us the concept of self-efficacy, where we see that if we don't believe in something, we tend not to try, and he asks us to examine hidden assumptions about what is 'possible.' Langer's work removes the blindfold. Her experiments over decades demonstrate how our internal models of aging and of health physically affect how our bodies respond. Langer urges us to be *mindful* each day about what we take for granted from our culture, and to question where there might be another viewpoint and another path.

"To retrace our steps today, we can encourage our emerging curiosity, discern our passion or longing, and then live our future into a fulfilling reality. However, to accomplish this, it is essential that we *believe* we can do this. Without that belief, we are destined to remain in our own private little status quo. Most of us have at least one inner character over in a corner, looking at any new possibility, and quietly saying, 'Oh, I could never do *that.*' That thought is a *belief,* not an absolute fact. While curiosity can be cultivated and passion must be discovered, our *beliefs* are completely within our control."

I emphasized this distinction to the group: "Frequently, when a particular dream or opportunity comes to mind, if we cannot simultaneously see *how* it can be accomplished, an inner character says we 'can't' do it. The reality is, it might well be possible, but we shut off that option when we *believe* it cannot be done. Setting aside the *how* question until it is actually needed is the best way to keep moving forward."

"Or we believe," Martina interjected, "we 'couldn't possibly' rise to the occasion. Sorry to interrupt, but I just noticed my own inner character piping up as you were speaking, and I wanted to call her on it."

"Another good catch," said Alicia.

I continued. "Anyone who is paying attention today would agree that disruptions of systems we until now took for granted will continue to cause chaos all around us. To find a life-giving way to live amid this rapid change means, in our metaphor of Prigogine's insight, that we must find ways to create islands of coherence. The gift of the metaphor is that it provides tangible hope that can bring concrete shape to the foundation for our belief, our self-efficacy.

"Retired professionals who are able to discern their calling and take steps to turn their personal future into reality will, I suspect, *of necessity* have to find themselves creating those islands. Dissolving our illusions of insignificance, to come back to Otto's observation, is an essential early step."

Himari took an audible deep breath. "I am beginning to put words to my longing. This is brand new as I speak it. I feel called to create an island of coherence. I can't say yet where or how, but this just feels right, at a really deep level. *What* I actually end up doing remains to be discovered, but one of these islands will be the foundational structure under building it so it can shift an entire system! I have no clue about the specifics—yet—but stay tuned!"

Shirley was watching the faces in the circle. "I have a hunch this will turn out to be true for several of us."

"Maybe all of us," Martina said.

I let the silence hang for a long moment as the implications began to sink in for everyone.

Then I continued. "As we begin to take steps out into the world to try some experiments, you can help each other at our meetings to check on the state of your belief system, and whether something is shifting."

"Do you mean keep each other honest?" Himari asked.

"Exactly. Nearly everyone has a smaller image of what they are capable of when measured against what they are actually capable of accomplishing. Living up to your potential, or I should say, your *capability* in your new calling, is both a joy and a challenge. That's why we're in this together.

I paused with the group before moving on. "Remember," I said, "curiosity, passion, and self-efficacy aren't just ideas to think about. They only become real when you practice them from the grounded stance we learned earlier—your liminal space. Use your anchoring gesture to remind yourself that open mind, open heart, and open will are available to you right now. From there, the future that wants to reach you comes into view more clearly."

I let the silence stretch long enough for them to feel the weight of that reminder. "Curiosity stretches your horizon—your open mind. Passion, or longing, keeps you awake to what matters—your open heart. And self-efficacy is the belief that gives you the courage to take a step when the world around you feels uncertain—that's your open will. Together, they form a bridge—from what we hear within to what we dare to live."

"We are now ready to turn to the secret sauce. At our next meeting we will uncover our Superpowers, and you will begin to test my theory that the most fulfilling retirement is one where you can find or create a new context to practice your Superpower. That promises to be the place where your Superpower is most life-giving and where you help create an island of coherence amidst the chaos."

Highlights

More Essential Practices to Assist Us – In addition to the concepts and practices of attending to inner characters and embracing liminal space, actively listening to our emerging future, and developing open mind, open heart, and open will to help us connect with Source, here are three other essential practices and a related concept that deepen our abilities to create our new way forward:

- **Curiosity.** A voluminous curiosity is essential to hearing a calling that lies outside the boundaries of our same-old, same-old expectations. It requires conscious effort to stay curious. It is a daily practice. Writing down thoughts and whimsies significantly boosts the results.
- **Passion.** We can notice and acknowledge passion. We cannot drum it up if it isn't there. Passion includes old favorites and subjects long forgotten or cast aside. It is our duty to our future self to uncover and nurture them.

- **Self-efficacy.** Self-efficacy is based on our belief systems. We must guard against our tendencies to "downgrade" our capabilities in our mind. We can give permission to trusted friends and colleagues to question our self-limiting assumptions, or they may take the initiative to offer encouraging feedback if we resist or falter.

- **Islands of coherence.** This concept is related to self-efficacy and our belief. It provides a metaphor for hope in our capabilities, in our self-efficacy. As a practical aid, meeting guidelines for "island" or "circle" gatherings give us how-to, in-the-moment methods for developing our inner coherence and our coherence in groups.

- (See the <u>Sourcebook for Chapter 6</u> for additional resources on these practices.)

Exercises: Where I Am and Where I Want to Go

1. **Journal Reflection:** Complete the same curiosity and passion exercises the group worked on, as described in the chapter.

2. **Journal Reflection:** Describe briefly in your journal what you believe regarding your own ability to influence events and outcomes. Do you believe there could be circumstances where you are able to influence events and outcomes? Or do you believe you are more helpless to influence outcomes? Use a score from 1–10 to summarize the picture you have drawn. Make specific notes on how you want to work on this issue. Talk with your inner characters who have opinions on this. Is one particular character more skeptical or feeling helpless? Your Liminal Space can inquire into where the hesitations and fears lie. If you are part of a Prime Time group, these concerns could be the topic for part of an upcoming meeting. Compare notes. Ask for perception checks from trusted friends. Examine old assumptions

or fears that might no longer be relevant or helpful. Then revisit this area in a few weeks and see if your score has changed.

3. **Journal Reflection:** Add in your journal any additional goals you would like to set regarding developing your curiosity and noticing your passions. Might further development in these two areas affect your sense of self-efficacy?

Prime Time Milestones

Take a breath. Pause. What are you noticing at this point in your journey? As you reflect, write your thoughts in your journal.

Insight. I see something new…

Sample response: *The spark isn't gone—it's just buried. I can still learn, grow, and pursue things that matter to me.*

Shift. I feel something changing…

Sample response: *More hopeful. Less stuck. Like there's movement where there was stagnation.*

Step. I'm ready to try…

Sample response: *I'll pick one thing that excites or puzzles me, and take the next small step to explore it.*

Chapter 7

Finding Your Superpowers: They've Been There All Along

The meaning of life is to find your gift. The purpose of life is to give it away.

—Attributed to Pablo Picasso

I could feel the electric charge in the air as I walked into Alicia's home for the next meeting. Everyone was standing around the kitchen island, seemingly all talking at once.

"You're here at last!" Alicia said. "Let's sit down and get started. We want to talk about our Superpowers."

When I'd met with the group for the first time, I told them my story about how I discovered that guiding groups like this was an aspect of my Superpower. But I hadn't grasped until this moment just how much they regarded this week's topic as the secret sauce of our journey.

"Let's start with the big picture," I began. "Picasso called finding your gift the meaning of life. I adopted the term Superpower instead of 'gift' because too many people think only other people are gifted. Borrowing a term from a Marvel comic book seemed just frivolous enough to invite people into a bigger tent. Saying, 'You have a gift,' evokes an 'aw shucks' response. When I proclaim, 'You have a Superpower,' people get curious."

You've Spent Decades Honing Something Rare

"You may not even be aware of it," I said to the group. "Your Superpower is just *what you do*. It may be that you see patterns before anyone else does. Or you cut through chaos and know instinctively what needs to happen next. Or, like me, you draw the best out of people who can't see their own potential.

"Whatever your specific ability is, it's a Superpower. It is the thing that has made you invaluable in your field.

"And now, the world expects you to walk away from it, just because the paycheck clicked off."

I reminded the group that we had talked about how retirement, so they tell us, is for stepping back. Slowing down. Unplugging. As if the only thing left to do is fill time—travel, golf, "enjoy life." As if the years ahead are just some extended intermission until the credits roll.

But that's not how it has to work.

"Everything you've built—your expertise, your insight, your way of seeing the world—was never meant to be mothballed. The work that matters most is still ahead of you. It's waiting for you to claim it, to shape it. As Picasso said, *the purpose of life is to give it away*. You are here today to put it to use in ways you've never had the freedom to explore before.

"Think about it. For the first time, you are no longer bound by office politics, by corporate demands and metrics, or by someone else's definition of productivity. You don't have to answer to anyone's agenda but your own unless you choose to. You have the freedom to create an experiment, to dive into work that fuels you instead of depleting you. You can build something that matters—not because you *have* to, but because you *want* to. You can contribute to what *you* most care about.

"Feel the gratitude. You don't need to keep grinding away at what you did before. You are here on this journey in your Prime Time because you sense that you need to step decisively forward into your new future. Your Superpower hasn't expired. It hasn't faded. It's here, in your hands, as important as ever. The only thing different is that now, you get to decide where you direct it.

"I know I am ranting a bit, but I feel strongly about this. The risk here is you *shrinking*, dismissing your own potential because the world has told you this is the part where you should fade out. They may not come right out and say it, but the world still expects you to have a *short life*. Not short in years, but short on relevance. Short on purpose. Short on impact.

"They expect you to believe that by the time you hit this phase of life, the best of you is behind you. That whatever you've built, whatever you've mastered, whatever fire you've carried—it's time to let it burn out. They expect you to downsize, to retreat, to become smaller.

"Your Superpower is the tangible and specific way that you make sure this doesn't happen. It's your means of focusing your strategy and your efforts going forward."

Alicia broke in. "I am really inspired by what you are saying, but I have to ask. Could you say more about what you mean by our Superpowers? It still feels like I've been dropped into a graphic novel."

"Of course. Fair question. I borrowed this metaphor from pop culture as a shorthand way of describing something that is actually real in our lives. If you are picturing capes or gold cuffs that deflect bullets, that's OK. The important point about why I chose this particular word is that I wanted to make a distinction from the ordinary personal and professional skills and capabilities—the résumé stuff. I will elaborate in a moment about how it is distinctive, but the short answer is this: You do your Superpower so well, you don't even realize you are doing it. Many people, once they have spotted it and named it, admit they do it on auto-pilot. It's your magic. Your in-the-flow talent. Your gift.'

"The secret sauce is this: something special happens when we find a new context to exercise that Superpower. Something empowering happens when we can plug it in again. This can be incredibly energizing.

"Superpowers are a big piece in the puzzle for creating a whole new paradigm of life after sixty. Superpowers are the leverage we need to wake ourselves up from the mirage of eternal vacation."

Superpowers Defined

"In our careers, there have been times and places where we excelled beyond the norm of those around us, and sometimes we've outdistanced our own expectations of ourselves. A particular skill or activity or way of being in the world has seemed to come easily. Many professionals report that such a skill doesn't feel 'super,' just 'normal' to them. But when pressed, they must admit, 'Yes, I am really good at that.'

"We miss living that way when we retire. It's natural to connect that ability with the context where we practiced it. We assume we need the company where we worked, or the lab, or the medical center, or a certain team, in order to accomplish it. And so, we quietly mourn its loss. Or we just wonder why we are depressed. Furthermore, as valuable as classical volunteering is to the community—walking dogs at the shelter or writing checks to the opera or even handing out food at the food bank—these tasks rarely tap into our desire to share the depth of what we have to offer."

I saw several nods in the group confirming this feeling.

"I challenge you now to use your open mind skill to set aside some old assumptions. Our first task is to identify what your Superpower is, especially since it is not always obvious to us. Then you will need open mind again for the second step—along with your curiosity—to find or develop new contexts where you can exercise your Superpowers once again.

"In your professional lives, as I said, it may have gone unnoticed by you, but colleagues will frequently have been much more aware of your Superpower. They can be a resource to help you spot what your Superpower is. I'll explain more on that soon. Going forward, your Superpowers can transform a somewhat passive entertainment-based retirement into the lively, purpose-filled life you are seeking. When you find a new context to exercise that Superpower, you will blossom into who you are called to be for the coming decades."

Here's the Problem

"Before we get specific about Superpowers," I said, "we need to step back for a moment and ask again, why are we talking about Superpowers in the first place?

"Here is the problem we are up against. Many professionals, particularly the ones whose jobs are highly dependent on a certain infrastructure (e.g., surgeons, lab scientists, judges, high tech, upper management, etc.), do not believe they have anything to offer once they retire.

"*Superpower* as a metaphor provides a way for these people to begin to identify what personal qualities and capabilities they have that can transfer to new settings and contexts. The metaphor of Superpower is a path to believing in themselves again, once 'the job' is removed from their lives. And it is a path to remaining as a contributing member of a world that needs all the help it can get."

Getting Specific

Martina said, "I don't doubt that some of you have Superpowers, but I just don't see it for myself. I just showed up and did my job."

"Actually Martina," I responded, "your reaction is fairly widespread. In the past few years, I have asked many people what they think their Superpower is, and they often can't see it. Then I ask them to consult their closest colleagues. The people they worked with can see it, and they can point it out to help them understand what I'm talking about."

Herding Cats

Samuel said, "Martina, I think I know what Marie is getting at. Earlier you mentioned that although you worked in the rather fixed structures of state government, what you seemed to be able to do really well was what you called 'herding cats.' I suspect that may be one of your Superpowers. Does that resonate?"

Martina stared at the floor for a minute. "Hmmm. Very interesting. I suppose you could be right. People were often surprised when I'd get a policy changed or get a bunch of people on different sides of an issue or procedure to come together on a creative compromise. Is that what you mean, Marie?"

"Yes, it is, Martina. And you have inadvertently made an important additional point for us. We can all visualize you doing that in state government, and more important, we suspect that we could begin to imagine you exercising that Superpower in other situations that have nothing to do with state government. That is exactly our challenge. How to use it again in the life we are now inventing. Can you see that possibility?"

"Well yes… yes and no… well, sort of," replied Martina. "But I knew everyone. I could instinctively see how to bring them into consensus on matters that concerned us. I don't know anyone now, really, here in Santa Fe. Except family, and they are long past looking to me for leadership." She chuckled at the absurdity.

Shirley said, "But isn't that part of our search? To begin to uncover other situations that we can't even name right this moment, where you could, in your case, get to know the parties involved? Help them see their common ground? From where I sit, that skill, that Superpower, is needed just about everywhere."

"You all seem to be seeing something I can't," Martina said. "Maybe if you could give me an example of what that could look like."

Samuel jumped in. "I don't want to scare you, Martina, with the enormity of the task, but let's take as an example the ongoing controversy over the monument on the Plaza. Paul, I'll give some background since you haven't been here long. The monument pull-down trend landed here and a memorial to some Civil War soldiers was pulled down by a crowd at the Plaza. Immediately one group wanted it restored to its former glory. An unfortunate phrase on the plaque mentioned the soldiers' fight with 'savage' Indians. Local pueblos understandably objected to literal restoration. Some well-meaning soul suggested a water feature instead. Environmentalists called that a waste of water in our desert climate. The city put a protective plywood shield around the base, and everyone found that offensively ugly—and a daily reminder that 'their' wishes were not being honored. Martina, we might call this an opportunity to see how the milling cats might be herded."

"I follow you," she said, "but how could I come up with an answer when so many others could not?"

Himari said, "I think what Marie and Samuel are saying is that when we wade in and practice our Superpower, unexpected, good things can happen. I heard you say, at your state job, 'I knew everyone. I could instinctively see how to bring them into consensus on matters that concerned us.'"

Before Martina could respond, Alicia said, "Click! She knew everyone! That's the key. We don't just barge in as the Retired Smart Person to dispense wisdom. We *get to know people.* We have the leisure time to do this now. We don't just show up because some executive sent us. Martina, I have a hunch that if you found a situation where you cared about the issue, or about the mission or the people involved, and you got to know them, you could work your magic of consensus building again. The magic is, the people themselves figure it out once their relationships to each other change."

"I'll vote for that," Paul boomed.

I let all this sink in for Martina, knowing it would take some time for her to digest. I asked if anyone else might have an inkling of what their Superpower might be.

What Do Superpowers Look Like?

"Could you say a little more about what to look for? Characteristics, I mean?" Samuel asked.

"Certainly. I'll elaborate. You might recall the times or places during your career that really gave you juice, so to speak. Times you felt in the zone. Times you felt so *on* that you were unaware of time passing. Or situations you eagerly looked forward to because you knew ahead of time that you had it nailed. Does that help?"

> *Exercise: In your journal, jot down examples of when you experienced this feeling of being in the zone, knowing you would ace the task at hand.*

Your Turn

"Yes," said Samuel slowly.

Alicia spoke up. "I think I know what you are pointing to. At my company, people often thanked me for bringing joy and humor into situations. I didn't do it for this reason, but I know I got a lot done by setting that tone. I do feel lots of joy as I go about my life, so I suppose you could say that is a Superpower."

"I would describe it slightly differently," Shirley said. "Judging by the way that I have experienced you, I'd say you *spread* love and joy."

Three others simultaneously said, "Yes!"

"The ayes have it," Paul declared.

Shirley added, "Seeing that Superpower bringing value almost anywhere is easy, but I wonder if, in Alicia's purposeful place, when she finds it, something deeper will be going on too. Marie, you've thought about this lots more than we have. How would you respond to that?"

"My experience says that Alicia's bringing love and joy will be *especially* valuable in the new context where she finds herself. But what is this deeper element? I suspect it will have something to do with Alicia's calling, the situation, that moment, where life has prepared her all along to now share her Superpowers.

Perseverance and Resilience

"When we start looking through the research literature to see how Superpowers might show up, Alicia, I see another quality in you. Angela Duckworth, an author and psychologist at the University of Pennsylvania, calls it grit and perseverance. We could also call it resilience. The Superpower is going beyond challenges and thriving where others fall by the wayside facing those same challenges."

I took a breath and continued. "I am suddenly a little nervous to elaborate because I fear this is going to sound like a cliché. Alicia, please know I mean this from deep in my heart. You have overcome a stunning number of obstacles, ever since you could walk…or run. South Central LA is still home to thousands who have not been able to do what you have accomplished. The words *grit* and *perseverance* only begin to describe the Superpower you will bring to your next assignment, should you choose to accept it."

Alicia put her hands over her heart, bowed her head, and remained silent, smiling shyly.

Guessing and Groping Are Part of the Search

Himari started to speak, then hesitated. "I'm not sure about my Superpower. I know that I was fairly successful at getting funding for some experimental projects and initiatives. I think that had to do with people having confidence in what I was advocating for. Or maybe confidence in me? I think my former colleagues would say I was good at getting people to trust me. But I don't know what to call it."

"Chief fundraiser!" Alicia muttered with a grin.

"That is certainly one likely arena for this Superpower," Shirley said. "But I think the question for Himari is, does doing it bring you joy and/or satisfaction?"

> *Exercise: In your journal, jot down what brings you the most joy and satisfaction.*

Your Turn 

Himari tapped her pen against her journal for a moment. "Hmmm. Good question. Yes, I think it did. Lots of satisfaction with the results, certainly, but also…hmmm, not exactly joy, but a warm feeling as I talked with people and they responded positively. I'm not sure we've hit the center of the target yet."

Adaptive Expertise

I asked the group, "Are any of you familiar with the term 'adaptive expertise'? It emerged in the early 1980s from the research of cognitive psychologists Giyoo Hatano and Kayoko Inagaki. Himari, it might be helpful for you to look into their work."

"Do you think it has something to do with my Superpower?" Himari asked.

"Yes, it might. They made the important distinction between *routine* expertise and *adaptive* expertise. The latter suggests a deep understanding of the concepts and principles below the surface, and it allows the person to adjust their approach in different situations. In short, the Superpower is to perform well in unprecedented or unfamiliar situations. Himari, I sense that this could be another of your Superpowers."

I explained to the group, "With all of these Superpowers as we work with them today, we don't have to pin down an exact description. We are just going for the general idea, for something to work with as we move forward. Clarity will come later. Anyone else?"

Social Intelligence and Sensitivity

Shirley said, "I like calling it a Superpower. Somehow that adds to my confidence that I am on the right track. I seem to have the ability to see people's potential. It's almost as if I can see their future unfolding. Once in a while it's almost eerie, in a good way. It's definitely part of my intuition."

"That's why we invited you to this group!" Samuel grinned, as if he had been the one there from the start.

"If we continue tracing lines," I continued, "from what we see in our colleagues to the research literature, I would nominate Shirley as having high social and emotional intelligence. We're familiar with Daniel Goleman's framework for this from his books on emotional intelligence, but in Shirley's case, I see her also demonstrating what psychologist Elaine Aron called high sensory processing sensitivity in her book *The Highly Sensitive Person*. The Superpower is processing information more deeply than others do and noticing subtleties that escape the rest of us. This feeds in perfectly with social and emotional intelligence."

"And it's a great fit with the dream Shirley has been spelling out," added Martina. "Paul, what about yours?"

Tacit Knowledge and Insight

"I see patterns that no one else can see," said Paul. "I can be in a meeting, or even an informal gathering, and people will be discussing an issue. They are all over the map. Each person offering an observation, or just an opinion. It slowly dawns on me that there is a thread, or an underlying coherence. I can see patterns in larger systems. When I spell it out, heads turn, so to speak, and people nod, as though something new has been added. I feel like I'm just pointing out the obvious, but clearly no one else has seen it until I spell it out. In an informal group, it's just satisfying to have order brought out of the chaos. In a meeting with an objective, it usually moves people forward toward the action they need to take."

Several in the room looked puzzled, so Paul continued. "I've been reading in the local paper about a large solar array that is planned for south of the city. In the closest subdivision some homeowners are fiercely objecting. I watched an obvious polarity playing out, getting sharper every week. The county commissioners, whose approval was needed, kept postponing the decision. The pattern I noticed by its absence was that no one mentioned, even in the Letters to the Editor, what might eventually be installed in that vast field if the solar project was prohibited. I could think of a lot of more objectionable uses for that land, perfectly legal, but things you would never want to live downwind from. In short, the pattern I observed was a boundary being drawn around the debate, and no one thinking to look beyond it at the wider situation."

"That is definitely a Superpower, Paul," Martina said. "I wish you'd been in my meetings all those years."

I suggested a book to Paul to give him a wider understanding of his Superpower: *Seeing What Others Don't: The Remarkable Ways We Gain Insights* by Gary Klein, a psychologist, researcher, and consultant. His work, done over decades, describes how people observe and learn and make decisions accordingly, often without being aware of how they are doing so. As with other Superpowers, many people have some ability in this area, but having a Superpower means you are a natural master with it.

Samuel spoke up reluctantly. "I'm still not sure about my Superpower. I'm going to have to check in with some old colleagues. And maybe ask my wife. I'll let you know what I uncover."

Metacognition

"Samuel," I offered, "I can suggest a couple of possibilities for you to consider. One is called *metacognition*. It is the ability to think about how you are thinking. I wonder if this is something you tried to teach your students over the years, with varying levels of success."

"I suspect you are onto something," he said. "Carry on."

I explained that John Flavel laid the foundation in 1979, and since then others have expanded on his work. Donald Schön, a professor of urban planning and education at MIT, described the importance of reflective practice; he called it "reflection-in-action." It is the ability to consciously think about what one is doing while doing it. He also described "double-loop learning," which refers to not only correcting errors within a given framework but also questioning the underlying assumptions and goals of that organization or framework, enabling deeper learning and adaptation to changing circumstances.[20]

I reminded the group also of Peter Senge's example of the tangible and practical technique of "sitting up in the balcony" above whatever scene we are engaged in. This form of metacognition allows us to both participate in a meeting and observe ourself and the others from a more "detached" but often more astute perspective.

"This is a helpful look," Samuel said, "at what I may, in fact, have been doing for decades, but, as you mentioned earlier, I was taking it for granted. At the same time, I know many of my undergraduate students really struggled with this. I'll ask a few people who know me and see what they say about Superpowers. But you said you had two ideas."

"Yes, the second is just a guess, since I don't really know you well yet. It's called *positive deviance*."

"Oh, I like it already. Go on."

Positive Deviance

I told the group that the idea originated from Jerry Sternin, who worked in international development. The core idea is that certain individuals find unique and effective solutions to difficult challenges, usually using existing resources with a new point of view. These "positive deviants," those with this Superpower, often excel in unconventional ways. He and Richard Pascale at Stanford Business School, along with Monique Sternin, authored *The Power of Positive Deviance: How Unlikely Innovators Solve the World's Toughest Problems.*[21]

An exemplary story: In certain Vietnamese villages, researchers discovered families with noticeably more well-nourished children. They were incorporating shrimp and sweet potato greens into meals. When the researchers highlighted and taught these practices to others, they saw widespread nutritional improvements.[22] Another story: Some hospitals reduced infection rates by identifying and emulating the unconventional hygiene practices of certain staff members, leading to overall better patient outcomes.[23]

"Samuel," I said, "I have noticed you frequently look at situations from a different perspective than others do, so it may be that you will recognize a Superpower along these lines, somewhere in your lifetime of experiences. For example, I can imagine you hanging out at the interfaith homeless shelter to see how you might be of service. You begin to notice that one of the volunteers seems to be noticeably more effective in eliciting cooperation from the guests. Because you are adept at looking beyond the obvious, you observe that this volunteer practices consistent gestures of respect, asking permission before speaking, not touching without assent. You then ask reflective questions of other staff, and the practice of upgraded respect begins to spread.

"I am not suggesting you should work in a homeless shelter, though you of course could. I am illustrating how noticing positive deviance and asking reflective questions as Superpowers could translate into *tikkun olam.* It's 'applied philosophy' at its most granular finest."

Dormant Superpowers

"Or," I suggested to the whole group, "it may be that you have a Superpower still in development.

"Let's not assume—watch those assumptions!—that all our Superpowers are wrapped up with a bow during our career years. Consider the possibility you had nearly invisible seeds of a

Superpower, but it simply could not develop fully in a professional context. Now, with our expanded freedoms—time, options, intent—these Superpowers can sprout and grow into a new effectiveness. The arts are the most visible example.

"I am thinking of a statewide disabilities program administrator from Montana who took up watercolor once he left that position. I find his Instagram posts of his artistic experiments to be quite remarkable. He captures the spirit of his subjects in watercolor in a way you seldom see from new artists. I suspect that a lifelong career of deep compassion is what is showing up in his works on paper.

"The arts are tangible, but new forms of leadership and collaboration, for example, are worth watching for. Without assignments and job titles, you may not notice them emerging at first, but be alert to such possibilities."

"Different ways of herding cats come to mind," Martina noted.

Full-Time? Part-Time? Focused Time.

"This brings up one more nuance to our discovery of our Superpowers," I said. "You do not necessarily have to engage your Superpower in a terribly serious endeavor, and you certainly don't have to do it full time, even as a volunteer. Or, you can decide to go full out in your Superpower in a really fun—what we might call 'recreational'—way. Just keep in mind that there will be a direct correlation between how meaningful the activity is to you and how satisfying it will be. For the budding Montana artist I just mentioned, he told me that it means a great deal to him to attempt to visually capture the *soul* of a scene or a person in his at-first-glance simple sketches. It is the *meaning* he finds in this activity that brings him deep satisfaction.

"A body of research is also showing that the *effort* you put into an activity positively correlates with the satisfaction you experience. Our Montana artist does not spend endless hours with his watercolors, but while he is there, he is fully present. You might say he is making a great effort to turn out his paintings, though his brushwork appears effortless. This intense application of his focus and prioritizing his time both contribute to the deep satisfaction he experiences. We need to reframe our professional assumption that full-time exclusive attention is the only serious way to live a satisfying life."

Closing the Loop, Connecting the Dots

"You now have a preliminary view of what your Superpower might be, or a path for how to explore it. To close the loop—and *this is important*—it is quite possible your new purpose or your calling is centered around your Superpower. But please don't get tangled up in which of these labels you should be trying to shoehorn your life into. Regardless, that 'gift' will hover at the center of what you feel impelled to create, and your new purpose or calling will include your Superpower. Here you will discover as important a guidance system as any we have considered—with the powerful exception of connecting with Source as your most central way of discerning your future.

"Let me summarize some of the skills and practices we have touched on so far," I said to the group. "This will help us connect the dots. When we sit in liminal space, with our open will (this is presencing), we can enhance our curiosity and observe our passion, as well as listening for our personal future. From that stance, we can begin to visualize what an island of coherence might look like—gathering a few kindred spirits to regularly practice clarity and discernment together by intentionally focusing our attention using a proven format. Participating in such a group boosts our self-efficacy, our ability to believe that new futures are possible for us personally. Then the secret sauce: we add our Superpower to that picture and see what might emerge."

"Actually," Himari said, "I can see now that liminal space is the *spiritual* secret sauce, and Superpowers are what we might call the *psychological and social* secret sauce."

"Excellent observation! Thank you. And as you can see, *taking the intentional time to place your awareness in these states* is the 'secret' to the secret sauce actually accomplishing the job for us. I suggest you do this repeatedly. Grow a new habit. Create quiet moments, both as part of your morning practice and on specially created occasions such as mini retreats. This is how we grow into unexpected places that will change the course of our lives."

Highlights

Your Superpower – Your new purpose or calling will include your Superpower. You have spent decades honing something special that comes from an innate gift and capability within you. Why would you want to "retire" that?

- **Superpowers defined.** You are engaging your Superpower when you're doing an activity and operating "in the zone." Time passes, and you don't even notice. You "nail" the task effortlessly while others have to spend a lot of effort just to complete it. Activities that use your Superpower are things you like to do or situations you like to be in—experiences that "give you juice."

- **What do Superpowers look like?** Superpowers take on a wide range of qualities, but all of them go beyond what we think of as résumé material. Some Superpowers as exemplified by the characters in the chapter include the following:

  - **Herding Cats** – Martina's Superpower of consensus building
  - **Perseverance and Resilience** – Alicia's Superpower of overcoming challenges

- **Adaptive Expertise** – Himari's Superpower of performing well in unprecedented or unfamiliar situations
- **Social Intelligence and Sensitivity** – Shirley's Superpower of social and emotional intelligence, of processing information deeply and noticing subtleties
- **Tacit Knowledge and Insight** – Paul's Superpower of seeing patterns no one else sees and reflecting them back to the group—when people can see patterns in the chaos they experience, they can begin to come up with solutions
- **Metacognition and Positive Deviance** – Samuel's Superpowers of thinking about how he is thinking, thus gaining more insight and a more complex perspective, and using that unique perspective to notice and come up with innovative observations and solutions

- **Figuring out your Superpower** – You may not immediately know what your own Superpower is. Don't forget that guessing and groping as you explore possibilities is a normal part of the search. Look at the examples of the characters, their process for thinking about their Superpowers and the Superpowers they end up identifying with the help of the group. Oftentimes, others can see our Superpowers better than we can. That's where a group or colleagues can help. Ask colleagues for feedback and think about their responses. It's also possible your Superpower has been dormant because of career or other restraints. Now that you have the freedom of time, intent, and options, be alert to the seeds of your Superpower that are begging to be developed. When it comes to discerning your future, we've already discussed multiple tools to help us devise a path forward.
- **Liminal space is the spiritual secret sauce, and Superpowers are the psychological and social secret sauce—** Liminal space is the pathway linking our Greater

Wisdom, our Source, with our everyday experience. Our Superpowers provide the strongest link between our Self and the world we serve. Underlying both is the fundamental practice of taking intentional time to pay attention and of course noticing *where* we are directing our attention.

Exercises: Identify Your Own Superpowers

I have described specific types of Superpowers in this chapter, but these examples are by no means a complete list. I offer them in the narrative to stimulate your powers of observation and discernment so you can identify your own Superpowers, whatever they may be.

1. **Action Step:** In the <u>Sourcebook for Chapter 7</u> you will find an expanded list of potential Superpowers, reflecting a wide range of talents, skills, and personality traits. Study the examples on that list. Reflect on your own experiences for clues to your unique strengths, to prepare you to apply them in a new context during your Prime Time. But don't overthink it. Look for what seems to come easily, or what you even take for granted.

   Also remember, a Superpower could still be *emerging*, ready to take shape in a new arena. Watch for the right cause, project, or opportunity to draw it out.

   If philanthropy might be part of your *Prime Time,* don't miss the section on Emerging Superpowers in Purposeful Giving in the "Expanded Superpowers" list in the <u>Sourcebook for Chapter 7</u>.

   If you are still unclear about your Superpower, try this second exercise. It is a tangible way to get closer to describing your Superpower.

2. **Action Step:** Contact two or three of the people who knew you best in your career. Explain to them what we mean by *Superpowers,* then ask them if they can describe yours. You

will find their feedback quite useful as we move ahead. And you may be surprised to find that they seem to know you better than you know yourself.

Prime Time Milestones

Take a breath. Pause. What are you noticing at this point in your journey? As you reflect, write your thoughts in your journal.

Insight. I see something new…

Sample response: *My real strengths may not be what was on my résumé. I'm beginning to spot deeper capacities in myself.*

Shift. I feel something changing…

Sample response: *Intrigued. A little proud. Like maybe I'm more resourceful than I've given myself credit for.*

Step. I'm ready to try…

Sample response: *I'll ask someone who knows me well what strengths they've always seen in me—and I'll listen.*

PHASE IV

From Epiphany to Action

CHAPTER 8

Invent the Future You Want to Live In

*Do not go where the path may lead, go instead
where there is no path and leave a trail.*

—Ralph Waldo Emerson

"Houston, we have a problem," I said in my most serious deep voice.

The group was just settling in, finding a place for a cup, pulling out a pen. Heads popped up when I said this.

I looked slowly around the room, meeting each person's eyes.

"Every one of you in this circle holds a mental model of your world that you are largely unaware of. You think like job seekers. You have worked for medium or large organizations that prepare written job descriptions with a staff that hires people for those positions. Agreed so far?"

Heads nodded.

"And this is a problem?" said Alicia. "I don't get it."

The Challenge—Temporarily Disguised as a Problem

For all these weeks together, we have talked about you finding new places to re-engage your Superpowers. Unfortunately, the world is not going to change rapidly enough for you. Some organizations will be clever and alert enough to recognize this talent resource. They will invent job-share roles, look for part-time volunteers of depth and substance, or create all-new opportunities. But not quickly enough, and most will do nothing at all. You are going to have to create your own opportunities, or a small group of you will have to get together to create them. To accomplish this, you are going to have to learn to think like an entrepreneur.

"Now, before you jump to conclusions about that word, let me clarify. I use the term 'entrepreneur' as a shorthand term for anyone who creates something where there was nothing. I don't mean you should go build a whole company—though you could, if that's your passion and your calling. I mean you will need to spot unfilled needs and unnoticed opportunities. You will have to have enormous confidence in your own ability to add value with your Superpower, even while others are not yet seeing it. And you will have to be persuasive about that passion and capability."

"OK," Alicia said. "I think I get it." She glanced around the circle. "I'd say offhand that I worked for the most entrepreneurial company of any of us here, but when I joined, it was already a functioning company with an HR department and they hired me to do a specific job. I had a certain amount of freedom to initiate programs by the time I was a product manager, but I still had a 'job' that everyone understood. So I suppose it's safe to say that I probably have a whole pile of unconscious assumptions gathered around that history."

"In emergency medicine," Paul chimed in, "we had to make it up as we went along in some instances, but there were still long lists of protocols that we were trained to follow."

Himari said, "Maybe we need to compile a quick list of what we even mean by this entrepreneurial mindset, so we know what we are talking about—and what we need to learn…and unlearn."

Alicia jumped up and retrieved her laptop. "I'll just ask ChatGPT for a list. It doesn't need to be 'scientifically verified,' just something that will point us in the general direction. Having something in our hands will help us discuss this more coherently. Just give me a minute."

"While Alicia is doing that, let me make one more observation. If it turns out that your passion and your calling lead you to go solo with a project, or recruit just a small team to do it together, you will still need to convince your target customers or clients of the value of what you do. If your new context involves an existing organization, there will be lots of other people with a job-holder mindset whose first reaction will be something like, 'You're crazy!' You can't let this kind of reaction bother you. Long ago a friend and mentor said to me, 'There is no such thing as *no*—they just don't understand yet.'"

Alicia stepped over to her printer at her kitchen desk and brought a stack of paper back to the group. "Here it is. It's not 'the definitive work,' but it will get us started."[24]

The entrepreneurial mindset thrives in ambiguity, opportunity creation, and self-directed action. To think more like an entrepreneur, you will want to develop some or all of these core personal qualities and mental habits.

1. **Opportunity Recognition** – You see problems as opportunities and identify gaps in the market or needs in the community.

2. **Self-Efficacy (Internal Locus of Control)** – You believe that your actions directly influence outcomes. You don't need to wait for external validation or direction.

3. **Risk Tolerance and Comfort with Uncertainty** – You take calculated risks, understanding that uncertainty is a constant. You have learned to make decisions without full information.

4. **Creativity and Adaptive Thinking** – You think outside of existing frameworks and are willing to test unconventional solutions.

5. **Resilience and Grit** – You have the ability to persist through failure, setbacks, and criticism. You can iterate and learn rather than giving up.

6. **Initiative and Proactiveness** – You do not wait for permission or direction. You take action and refine as you go.

7. **Resourcefulness** – You can make the most of limited resources, leveraging relationships, knowledge, and unconventional solutions.

8. **Persuasion and Influence** – You have the ability to sell an idea, whether to customers, partners, donors, or potential collaborators. You build networks of people who can help.

9. **Comfort with Experimentation and Learning** – You are willing to test ideas in small ways, learn from results, and pivot as necessary.

10. **Ownership Mentality** – You have a mindset of accountability. You take neither success nor failure personally. You don't blame failures on external factors. You are willing to take responsibility for what is happening.

In contrast, the job-holder mindset frequently depends on external direction, predefined roles, a stable work environment, and structured expectations. The shift to an entrepreneurial mindset requires both cognitive and emotional adaptations.

Claiming What Is Already True

As the group read through the list, Martina remarked, "I don't think I could do all these things."

Samuel countered, "I don't imagine we need to adopt *all* of these beliefs and behaviors in order to be successful in our new calling. I see this as a list of signposts. Indications of ways we could stretch and grow, each in our own way."

"I appreciate that comment, Samuel," Himari said. "The scientist in me feels like a ChatGPT list is somehow cheating. But as Marie said, this isn't about peer-reviewed activities. We are all learning, experimenting, and challenging the status quo. This list is comprehensive *enough* for me to use it as a learning tool."

"This isn't just for business founders," Paul added. "These qualities can help anyone who wants to design their own new opportunity, in any realm."

Shirley said, "I wonder if some of us might already have some of these traits. Could we glance back down the list and see?"

Several voices murmured, "OK," "Sure," and "Let's do this right now."

Your Turn

"I'll claim resilience and grit!" Alicia said enthusiastically. "I learned that about the time I learned to talk."

"I think I'm pretty resourceful," Martina chimed in. "That explanation was almost my whole job as head of a statewide department." She paused, realizing the irony. "That was my job description. Ha! Himari, what about you?"

Himari hesitated, then said, "I suppose I'll have to claim self-efficacy, though I never would have used that actual term before. In medicine I certainly could see the results of my decisions. On a day-to-day basis, there was rarely time to wait for either external validation or direction. Paul, how did you experience your more immediate immersion in emergency medicine?"

"I'd say ownership mentality is a good fit. No question I was used to taking personal responsibility as I went. If I had tried to always be blaming someone else, or other circumstances, I doubt I would have lasted long."

Himari turned to Samuel. "I still have a rather vague picture of what your work days looked like, Samuel. Do any of these feel like a fit?"

"Yes, actually, there is one," Samuel answered. "I am very comfortable with uncertainty, though I'm not sure I connected it much with risk tolerance, unless you think proposing unpopular theories is a risk—or trying to sustain the interest of nineteen-year-olds."

Shirley said, "I'd say putting forth minority opinions is often risky. We'll give you this one, Samuel. And yours seems to share space with mine. I am pretty comfortable with experimentation and learning. This description is me: *willing to test ideas in small ways.* I probably learn better when my mistakes aren't on the front page. Well, that has never happened, so that proves my point—as does the fact that I am sitting in this group."

Shirley turned to me. "Marie, can you claim one of these on the list too?"

"Yes, I am pretty confident that creativity and adaptive thinking is what I do most days. And you all are the guinea pigs for my willingness to test unconventional solutions."

Everyone laughed.

"I'd be curious to know," I continued, "if each of you has spotted at least one thing on the list that you'd be most drawn to develop more for yourself. I'll give you a moment to ponder this. Listen to your inner voice."

Your Turn 

Choosing a Growing Edge

"I could probably pick two or three that I need to work on," Shirley said, "but I'll start with persuasion and influence. I'd like to get really confident in my new ideas, whatever they turn out to be. I'll need to stand up for them so others can believe in them too."

Samuel gestured at his paper. "I'll take on resourcefulness. I know I'll need to make the most of limited resources at first. I'd like to learn to be really clever in this way, having worked with quite intangible matters for so many years."

Himari chimed in. "I feel that way about risk tolerance and comfort with uncertainty. I know whatever I end up doing will push some envelopes, and although I don't know if 'comfort' is the best descriptor, I do want to learn to be able to tolerate risk in new areas, not just in pushing for a larger departmental budget."

"Adaptive thinking is my next hurdle," Alicia said. "I think I've been pretty creative over the years, but going way outside existing frameworks is still making me nervous. I've been very creative *inside* a very specific industry, with its unspoken rules and traditions. I want to grow and take risks beyond that."

Paul said, "I'd like to learn to better spot gaps and unmet needs. In my career the needs have seemed so clear. Real no-brainers. I want to stretch. I think I do see patterns, I just don't recognize them as *opportunities* because I've always had a full plate before. Now it's different. Like Himari said, time to push the envelope. So I'll claim Opportunity Recognition."

"Here I am going last again," Martina said. "No irony here: I am choosing initiative and proactiveness." The group chuckled, then encouraged her on. "I really need to not expect to wait for permission. Well, it's not so much permission, I've just always liked to see which way the wind is blowing before I speak up. Sometimes I *have* the new idea, but I don't always say it out loud right away. So this will be a shift in my self-image, as well as a new set of action steps."

The group turned to look at me, gesturing as if to say, "Out with it."

"OK," I said. "I'll pick one. I confess I still need work on self-efficacy. I have raised the bar for myself quite a bit by committing what we are learning to a book. Teaching groups of clients is one thing, but no matter how successful those clients are, putting it all into print for thousands more to read…well, let's just say that believing this can all take hold in a bigger way is still a work in progress. But I am energized by the possibility."

As we talked about these qualities, it occurred to me that something like a self-inventory might be useful. I explained this and asked the group, "What do you think?"

Paul asked, "What would a self-inventory look like?"

Alicia burst in. "I'll just ask ChatGPT to give us one we can take home tonight to work on! It's good at formatting clusters of thoughts. As we said, this isn't meant to be peer-reviewed science. I, for one, would like just a simple map of where I am and where I might want to go with these entrepreneurial mindset qualities and capabilities. Would you all like that?"

She glanced around the room to heads nodding affirmatively, so she picked up her laptop again and started typing a prompt. As the others continued to compare notes on the various qualities, she was soon handing out "The Entrepreneurial Mindset Self-Assessment and Development Guide." [25] (See <u>Sourcebook for chapter 8.</u>)

Your Turn 

I thanked Alicia for taking initiative and suggested the group could compare notes on their results at a future meeting.

Glimpsing a Wider Vision

"You know," said Paul—he paused for a long moment, gathering his thoughts—"I am seeing another pattern here. Maybe I'm better at this than I thought. As we were talking about other people reading the book and gathering in groups, I am feeling a shift. We thought we were just trying to figure out our own next step in our lives, but I can see now how we are actually part of something much larger."

"I think I see what you are pointing to," Himari responded. "As we try to figure this out, this redesigning our lives, we are not just helping ourselves, we really are creating a path for others to follow or to walk alongside on similar new paths."

Martina said, "This is all sinking in for me. If I wait for someone else to offer me a perfect opportunity, I could wait forever. If I can figure out a way to build it myself, I am helping change the game."

"I'm getting chills down my back," Alicia whispered. "The good kind. Maybe this isn't just about reinventing our own lives. It's about shaping what is becoming possible for a whole generation."

Highlights

Entrepreneurial Mindset. Superpower opportunities are in short supply—we will have to create them ourselves. This requires an entrepreneurial mindset which can include the following characteristics, each of which came alive in the conversation:

- **Opportunity Recognition:** You see problems as opportunities and identify gaps in the market or community. Paul realized that his career had trained him to respond to obvious needs, but now he is learning to notice subtler gaps in the world around him—and that these might be invitations, not just curiosities.

- **Self-Efficacy (internal locus of control):** You believe that your actions directly influence outcomes. You don't need to wait for external validation or direction. Himari shared that, in medicine, waiting for outside permission was not an option—she had long operated from the belief that her decisions mattered. Now she is seeing how that same belief will serve her in designing her next chapter.

- **Risk Tolerance and Comfort with Uncertainty:** You take calculated risks, understanding that uncertainty is a constant. You have learned to make decisions without full information. While Himari was once confident managing risk within institutional boundaries, she now names her growing edge—learning to stay steady in the face of the open-ended risks of personal reinvention.

- **Creativity and Adaptive Thinking:** You think outside of existing frameworks and are willing to test unconventional solutions. Alicia recognized that her creativity had flourished inside a structured industry—but now she wants to unhook from those frameworks and invent freely, with more willingness to question her past constraints.

- **Resilience and Grit:** You have the ability to persist through failure, setbacks, and criticism. You can iterate and learn rather than giving up. "I learned grit about the time I learned to talk," Alicia quipped. Her early and enduring toughness gave her the foundation to persist through new challenges, a trait she knows she can lean on again.

- **Initiative and Proactiveness:** You do not wait for permission or direction. You take action and refine as you go. Martina surprised herself by choosing this quality as her growing edge. Though accustomed to leading from behind the scenes, she is ready to speak up sooner and act without waiting for consensus.

- **Resourcefulness:** You can make the most of limited resources, leveraging relationships, knowledge, and unconventional solutions. Samuel named this as the quality he most wants to develop now. After decades spent in abstract thinking, he wants to become savvy and practical with limited tools—clever in action as well as theory.

- **Persuasion and Influence:** You have the ability to sell an idea, whether to customers, partners, donors, or potential collaborators. You build networks of people who can help. Shirley chose this as her frontier skill—she wants to become more persuasive so she can champion her own ideas with confidence, and help others believe in them, too.

- **Comfort with Experimentation and Learning:** You are willing to test ideas in small ways, learn from results, and pivot as necessary. Shirley also saw herself in this mindset already—especially the part about learning best through small tests and iterations, out of the spotlight. This gave her confidence that she's further along than she thought.

- **Ownership Mentality:** You have a mindset of accountability. You take neither success nor failure as personal. You don't blame failures on external factors. You are willing to take responsibility for what is happening. Paul said this was the air he breathed in emergency medicine—you take responsibility, full stop. Now he brings that same clarity and readiness into this next, less scripted chapter of his life.

These qualities aren't all-or-nothing traits; they are postures we can each grow into, just as the characters in this circle are doing. The key is not to become someone else, but to claim what is already true—and choose which edge to stretch next.

Exercises: Where Am I on the Job/Entrepreneur Spectrum?

1. **Action Step:** If you have not already done so, go to the <u>Sourcebook for Chapter 8</u> and take the entrepreneurial mindset self-assessment. Set yourself a goal of at least one area you would like to improve. Make a note in your journal regarding how you could be more alert to opportunities to practice this skill. This awakens your unconscious to watch for situations and opportunities that you previously would not have noticed.

2. **Journal Reflection:** From the assessment, make note in your journal of the area where you are already strongest. Here is a journal prompt for the coming week:

   In what ways might my strengths in this area overlap or reinforce my Superpower?

   Keeping this in the front of your mind will help alert you to recognize potential situations where you might engage your Superpower.

Prime Time Milestones

Take a breath. Pause. What are you noticing at this point in your journey? As you reflect, write your thoughts in your journal.

Insight. I see something new…

Sample response: *There's freedom in not knowing. I don't have to be an expert to begin again.*

Shift. I feel something changing...

Sample response: *A little nervous, but also energized. Ready to stretch.*

Step. I'm ready to try...

Sample response: *I'll let myself be a beginner in one area this week—without apology.*

CHAPTER 9

Crystallizing Your Calling: A Workshop to Discover What's Yours to Do

Crystallizing happens from the deeper place of knowing…"visioning" can happen from just about any place, even from… downloading.

—OTTO SCHARMER[26]

The scene is a Berkeley High School chemistry lab in 1959. Mr. Crandall carefully carries a large glass container from his supply room and sets it gingerly on the front lab table, inviting us all to gather around. He explains that the clear liquid inside is supersaturated. He takes some tweezers and picks up a tiny speck. He drops it into the solution.

Slowly the speck seems to grow icicles, or are they snowflakes? As we watch, in a silence not characteristic of seventeen-year-olds, the white structures begin to spread with irregular but patterned intent. Before long, the whole container is filled with something white and beautiful and not at all self-explanatory.

This is crystallization. The substance transitions from a liquid to a solid. Its atoms or molecules arrange themselves into a specific, repeating pattern, forming a crystal lattice. To the naked eye, it looks like magic. It is an inspiring image for a journey into the unknown.

As our group in Santa Fe gathered to discover what would come next, now that they had sketched out their Superpowers and identified how they would augment their entrepreneurial mindset, I decided that crystallizing would serve as our metaphor for the next step in the process of discerning our calling.

Note: This chapter is primarily a workshop, in the sense that you, the reader, will be invited to do extensive reflecting and writing, right alongside the group at Alicia's house.

Mind Map

"In order to allow this discernment to emerge," I explained, "we will want to hold our journey-to-date visually in front of us. We will do this with a simple mind map." I passed out paper from an art sketch pad. Any large paper will do, but it needs to be at least 11"×14" in size.

"At the top, write your own name and the word 'journey.' For example, mine would read Marie's Journey."

"Randomly draw nine or ten tennis-ball-sized shapes around the page. They can be circles or messy rectangular blobs—whatever you wish. Choose the first shape, the one nearest the center, and label it 'Liminal Space/Connect with Source.' Leave plenty of room to write more within each shape. Somewhere on the top half of the page, label one shape 'Inner Characters' and the next 'Open Mind, Open Heart, Open Will.' Label three more shapes near each other as 'Curiosity,' 'Passion,' 'Belief.' Label the next shape 'Superpowers.'"

Your Turn 

"Now, take some quiet time to breathe, center in your own liminal space and then write some key insights in each shape— what you have learned or what you want to explore further in that area. You can write outside the lines if you wish. Then, around the perimeter, you can also write a few lines of what larger or additional lessons you have learned or are questioning. For example, you may have thoughts about culture, longevity, and expectations. You can also add a small symbolic sketch that represents the lifeline you drew earlier, with your current age starred along the line. Everything you write should be personally meaningful *to you*. Your goal is to capture *your own journey*, not to fill in a theoretical model as 'an assignment.'"

Your Turn

"Next, we will take a journey through time in your journal. I've adapted these questions from the Presencing Institute Toolkit.[27]

Time Travel

1. Close your eyes, breathe deeply, and go back to a time when you were a late teen or young adult. Picture yourself in a particular place where you will have a chance to quietly ponder for a few minutes. Now look at your current situation from the viewpoint of that younger self. What does your younger self have to say to you?

I gave the group some time to reflect and write. Minutes passed, and then Alicia asked, "I'm not sure if I understand what my younger self is supposed to be seeing or thinking. Marie, could you give us an example from your own life? How did you answer this question?"

"Fair enough," I said. "I'll give my example only to loosen up your imagination, not to say this is how you should do it.

"My younger self is in her first apartment after college in Berkeley. It's a Saturday and she is home from work with some free time. When I ask her what she has to say to me now, she is clueless. She cannot even imagine, of course, what I am doing today, six decades later. But then she remembers that in college she had a dream to someday publish a book with Harper & Row, so she is excited for me that the company that published my first book, in 1983, was bought several years later by Harper. She smiles at this and thinks, 'How funny is that?!'

"Then my mind jumps to my still-young self at thirty-three. I am sitting on our yellow couch in Portland, Oregon. Thinking about me now, she realizes that she has been feeling called to *go where the church isn't yet.* She is awed by the scale of my current vision to transform the whole idea of 'retirement.' So she simply says to me, 'You go, girl!'"

I asked Alicia if this was helpful.

"Yes, it is," she said. "It shows me that whatever pops into my head is cool. I should just let my imagination wander and see what comes up. I can also see how we might notice that some of what we are doing now has been building for quite some time, or had seeds long ago."

I had the group take some more time to play with their mind pictures, and then gave them the next questions.

2. Now imagine yourself in the last days of your life. For our exercise, let's assume you are clear-minded enough to respond to this question. Look back on your entire life's journey. What would you want to see? What specifically would you want to be leaving behind? What footprint? What legacy?

3. Still in that future point of view, what advice would your older self give to you now?

"Take more walks! Lift more weights! Eat more vegetables!" Samuel shouted, then grinned around the room as people laughed and rolled their eyes.

"That's brilliant, Samuel, but I think Marie wants us to push it a little farther than that," Himari said.

Samuel snapped a sharp salute to Himari.

Your Turn 

When they finished writing, I asked if anyone wanted to share anything particular from the three questions.

Himari spoke first. "I have been stunned by reports like the corruption that went on in Alzheimer's research. Drug companies buried results that did not support their medication. I have no idea yet where I can touch in, but my old self says I must find a way to put my Superpowers to work again."

Alicia said, "I don't have children of my own, but I want to become a 'grandmother' for lots of young women who will thank me for making a difference in their lives…well, not exactly 'thank' me, but will appreciate how someone gave them a chance. My younger self really connects with that because of the people who made my own path possible."

"I'll go next," Martina said. "I must agree with Samuel about taking more seriously the physical stamina issue. The thing that really hit me, though, in the last question is that my connecting with Source daily is what is going to save me from the disruption and chaos I am sure is going to continue. This must become my daily practice. Daily. As relentlessly as brushing my teeth. I don't want to get to that last day and regret having been thrown off course by whatever whim or evil somebody else is generating. A few years ago, meditation seemed to me like a nice option. I am past that point now."

I reminded the group that they could come back to these questions and answer them again, as many times as proves fruitful. Checking in with the younger self and the older self can be a way of taking a different perspective on what is happening currently.

Feeling Most Alive

"Your next journal question," I said, "is to close your eyes again and recall a time when you felt most alive."

> 4. Jot down a brief description of what was going on when you felt most alive, then close your eyes again and see if you can

come up with a second and a third time. Don't belabor this, but is there a pattern or a theme? Anything instructive that you notice? Capture in writing whatever you observe. What are these memories wanting to teach you?

After they wrote for a few minutes, Paul said, "I am back in the midst of a lot happening at the same time. Martina, you might call it 'chaos,' but for me that was most often my workday. I know now, looking at my mind map, that I have the ability to bring calm and a certain serenity to the people around me. I'd like to be able to make that contribution again."

"An island of coherence?" Shirley offered. "You have a gift, Paul, for convening islands of coherence."

"You are valuable to each other," I said, "when you help each other observe and name the things the person hearing you is too close to notice."

"That's true." Paul laughed. "I'm so used to that world, I hadn't even made the connection with our discussion about the islands. Thank you."

"Take a moment now," I said, "and go back to your mind map and enter wherever seems appropriate, what you want to remember about the whole idea of feeling most alive."

Your Turn 

When the group seemed to finish writing for the time being, I said, "It's time to take a break, and when you come back, we will take a very specific journey."

"Through the Gate"

As we resettled, I said, "Next I am going to read a guided visualization. If you have not done one before, it's quite simple. You just let your imagination follow along with the instructions as I say them. Don't edit or analyze, just 'go with the flow.'"

> *Note:* You can also listen to this visualization on your own. Simply go to: https://www.MarieMorganPrimeTime.com/gate/ There you'll find a recording you can play at any time. *Do not listen to it while driving.*

Before we began, I instructed the group: "As soon as you 'return' from your trip through the gate, it is vital that you immediately jot down in your journal what you experienced, so please have it and your pen at hand before we begin."

After the guided visualization I explained what to capture in their journals. "Note such things as what you saw at first, what happened after your first steps, second steps, and so on. What messages do you glean from this experience? No need to examine or critique it now, just record it as you experienced it.

"Earlier, in chapter 5, we talked—somewhat theoretically at the time—about what it meant to have a spiritual practice for listening to the emerging future. You might consider the gate journey as an immersion in that special way of listening. If it seems helpful, you might pause now and revisit that section in chapter 5, reading it in a new light. And do keep these principles in mind as we do the next exercise on calling and intention."

Calling and Intention

As the group wrapped up their journaling, I said, "You are back in the present moment now, after all that time travel. I invite you to recenter yourself in your liminal space. Take as long as you need to settle down your memories and inner characters, and do your anchoring gesture to feel your largest, most wise self present in the room. We are going to start imagining and then writing about what we want to create over the next three to five years. Recall everything on your mind map, and then respond to as many of the following questions as you wish. Be as specific as you can, as visual and concrete as possible. Focus on writing and capturing what is present. Don't be tempted to overanalyze.

5. Sentence Completion:

My younger self or my very old self said this and it resonated in a new way:

____

I am so curious about _______________________
that I can't not explore it.

My passion is leading me toward _______________________

Some of the elements of the future I want to create include

____

My Superpower in action might look like this, in a new setting

____

Something here has been brewing for a very long time: _______________________. It looks or sounds like

____

I can actually hear my future whispering something that would have seemed "unthinkable" before we began this journey. It is saying

____

Here is one new intention a whispering voice is inviting me to set:

____

If I were to make a particular contribution during my remaining time here on the planet, it might be _______________________

____

Now summarize:
Right now I hear a call from the future to _______________________

____

Revisiting Letting Go and Letting Come

I said, "We discussed the theme of letting go and letting come in chapter 5, but check now on what you have just written in exercise number five, the sentence completions. Is there something you will need to let go of in order for these calling nudges and clues to come to life? Are there still habits or a certain mindset or a lurking inner character that needs to be asked to take a sabbatical? Record these in your journal."

Your Turn 

"Listen carefully now for the seeds of tomorrow. What might be whispering to you to coax it into being? Is there something in question five that will need special urging or shepherding in order to come into reality? Perhaps a new practice that you will want to introduce in order to sponsor that new thing? Is there a needed belief or action to help you form or join an island of coherence? Jot these down."

Your Turn 

"It is time to get even more specific. I want you to picture the next three months IRL—in real life. Otto uses the term *prototyping*. You don't have to start immediately on your final and always *big thing*. You just need to pick a starting place. Even a tiny thing. Somewhere you can show up, something you can do that will be a first, experimental step toward what you have captured in writing today.

Brainstorm Some Starting Points

I said, "Start a brainstorming list in your journal, and then I will invite you to pair up and share your list out loud. Number down your page one to twenty-four, and then start filling in whatever ideas come to mind that take you one baby step closer to the calling(s) you have described." Then I presented some questions to get them started:

- Where are some places you might visit to explore what the people there are up to?
- Who are some people you could interview to see what they are doing?
- What is some research? In other words, things you want to find out to see if you are even actually interested in a certain area? For example, if you are curious about rebuilding bird habitats on ranches, do you need to do a web search to learn if someone is already doing that?
- What are some calls you could make?

"It doesn't have to be logical. You don't have to know ahead of time where it will go or what it will yield. Some should be ludicrous. Be curious! Erase 'feasible' from your vocabulary for now. Just list *actions* you could take." I gave them some more examples:

- Call a distant uncle, the rancher in Wyoming, and run your ideas by him.
- Draw with colored pencils a scene of cattle grazing and birds flying and singing in the trees.
- Schedule lunch with your friend Suzanne who is an avid Audubon fan to brainstorm with her.

"If you run out of ideas, put your idea number six and your idea number fourteen together and see what that suggests. Mix and match. Add more.

"Now pair off and help each other add another ten. Adapt some of your partner's ideas to your subject."

Your Turn 

Prototypes

The pairs started to come to a stopping point, so I said, "Return now to your liminal space and quietly consider your long list. Put a star next to any that have a magnetic energy. And ones that make you smile. Or laugh. Circle *five* of your most compelling or curious ideas."

I instructed the group to write out *each of the five ideas separately* in their journal, making informal columns with these headings across the page:

Subject or Calling Action to Take When? Who Is Involved?

"Also note what specific thing or things you will do to get it rolling. In other words, add specifics that will enable you to immerse yourself and create a new reality, however small.

"Finally, select *one* of these five to start on, and circle the *date* you will begin it. Make it sooner rather than later."

Your Turn

Who Can Help?

Once everyone in the group had selected the thing they wanted to work on and the date they would begin, I said, "To strengthen your ability to create this future you are sketching out, on a new page start a list of *people* for each of your five items, beginning with the one you will be doing first." Then I presented the following questions to get them thinking:

- Who can help you bring this new future into reality?
- Are there people with particular resources or knowledge you could call on?
- Is there a core partner you could enlist?
- Are there other potential partners with similar interests? Or even time on their hands?

- Who might have a latent Superpower you could enlist?
- Who might be interested in a small island of coherence around your action step or project?
- Who could help you think of more people who could help?
- Be sure to ask every person you call on to *think of one more person* you could speak to.

Crystals and Pearls

When the group reconvened after a break, Alicia was bubbling with excitement. "I can't wait to hear what everyone learned from this exercise."

"Then we nominate you to go first." Samuel mimed his stern face.

"OK, I guess I asked for that," Alicia said. "I am amazed how clear my picture of my future became by the end. It does actually feel like a calling! I confess I was doubtful that would happen." She glanced at me sheepishly, then brightened again and asked me how she should describe what she had just learned.

"Just hit whatever highlights seem most significant to you," I said.

Alicia's Calling: Free to Be Me

"When I was young," Alicia began, "running sprints was the place I felt most alive. Later at UCLA, the track team was where I felt safest. It was the most predictable environment in my daily world. My 'young woman' said to me today, 'You've come a long way, baby! Be proud of your accomplishments.' Then my old, old self admonished me, 'Be an example for other girls and young women who need hope.'

"Then old me urged me to get back into some kind of sport, either running or maybe even learn something new. 'There are no more corporate board rooms and air-conditioned offices,' she said. 'Get moving again.'

"The pattern I began to see is this—I am at my best when I am comfortable with my body and it is doing what it was designed for.

"On my mind map my inner characters all understand now that we are free to be my own real self. I don't have to constantly bring order out of chaos. No one is my boss. I have no accountability to corporate goals. Free!

"I need to *let go of* any remaining unconscious corporate expectations and also any hyper-adrenaline impulse to prove to myself I have escaped poverty.

"Should I tell about the gate?" she asked me.

I nodded.

"It took my breath away. I saw a whole bunch of girls clustering around me, all excited. They seemed as if they were looking to me for inspiration.

"My Superpower developing in a new context is finding a way to help young girls keep their confidence in their bodies as they turn into teenagers. *I am curious* why so many girls lose their body confidence around age twelve. How can that be overcome? Surely someone is working on this question. I need to find out.

"When the future whispered in the exercise, I immediately thought of Serena Williams buying ownership in the Toronto Tempo, the first Canadian WNBA team. I have no idea how to interpret that image, but it was vivid.

"I am setting an intention to research this, the evolution— and devolution—of girls' body confidence. And a resonance with the advice I received is that getting back into sports myself has something to do with this. Two of my five *action steps* are to go for a run in the morning and to do two or three hours of internet research tomorrow afternoon.

"My summary of my calling right now is *to research and then design a program that will help girls maintain their body confidence through their teen years and into young adulthood.*"

Alicia stood and took a bow. Applause filled the room.

I said to the group, "We will talk more about the action steps and who can help us after we have heard from everyone. It may be that overlaps in stories will evoke ideas of how we can help each other. Who's next?"

Shirley: Wildness, Wilderness, and Art

Shirley spoke up. "What an amazing process. It surprised me. I could not have guessed what popped up if I had just sat down and tried to think about it on my own.

"I was most myself at seventeen when I was underwater in Hawaii, scuba diving. That young girl called me to remember how much I love the ocean but also the wild mountain wilderness. I realized as she spoke how much the spirit of those places runs through me. It has no language. It's pure experience.

"My oldest self reminded me of Thoreau's words: *In wildness is the preservation of the world.* She challenged me to somehow, through my art, find a way for others to experience this. Her advice to me was that my contract termination was a gift. She said I need to get back out there where it is wild while I still have my health and see what wildness wants to say through my artistic self.

"My Superpower helps with this through my sensitivity to what others are experiencing, and my seeing their potential for transformation in this setting.

"Through the gate caught me by surprise. I saw small groups of women who long to experience the spirituality of wildness. They aren't the usual outdoor types.

"On my mind map I see my inner characters Lone Ranger and Team Player learning to collaborate and give each other respect, but

I see now that it is my Liminal Space self who takes the women into the wild.

"My 'unthinkable' whisper saw a group making a mystical art project *together*. That blew my mind, looking on as Lone Ranger!"

Shirley looked at Alicia. "This art-making image feels to me about as likely as owning a WNBA team, but I am learning to entertain unthinkable thoughts. And my younger self also advised me not to overthink things, so this is an intentional stretch exercise."

"My summary of the calling: *Find ways for women to experience the wildness as a spiritual presence, and let art be actively part of it*. Listening to the future as a spiritual practice is perfect for this because my practical self wants an instant strategic plan, and I can see now that this would not be the way to proceed. This is new territory. Ha ha. Like wilderness!"

I emphasized to Shirley and the group that their calling needed to be allowed to blossom *before* we start worrying about *how to*. Being unable to see *how* at the outset has killed many dreams. We know better now—take it in a different order.

Himari tentatively raised her hand. I nodded for her to go ahead. She said, "Shirley, several weeks ago you spoke of a dream to start an institute to teach what we are learning here. I notice this did not show up in your report today. Have you noticed this?"

Shirley took a moment. "Yes, I did notice that. My first thoughts on that are, if I am honest with myself, administering and managing are nowhere near my Superpowers. I would call the institute a 'dream' but not a calling. What I just described to you today touches my soul more deeply. I'll take some time this week to ponder this further, but I think I've given you the essence of my insight."

Himari: Letting Come to a Conceptual Breakthrough

Himari went next. "I'm glad we are talking about this not being the day for discerning exactly how to accomplish our calling," she said. "In an earlier life, I might have been reluctant to try something new if I couldn't answer all the how questions immediately, with some sort of CFO inner character sitting on my shoulder.

"I time-traveled back to high school, hanging out with two girlfriends. I studied hard, but compared to later, it was still a carefree time. Today my young self pointed out to me what the lifeline exercise displayed, that I spent ages eighteen to seventy-one doing one thing: excelling in medicine. That's half a century. Now I have seventy-two to ninety-eight. That's another quarter of a century. She advised me to take at least a year, maybe three, educating myself in my new endeavor. That was a new thought! My first instinct would have been to just dive in. But compared to my previous years of medical education, two or three years will be a breeze.

"My pattern for feeling most alive has been to bring new ideas to disparate teams to create unexpected results. But my Superpower is being *adaptive*. So I understand now that what I do next won't look like what I did before.

"I have a growing curiosity about bringing better medical care to the vast rural areas of the American West. We joked earlier about what sounded like an 'unthinkable' idea—me as a Navajo shaman. And I want to start using the word the people call themselves, the Diné. But the Diné Nation is not New York or San Francisco, with a major hospital ten minutes away. It can take four or five hours or more to drive across their lands. I am getting passionate about finding a conceptual breakthrough.

"I can see now that I need to *let go* of mounds of assumptions about medicine needing a vast infrastructure to support its results. I am setting an intention to open to the *letting come* insights that may beckon me. I am greatly encouraged by the ingenuity my parents and their communities showed. Placed in empty barracks against their will, they soon established schools, churches, temples, newspapers, sports teams, and a rich variety of recreational programs. I learned as an adult, for example, that by April 11, 1942, the Manzanar Free Press began publication.

"When we talk about where to start and who might help me, I'll need your ideas."

The group nodded their willingness, and then after the break, Paul suggested to Martina that she go next.

He said, "Samuel and I were comparing notes just now, and we found some themes in common. We would like to present our findings together once you're finished."

Martina: Find a Third Way Beyond Structure/No-Structure

"I'm happy to support whatever subversive plots are afoot," she said, smiling. "My time travel took me back to my first year in college. In my newfound freedom I wasn't as wild as others might have been, but I felt freer to be myself than I had imagined was possible. I no longer felt like an appendage to centuries of family history. That young woman said to me today, 'You are so good at getting people organized and moving toward the same goal. Don't take that for granted.'

"I noticed two times when I felt most alive. The first was the campus experience. The second was when we put in place a whole new voter registration system for the state. I tried to see if there was a pattern there. And I'm not sure…" Her voice trailed off.

"When I went through the gate, I almost laughed out loud. In front of me was a massive structure of bamboo scaffolding. Have you seen photos of how they build skyscrapers inside these in Asia? It's remarkable. I am realizing that my new calling won't have to worry about creating my own structure. I sense that I will come across a *light* structure of some kind where I can join people in reaching their goals. This seems quite different from creating structure out of nothing.

"I interpret that symbol to mean I don't need to learn *all* the entrepreneurial mindset items we discussed. A little more open-mindedness will go a long way.

"My elder self tried to explain to me, and I am just now grasping it, that I also need to let go of my Secretary of State worldview just as I let go of generations of family expectations. Both steps mean cutting the tie. My error has been to draw a black-or-white polarity in my mind—either a formal, official structure *or* lying on the couch in my bathrobe.

"Here is my summary. My calling is to discern a third way that takes action. There will always be plenty of informal situations—those herds of cats—needing to move in a more focused direction.

"I can see now that, first, I need to trust those good places will show up and will need my Superpower. Second, trust that I don't have to be in charge or have a title in order to use my Superpower. I can inquire, teach by example, nudge, and most of all build relationships with people. The 'scaffolding' will take care of itself.

"I also intend to visit a neighbor near me who has bamboo growing in the yard. I am going to knock on their door and ask to clip a few pieces to arrange in plain sight in my living room, to remind me of my new calling."

I thanked Martina for her story and for the inspiration we could all follow to find a physical symbol of our future and place it where we will see it every day.

Himari picked up on the idea. "Oh my God! I already own a Navajo rug. Perfect! I'm going to bring it out and hang it in the living room."

Shirley said, "I wonder if I should get an aquarium? Hmmm. Maybe not. Fish in captivity isn't quite the sense of wildness I am after."

"Yuh think?" Paul said in his best Leroy Jethro Gibbs voice.

Samuel and Paul: Collaboration and Coherence

Samuel took up the theme. "I have no idea what sort of symbol will arise from what I am about to say. Maybe a suggestion will emerge. My time travel took me back to Columbia University, where I immediately immersed myself in philosophical questions and debates from which I have never fully emerged. I felt most alive once I began teaching and engaging other students like myself. Intellectually jousting with bright students, bright people of any age, is a high form of recreation for me.

"Naming my Superpower as 'metacognition' seemed like a perfect fit. I am still contemplating how my inner characters of Bella and Sarah are coming to terms with what we are learning here. I can see how allowing them to remain a polarity is the least helpful option.

"The gate, however, brought a surprise. Well, it was a surprise and a perfect fit simultaneously. When I stepped through the gate, I saw what my mind understood to be an island of coherence. I can't give you an exact picture of what that looked like because it was just a group of people sitting around a living room much like this one. But seeing it, I somehow *knew* it was an island of coherence. People were talking together about the disruption and chaos all around them. They were discovering ways to become personally centered and at peace—without losing their motivation to act to bring about constructive outcomes.

"I can't report to you what exactly they talked about. This will be the how-to step that we realize comes later, after the vision and calling itself is clearer. That's OK.

"What has been brewing for a long time for me is a departure from the university setting. This is a big letting go. For many years it was my responsibility to give students a solid foundation of what philosophers have discussed over the centuries, and how they reached the results they did. Now I am free of that. Here is what my very old self pointed out to me. Over those years I think I had a secret inner character who was impatient with having to stay within a certain curriculum, even one I wrote myself. Now I am free to consider only questions that *really matter* to me and the people I speak with.

"Of course there was a certain security—Martina you'll appreciate this—in teaching that expected curriculum. But now no one can fire me. I do not have to publish to satisfy some committee passing judgment on me. It is dawning on me, as we work together here in this group, that my future is inviting me into a vast and exciting new space.

"I am also enamored with the concept of positive deviance. The more I think about it, what an assignment! Watching for things that are working that no one has noticed yet."

Samuel paused for a moment, reflecting. "Can an assignment be the same as a calling? Maybe only to us professor types. For myself, I welcome the challenge."

He gestured toward Paul. "I am going to yield the floor now to Paul because, as he mentioned, we stumbled onto some common ground as we were talking at the break."

Paul: Inviting Coherent Silence

"I'll start with my gate experience," Paul said. "Samuel and I found this immensely amusing. I saw a group of people sitting around in a living room. Only they weren't talking. They were sitting in what I could sense was a very intentional silence. It wasn't meditation, *per se*. I knew watching them that it was a discernment process. As I speak of it now, I would call it listening to a future that wanted the group to manifest it into reality.

"As you know, my inner characters are a work in progress. I cannot yet articulate exactly how they will learn to live in an integrated place between compelling calling and the day-to-day joy of family and discovering art. But I trust this is happening at an unconscious level already. My head just needs to catch up.

"As Samuel and I compared notes on the 'living room' that we each saw beyond our gate, we discussed the possibility of starting an island of coherence group here in Santa Fe. If we were to tag-team the leadership at the outset, I see him as the guide for helping people learn how to talk again, on a deeper level. And I see myself as the guide for how to be silent together.

"I know what you are thinking." He smiled. "You think Samuel has all the work here. But actually, helping people understand the presence, the spirit, if you will, of what they bring to a group before they say a word—this is rigorous work! He and I are going to sit down together this weekend and try drafting a set of guidelines for what participants might expect from an island group. We do not want to get ahead of ourselves with the how-to's, but we see this as a values-clarification exercise, as well as a getting-to-know-you time." He nodded, pleased with the realizations he had come to.

I congratulated the group. "Good work, everyone! Before we conclude today, I want to give you two more valuable tools for your progress. Several of you mentioned at the outset that you didn't want a trial-and-error path. These two methods deal with that specifically. But please notice, these are far more than tools. They each teach a state of mind. They teach us a way of dealing with the world that is uncommon to our current society. As you read about how they work, see if you can articulate what the unusual state of mind is with each one."

Action/Reflection: A Quantum Leap beyond Trial and Error

"As you move out into the world with your 'action experiments,'" I said, "you are going to want to evaluate how it's all working. Here is the significant difference from trial and error as most people practice it. Generally, people tend to say to themselves, 'Well that didn't work,' or 'Something here just isn't clicking for me.' Or they just get bored and stop showing up, with no critical evaluation whatsoever.

"Instead, I would like to offer you these two methods for evaluating your experiences and discerning what needs to happen next. You can repeat this process as often as you need it, as you narrow down to your best fit for doing your Superpowers in a new setting. Both of the methods are described at length in the Sourcebook for Chapter 9, but here is an overview."

The After-Action Review

I explained to the group that, adapted from the U.S. Army, this method of evaluation originates from the crucial need to improve each time a new action is planned. The fourteen steps in our version are in the Sourcebook for Chapter 9. Questions include the following: What was planned? What actually happened? How did it benefit the people present? How did it benefit the larger community? How did it benefit me? How did this situation utilize my Superpowers?

"This process may seem obvious," I said, "but I want to underline *how* you do it: The discipline of actually *writing out* your observations in your journal or on your computer will yield insights that simply 'thinking about it' will overlook. After you have tried two or three different experiments, reviewing your notes from each will illuminate patterns you could not see in the moment.

"You can do the after-action review in the quiet of your own home, but, by definition, we must do the clearness committee activity in a group."

The Clearness Committee

I described to the group how, developed by the Society of Friends (the Quakers) in the 1660s, this discernment method is based on holding your own wisest self in the highest respect. What distinguishes the clearness committee from most group meetings that try to help people is the insistence that the group *never* gives advice. The point is not to solve the convener's dilemma but to help them surface their own deepest wisdom more clearly. Committee members support this by asking only honest, open-ended questions—questions that arise from curiosity, not expertise, and that do not imply a preferred solution. No matter how brilliant a peer participant may think their advice is, offering it is counterproductive to the convener's ability to hear their own inner voice. Even a gentle suggestion—"Have you considered…"—can subtly override the inner knowing the convener is trying to surface.

Rather than including full instructions here or in the Sourcebook, I strongly encourage watching Parker Palmer himself before you embark on this process. [The <u>Sourcebook for Chapter 9</u> includes links to videos and written resources by Parker Palmer and his Center for Courage and Renewal. Or simply search for "clearness committee + Parker Palmer."] This is not just another tool. It is a discipline. It can be a spiritual practice. It is a gift we give each other, and it only works when held with care.

Acknowledgment of Gratitude

I want to express my deep appreciation to Otto Scharmer and the Presencing Institute. My experiences in Otto's workshops, his book *Theory U*, and the Presencing Institute toolkit have profoundly shaped my own journey. The reflective practices in this chapter—such as journaling across time perspectives, prototyping, and mind-mapping—carry echoes of that inspiration. What I share here has been reimagined through my own lens, with gratitude for the seeds they planted, and offered now in service of your life-reinvention journey.

As you begin to take action on your own calling, you may discover something unexpected: that your efforts—no matter how personal or modest—may begin to look like part of a much larger story unfolding around us. In chapter 10 I invite you to step back and glimpse that wider view.

Highlights

Activities to Crystallize Your Calling – In this chapter, you explore several powerful exercises alongside the group. Each offers its own slice of wisdom, bringing you closer to discovering what's next. Together, the exercises reveal a bigger picture:

1. **Mind Map**

   Use this visual tool to brainstorm potential callings by connecting your Superpowers, passions, and curiosities with real-world needs. It gives your unconscious mind permission to surface new ideas without requiring you to commit—yet.

2. **Time Travel**

   Ask your teen/young adult self for perspective, then consult your oldest self for wisdom and guidance.

3. **When Did You Feel Most Alive?**

   Recall a time when you felt deeply alive. What does this memory teach you about your Superpower—and about your future?

4. **Through the Gate**

   Follow the guided visualization and pay attention to what images or feelings of a potential future arise.

5. **Calling and Intention**

   Take time to articulate not just what you might do next, but why it matters—naming the deeper intention that gives your calling meaning and direction. Do the sentence completion exercise. What insights emerge here?

6. **Revisiting Letting Go and Letting Come**

   Before settling on a path forward, return to an earlier insight: What are you releasing—and what might be asking to come through now?

7. Brainstorm Starting Steps

Instead of waiting for clarity, write down possible actions—gentle, doable steps you can take to test or explore a new direction.

8. Prototypes

Choose a few small-scale, low-risk ways to try out your idea—not to prove it's "right," but to discover what feels alive in practice. Select your top five starting steps.

9. Ask Yourself

Use a set of reflective questions to sense whether an idea feels resonant, aligned, and energizing—or whether something is still missing. Ask yourself these questions: Who can help? When will you start?

10. Assessing Your Experiments

Pause to reflect on what each small experiment reveals—what surprises you, what works, and what doesn't. Learn not just from outcomes, but from your process.

After-Action Review

Step back after trying something and ask: What happened? What did I expect? What can I learn? Writing down your observations helps you see patterns and harvest insights you might miss in the moment—and without judgment.

Clearness Committee

Share your dilemma aloud with trusted listeners who ask only open, non-directive questions. Their role is not to advise or solve but to hold a space where your inner teacher can be heard. This discipline of collective listening protects the silence in which clarity often emerges.

Exercise: Take Action

1. **Action Step:** Just do it.

Prime Time Milestones

Take a breath. Pause. What are you noticing at this point in your journey? As you reflect, write your thoughts in your journal.

Insight. I see something new...

Sample response: *My calling may not be a lightning bolt—it may be something I've been circling all along.*

Shift. I feel something changing...

Sample response: *More grounded. A clearer sense of what matters most.*

Step. I'm ready to try...

Sample response: *I'll write down a few threads that keep showing up—and follow where they lead this week*

PHASE V

Personal Quest to Cultural Movement

CHAPTER 10

The Moment We Were Born For

*What if everything we are experiencing right now
is exactly the moment we were born for?*

The group gathered for their final scheduled meeting. They settled into their favorite seats, then grew quiet, looking at me expectantly. I let the silence settle for a moment longer. I looked around the circle into each face individually and began.

"We are at a tipping point. Not just us in this room, but this generation. We are the first generation in human history to have this much wisdom, this much expertise, this many resources at our disposal, and," I said slowly, "this much available time."

I admitted we are all painfully aware today how quickly disruption and, in many instances, even cruelty can spread. "If I may summarize human history in a few sentences, we have always encountered drought and starvation, plagues and wars, autocrats and dreaded conquests—even nuclear weapons have been with us for eighty years. Most recently human-caused climate change looms as seemingly the most all-encompassing threat yet.

"And Otto Scharmer has alerted us—as I mentioned before—to an even greater threat to our survival. Remember his chilling but inspiring words: 'Our number one challenge isn't biodiversity loss, climate change, polarization, countries falling apart, or AI. It is our widespread **illusion of insignificance**—the belief that there's *nothing* we can *do* about it.'

"Before you fall into utter paralysis at this scenario, I propose an alternative perspective. We have total power to adopt an alternative belief about our role in our future.

Attend to This Moment

"What if everything we are experiencing right now is exactly the moment we, as retired professionals and baby boomers, were born for?"

"What if we unknowingly trained our entire lives for this time?

"What if our most important contribution is still ahead of us?

"Not that we would do it alone, of course," I quickly added, "because we are called to join with the generations coming along behind us to employ our Superpowers in new ways and demonstrate what is possible.

"Will we waste this opportunity and let the invitation pass us by? Or will we hear our calling to entirely rewrite what it means to age in America?"

I paused to let this sink in, then suggested the group jot in their journals whatever was running through their minds.

"As you process this alternative belief framework," I told them, "you may notice that more than one inner character has a reaction. Capture these thoughts in brief notes so you can have further conversations later."

Your Turn 

They wrote for a few minutes.

Then Samuel exhaled. "Well, that lands differently. I don't know what I expected you to say today, but *that* wasn't it. 'Born for this…' My first thought was, *'Really? This mess?'* But then I thought—well, yeah. Maybe this is the moment when positive deviance isn't just tolerated, but desperately needed. Maybe we're not the oddballs anymore—we're the ones who can *see* what's quietly working and ask, 'How can we make this normal?'"

Paul joined in. "I've been tracking in the same direction. Patterns are fracturing—but also reforming in unexpected ways. I've noticed that where centralized systems are faltering, decentralized trust is rising. Neighborhood food shares. DIY power grids. Community-run clinics. It's like the old web is tearing, but there's a new net beneath it—and *we* can be the weavers. We're not out of time. We're *right on time*."

Martina looked troubled, but then smiled, her arms crossed. "Well, I know what herding cats looks like. That's basically been my whole life story. But lately I can't help but notice how the stakes keep getting higher. It's not just about organizing anymore—it's about organizing with soul. The kind of effort where people feel seen, not managed. I don't want to just coordinate volunteers. I want to coordinate *vision*. And maybe this is exactly the kind of mess I've been training for."

Alicia, her eyes shining, said, "I feel this in my chest, not my head. When you said it—'born for this'—something just…sparked. I've always believed in joy as a survival skill. But now I think joy might be a *leadership strategy*. There's so much grief in the air. So much bitterness. I want to walk into broken places and laugh with people again. Show them that love isn't a luxury—it's how we begin again."

"For me, it's about agility," Himari added. "Medicine taught me to adapt, but life—especially lately—has taught me to listen differently. What you're saying aligns with something I've felt: that we need to co-create new systems from the ground up. Modular. Local. Responsive. I don't want to rebuild the old world. I want to prototype a better one, in real time. And if I have the freedom now to do that, why wouldn't I?"

Shirley said, "I'm thinking about all the people who feel useless right now. Like they've missed their window. I want to tell them it's not too late. I want to remind them that their gifts are still unfolding. I spent my whole life helping others see their potential. Now I think it's time to help our generation see its *collective* potential. We've got what we need. What we don't have, we can grow."

Martina spoke up. "Are we at risk of wasting it? This amazing gift of time and our energy that we could easily take for granted?" She looked slowly around the room. "There is no law that says we have to disappear after sixty-five. But for some reason, a lot of us are still acting like there is."

Samuel chimed in. "A hundred years from now, people will look back and ask, 'What did the baby boomers do with the last thirty years of their lives?' I don't want my great-great-grandchildren to just laugh. Or sigh and roll their eyes at my memory."

Himari stood up, making a time-out sign with her hands. "Millions of us have been trained for leadership, innovation, and problem-solving—so why would we even consider disappearing just when the world needs us the most?"

Shirley said, "Self-consciousness—or maybe I mean self-awareness—is part of the picture. As a generation our identity was strong in the sixties. I wonder where that feeling is now. Our generation has always been a tuning fork for cultural vibration—starting with civil rights, women's liberation, environmental awareness, spiritual renewal. The tuning fork is being struck again. But this time, it's resonating with a new shared narrative. I wonder if we have the collective willingness and courage to take that role again."

Shirley gazed out the window, thinking it through, then she added, "I think this sense of identity is a useful way to think about it. Individually, a lot of us left our identities on our professional desks. Now we have the opportunity to take on a different identity. A group identity.

"We Are the People We've Been Waiting For"

We're in our Prime Time. Remember the bumper sticker from a while ago? 'We are the people we have been waiting for.' It's still true."

Paul leaned back in his chair, studying the ceiling. Finally, he spoke. "We can't say no. We can't drive by the just-wrecked car beside the road and pretend we didn't see it. We have to do all we can. Lord knows, the country and the planet need all the help we can offer."

"And it's not as though we don't have what it takes. Or the creativity to figure it out," Alicia added. "But I also want to underline something. We are for *choices*. More choices for our roles. None of us is saying that vacations or golf is bad or inappropriate. We just have to claim the space to do many, many additional things that go beyond the retirement stereotypes that have unconsciously kept us living a narrow strip of our potential."

The silence hung, in a good way, as they took in what had just been said. Some in the group were leaning forward, some sitting back. All were alert and focused. There was a different energy. Something had shifted—the mood was not as tentative. The idea that they were born for this moment was taking root, but I sensed that now they were circling around it, testing its strength.

Alicia sighed, but not in frustration. "I keep thinking about what you said—born for this. It's almost too big to take in. But I can't shake it. I mean, I've spent my whole life pushing to be seen, to be strong, to break through. Running was my way out, my way up, my way in. And now I am seeing that maybe the real race wasn't just to get myself out. Maybe it's to reach back and bring others along. I keep picturing all these middle-school girls on the verge of losing themselves. What if part of what I was born for is to help them stay whole?"

Himari nodded thoughtfully. "I've been sitting with that, too. You know, in medicine, we're taught to fix things. Solve problems. But some problems are too entrenched for that. Too entrenched to just dispense medications, for sure. The healthcare issues in the Diné Nation… It's not just about delivering more of the same. It's about reimagining the whole system—community-centered, rooted in their way of life. I keep seeing this vision of a clinic where the people come not just for treatment, but for gathering. A place where elders' wisdom is part of the healing. There is some of that already, of course. But there have to be more ways. They have preserved the old ways, but maybe I can bring something additional to that from Western medicine. Maybe that's what I'm being called to—taking what I know and offering to reconfigure it with their culture at the core. That would feel like honoring my life's work and letting it evolve."

Shirley smiled to herself. "I was out hiking yesterday, and it hit me. I was walking this narrow, rocky trail, totally focused on not twisting my ankle. But when I finally looked up, the view was—God, it was huge. Like I'd walked right into the sky. And I just thought… that's it. We spend so much time looking down, surviving. But what if I could help women look up? Help them feel their wildness, feel how strong they really are. Not the controlled, polite kind of strong. The wild, fierce kind. That's what the Rockies do for me—they remind me that life is supposed to feel vast."

Martina leaned forward, tapping her fingers together. "I keep coming back to that bamboo scaffolding. I thought it was nuts at first. I mean, we're talking high rises, right? And yet it holds. It moves with the wind, it flexes, but it doesn't fall. The more I think about it, the more I wonder if that's the key to defending democracy right now. Not rigid resistance, but flexible support. Building networks that can move and shift but still hold the weight of what we value. Voter registration is only one tiny piece. Personal relationships are what make herding cats possible. What if we could teach that way of thinking—how to build flexible, resilient structures, based on relationships with people we know and trust, that hold up under pressure?"

Paul looked thoughtful, then said, almost whispering, "Patterns. I keep seeing them. Islands of coherence popping up, almost like constellations—separate but connected. It's not about any one of us doing it alone. It's the connections that matter. If Samuel and I can build that space where people slow down, listen deeply, and learn to *see* differently, that could change the way people approach their own projects. I keep seeing it—contemplation as the foundation. Without it, we're just reacting. With it, we're creating."

Samuel chuckled. "You know, I spent years teaching people how to think critically. Now I'm seeing that it's not just about thinking better—it's about *being* better. Seeing ourselves as part of something bigger. I'm drawn to this idea of positive deviance—not just pointing out the problems, but highlighting what's *already working* and amplifying it. If we could create a space where people come and find that spark—wow, I think we might actually change something."

"And Samuel," I added, "it's not just about personal reinvention anymore. It's about creating the *conditions* that help the reinventions stick. It's like a farmer amending the soil. Conditions where people feel safe to explore, to speak their truth, to try things that don't always come with a tidy plan or a polished LinkedIn update."

"Thank goodness!" quipped Alicia.

Tipping Point and Critical Mass

The group settled in quietly, each still digesting the idea of being born for this moment. There was still a mix of excitement and caution in the room—as if they had glimpsed a vista but were still finding their footing.

Paul shifted in his chair. "You know, I read something recently about social-change tipping points. Sociologists say it only takes around twenty-five percent of people to really believe in something for it to become unstoppable. After that, it's like…cultural gravity. Or the tide. It just pulls the rest along."

Samuel raised an eyebrow. "Really? Just a quarter? So we don't need to convince *everyone*?"

I wanted to elaborate, sensing an encouraging leverage point. Culture shifts when enough people say, "This is what we do now," or, "This is how it's done now." Paradigm shifts happen not because everyone changes overnight, but because a growing number of people begin reinforcing a new story in small, visible ways. It's the moment when new behavior feels *normal*, not *brave*. And that moment only comes when we see each other doing it.

Paul added, "Right. It's not about getting everyone on board. It's about building momentum for that critical mass. And honestly, I think that's where we are with this whole *Prime Time* thing. *We're not waiting for permission to reimagine what aging looks like—we're just doing it.* The fact that it's already underway, even if the media doesn't notice, means we're closer than we think."

"And that's where the real-world magic starts to happen," I said. "Because once we see how individual transformation depends on social feedback loops, we shift faster. And more boldly when we see each other shifting. We start to realize we can do this, but not alone.

"When you think about it, we rarely change in isolation. We think we believe in individualism, but even when people talk about personal epiphanies, those moments are often sparked or sustained by seeing someone else *go first*. The human brain is wired to take social cues seriously—when we see a friend or peer stepping into something new with conviction, it creates permission, courage, and then momentum."

Alicia perked up. "I love that. Because every time I see one of those stories about a ninety-year-old marathon runner or the ninety-five-year-old female weightlifting champion, the media acts like it's this crazy anomaly. They put it in the feel-good news section, right? Like it's adorable or freakish. But what if it's not an exception? What if it's just…underreported? Or the beginning of a whole new way of being?"

Perception IS Everything

"There is a larger phenomenon going on here," I added. "A misperception gap. In the *UN Human Development Report of 2023–2024* they reported that sixty-nine percent of people around the world would be willing to sacrifice part of their income to contribute to climate change mitigation. Meanwhile only forty-three percent believed that *others* would do the same."[28]

"And it's not just our perceptions of *others* that hold us back. It's our internalized assumptions about *ourselves*—especially what we believe aging allows or forbids. Recall Harvard psychologist Ellen Langer's work (chapters 2 and 6), which has shown that these assumptions shape not just our outlook, but our biology. This isn't magical thinking—it's hard science. The mind and body are not separate. And when we change the story in our minds, our bodies, our behavior, resilience, and possibilities begin to shift too."

I explained that the misperception gap we are experiencing about aging has several contributing factors, including:

a. keeping silent about how we feel and the changes we are making;

b. stereotypes that keep us from noticing what is real now, what is actually true;

c. our own unquestioned assumptions;

d. media attention shaped in part by those stereotypes, so old assumptions are erroneously amplified; and

e. selective perception that skews what we "see" (once a yellow Volkswagen is brought to our attention, we suddenly start "seeing" them)—yet we still have choices about where we place our attention.

"So the tipping point can be accelerated when we can see what our peers are feeling and doing," Paul added. "Do I have it right? And we can accelerate the change by changing our own beliefs and assumptions."

Shirley nodded. "That's exactly it. It's not that these stories are outliers. It's that they don't fit the old narrative about retirement, so they are framed as oddities. But I see it all around me—people stepping out of the so-called comfort zone and doing something remarkable. They just don't make the news. And it's not always these big, dramatic achievements either. Sometimes it's the little things— helping a neighbor, mentoring one kid—that causes ripples."

Himari said quickly, "Ripples! That's what it is! You do one small thing, and you have no idea who it touches, how far it travels. Even a small effort—if it's authentic—can spark something."

I shared my own experience of a woman who approached me on the streets of Portland. She introduced herself, having heard me speak at an event fifteen years earlier. She explained that my story had inspired her to go back for her GED, then get into college, and eventually earn a PhD.

Samuel smiled. "That works as a great metaphor too, Marie. Take clear action and ripples happen. And more often we don't know what we have done. We can't see our ripples. Today it feels like we're reclaiming our Prime Time together. Owning it. Saying, 'We're not done. We're not winding down. We're stepping up.' It's a fine feeling, isn't it? And it's not just about being *able* to do something—it's about knowing we *should*. I mean, we've lived through enough to see what happens when good people sit back and wait for someone else to step up. That's not who we are. Not anymore."

"We've Got This!"

Himari nodded thoughtfully. "And this shared confidence—it's real. I'm seeing it in myself now. A few months ago, I couldn't have imagined taking on something as ambitious as helping the Diné community redesign healthcare. I was still thinking like an administrator, waiting for a system to change so I could work within it. But now, I realize we could build something entirely new with them—more flexible, more connected to their way of life. I don't have to follow someone else's blueprint. We can create it together."

I responded to Himari. "So I hear you saying that the real magic isn't just in believing in yourself—it's in believing in *us*. Our personal sense of purpose deepens when we realize others are on this path, too. It's the 'We've got this!' energy. Call it resonance. Call it collective courage. But when people feel part of something *shared*, that's when the tipping point gets real traction."

Martina leaned forward, more animated. "I like that—*We've got this!* It's not just optimism. It's knowing that we've got the chops, the experience, and the *staying power* to actually make this work. I keep thinking about that bamboo scaffolding—it's lightweight, it bends, but it's strong as hell. Maybe that's how we need to be—adaptable, resilient, willing to move with the challenges instead of bracing against them. We don't need the perfect plan before we start. We just need to put up the scaffolding and build as we go."

Alicia smiled. "I love that image—building as we go. That's what athletes do, right? You don't know how a race will unfold. You have to adjust, stay loose, respond to the terrain. I used to think I needed a whole strategy before I started anything big. Now I see it differently. I'm thinking of starting with just a few girls—helping them keep their confidence through those tricky years. It doesn't have to be a whole organization right away. In fact, it shouldn't, because I have research to do. And small experiments. Just one ripple at a time."

Shirley said, "I see now. It's not about having one grand plan. Sounds like it's about giving ourselves permission to follow the ripples. Start with what feels real, then see where it leads. I used to think big impact meant big effort—organizing whole retreats, getting funding. But now I'm thinking, what if I just start taking small groups out into the mountains? Let them experience that wildness and see where it takes them? Maybe simplicity is the key to starting."

Paul smiled at Shirley. "That's it, isn't it? We've been conditioned to think that impact has to be grand. But ripples work differently.

They start small, and then they spread. We don't need to change everything all at once. We just need to get started. Even if it's modest. Even if it's messy. We're still the right people for this moment."

Samuel grinned. "I don't want to beat this metaphor to death, but as those ripples spread, they start to *connect*. That's when you get that virtuous circle—one person sees another trying something new, and they think, 'Maybe I can do that too.' The trick is to keep the stories circulating. If we can get better at showing people what is happening, we can speed up the shift. It doesn't have to be a movement in the traditional sense—just a series of breakthroughs that become visible enough to catch on."

"At last! A constructive use for social media," Samuel observed, with just a sliver of irony in his voice.

Martina was nodding. "That's where younger folks can really help us out. They know how to make things visible—how to tell a story in thirty seconds and make it stick. We need to partner with them—not just to amplify our voices, but to show them that they are part of this too. It's not us *telling* them—it's us *building with* them."

Alicia's eyes lit up. "Yes! We're not the mentors and they're the students. We're co-creators. If we can model that balance between experience and fresh vision, it might just click. This is not an original idea, but I want to underline it here. We don't have to do it alone—just set the tone, and they'll add their own flavor to it."

Himari said with her dignified calm, "And that's why this is our Prime Time. We have the capacity to see where things could go, but also the freedom to experiment without worrying about careers or making a name for ourselves. That gives us a kind of lightness— freedom to be bold without needing it to be perfect. We can show up, try things, and let them grow organically."

Several in the group had been taking notes in their journals, and then the room went quiet again.

We Do Not Need Anyone's Permission

Himari spoke again. "I notice that we have shifted from focusing on personal development, which has been most of our conversation in past weeks, to a *movement*. I predict, however, that this will be a *de facto* movement, rather than the kind that holds marches and proposes legislation. We do not need anyone's permission. Compulsory retirement ages might be modified. Pension planning will be reshaped. But we can each make our own intentional decision about the purpose we put in place for our life. More choices will become available as more of us take this path. 'Normal' will keep getting wider and wider. As people are inspired by examples, they will get more creative in turn. It's that positive feedback loop again."

"If ever there was a time to lean in, this is it," Alicia said with finality.

Then she invited the group to replenish their refreshments and take a short walk outside for some fresh air.

Islands of Coherence

Martina resumed the conversation. "It sounds to me like we're all getting it—one bit at a time. But there's something else we haven't said yet. I don't think we can just scatter and go do our own thing. We've got momentum here. And mutual trust. We've found something that works. What if we keep this group going—turn it into our own island of coherence for the journey ahead? Somewhere we keep coming back to—like a base camp—while we're out there trying all these wild ideas."

Himari nodded. "That makes sense. We've mentioned this concept several times, but this is our last meeting. It's time for a clear decision. We will need each other as we set about reinventing our place in the world. We've got so much going on individually, but together we can help each other stay focused, stay grounded."

Alicia grinned. "Yes. And it's not just about accountability—it's about keeping this fire lit. I don't want to lose this momentum. I wouldn't want the spark to die."

Paul and Samuel exchanged a look. Paul said, "Islands of coherence makes a perfect model for what we need next—a small, intentional group that gives us some structure, support, and sacred space for this growth. It's not therapy, certainly not a coffee chat, not even an accountability club. It is something deeper. Call it a greenhouse for transformation, of ourselves and our world. And if we're serious about tipping the culture toward purposeful retirement, these islands aren't optional. They're essential."

He continued. "Let's make it official. Our own island of coherence for our Prime Time. Right here. A place to refine our practices and keep each other rooted in what really matters."

Samuel said, "Absolutely. And this time, it's not just theoretical. We're doing this. We're going to take what we've learned and test it out in the real world. If it works, we'll share it. If it doesn't, we'll pivot. Either way, we're not sitting on the sidelines and we're not playing lone wolf."

Then he added, "Let's be clear. We don't need a plan or guarantee before we start. Just some simple guidelines. We've already seen too much of life to wait for perfect conditions. We just have to step into this time, this calling—together. And as long as we stay connected, we'll keep each other moving. One ripple at a time."

Note: Revisit guidelines for circles of coherence in the Sourcebook for Chapter 5.

He looked to Shirley and Martina. They both nodded enthusiastically.

Samuel looked around the circle. "Then it's settled. We'll reconvene, but as a different group with a different purpose—an island of coherence. A place to keep this energy alive, keep each other accountable, and share what's working. And not just for us—if we do it right, we'll inspire others to start their own groups. Maybe that's our real legacy—helping people see that Prime Time isn't just a personal shift. It's communal and cultural."

Himari said, "I propose that this is what it means to be born for this moment—not that we have all the answers, but that we're willing to step up and help create them together."

Highlights

Power of Prime Time – We have total power to adopt an alternative belief about our role in our future:

- **What if everything we are experiencing right now is exactly the moment we were born for?**

  This powerful reframe invites you to see the challenges of our time not as obstacles, but as your exact assignment—an invitation, a purpose, and a calling to step forward.

- **We do not need anyone's permission.**

  We are no longer waiting for approval or instructions—this is the stage of life when we write the map ourselves and claim our own authority.

- **This journey is more than personal development—this is a movement.**

  What began as an inner search for meaning becomes part of a wider cultural shift—one that opens new possibilities for how future generations will view aging itself.

- **Our expectations shape our bodies—strength, cognition, capacity, and more.**

  This isn't wishful thinking; it's science. And when we shift our mindset, we help shift the culture.

- **We are the people we have been waiting for.**

  There is no cavalry coming; our generation holds the wisdom, resources, and freedom to lead where others hesitate. This realization also restores a sense of identity many lost in the transition out of traditional careers.

- **Tipping point and critical mass— we don't need everybody, just a starter crowd.**

  History turns when enough people act with clarity and courage; even a small, committed group can catalyze cultural change. (See the <u>Sourcebook for Chapter 10</u> for "Ways We Are Already Changing the Narrative.")

- **Islands of coherence are the seeds where we begin to bring sense out of chaos.**

  By gathering in trusted circles of clarity, purpose, and presence, we anchor meaning in turbulent times—and the image of islands gives us immense hope that something beautiful and lasting can grow.

Exercise: Next Steps

1. **Journal Reflection:** Review the parts of this chapter that resonate most with you. Write down the phrases most meaningful for you. Which aspects of the group's discussion in this chapter feel closest to the future you see for yourself? Can you write a very specific response similar to what the characters spoke in this chapter?

2. **Action Step:** If you are studying this book with a group, what will you decide to do next? You don't need a full plan. Instead, dare to say what you need from each other and speak about what commitments you would like to make to each other.

3. **Action Step:** If you feel called to experiment with an island of coherence, you will find the Presencing Institute's guidelines for what they call circles of coherence located in the <u>Sourcebook for Chapter 5</u>. There is an outline for a proven one-hour process you can repeat each time you meet.

4. **Bonus**: Paul and Samuel drafted an invitation, "An Invitation to Island Living" for a second group that they want to start, designed for people to support one another in challenging work environments. Their first draft of that invitation is below the milestones. It is one kind of group. There will be other kinds. We are all experimenting. If you feel inclined to start your own, write your own invitation or improve on this one.

Prime Time Milestones

Take a breath. Pause. What are you noticing at this point in your journey? As you reflect, write your thoughts in your journal.

Insight. I see something new…

Sample response: *This isn't just about me. My choices can help reshape what it means to grow older in our culture.*

Shift. I feel something changing…

Sample response: *More connected. A sense of purpose beyond myself.*

Step. I'm ready to try…

Sample response: *I'll look for one way I can contribute this week—using what I already carry.*

An Invitation to Island Living

*For those who sense another way is not only
possible—it is already quietly arriving.*

Welcome to this island of coherence.
It's not a destination—it's a practice.
Not a club—but a commons.
Not a path of certainty—but a space where the next step
reveals itself when we are still and listening.

If you wish to join us, bring a daily practice.
Whatever anchors you—silence, journaling, walking, breath, music.
Not perfection. Just intention.

Listen beyond agreement—as if the future is speaking through the other.
Be open to emergence.
This is not about knowing more, but sensing what
wants to be known—through us, as us.

Protect the field.
Your presence shapes the atmosphere. Call back coherence if it frays.
Unlearn with grace. Let mystery teach.

Offer what you carry.
No spectators—your voice, your silence, your
laughter, your questions all matter.

Hold it lightly, hold it holy.
Bring purpose, but not without joy. We laugh here.
We dance when the spirit moves.

Respect boundaries. Some truths are still
ripening—let them have their time.

Stay with the yes.
When cynicism knocks, return to the yes that brought you here.

This is not a formula.
It is a field.
If you feel it—welcome.
Bring your full self.
Let's listen for what's next, together.

What's Next?

Prime Time isn't the end—it's the Invitation

This moment can be the beginning of something much bigger.

If you're wondering what comes next, you're not alone. Many people find that *Prime Time* opens questions, energy, and possibilities that want a place to go.

Here are four ways to stay connected—choose what feels right to you.

➤ Add Your Voice!

If *Prime Time* spoke to you, reader reviews can help others decide whether this book is right for them.

You can find a direct link to the Amazon review page here: https://MarieMorganPrimeTime.com/review

➤ Subscribe to *Prime Currents*

Personal notes from Marie Morgan and *Prime Time*, delivered to your inbox.
Ideas, new thinking, questions, and cultural ripples for those of us reinventing what 60+ can mean.
https://www.MarieMorganPrimeTime.com/currents

➤ Share What's Stirring

Has *Prime Time* sparked a reflection, question, or story of your own? You're invited to share what's emerging for you—and to see how others are engaging this stage of life in thoughtful, creative ways: https://www.MarieMorganPrimeTime.com/addstories

➤ Feeling Called to Help Shape What Comes Next?

If you're a seasoned professional—facilitator, therapist, experienced coach, or changemaker—drawn to active leadership in this cultural shift, you may want to explore opportunities to contribute, co-create, or lead within the movement: https://www.MarieMorganPrimeTime.com/pro

You're stepping into a current
that's already moving—
quietly, steadily, and with purpose.
Let's keep going, together.

LIST OF CHARACTERS

Himari

A recently retired medical administrator from San Francisco, now building a life in Santa Fe. After years of structured service, she longs for purpose that is personally meaningful—not just socially sanctioned. She grew up in the shadow of her parents' courage after surviving a U.S. government internment camp during World War II, and now carries their resilience into her own search for belonging. Calm on the outside, she's quietly determined to forge a next chapter with substance and grace.

Shirley

A laid-off design team manager who thought she had one more year to plan. Fiercely independent, shaped by a lifetime of figuring things out on her own, she now feels unmoored. Joining this group is a bold but frightening step toward learning how to trust others at eye level and to stop going it alone. A devoted solo hiker, she's most at home in the wildest parts of the mountains—but she instinctively knows she can't navigate this next terrain alone.

Martina

A former Secretary of State in the Midwest, now returned to her deep-rooted New Mexico family. Her days are slower now, but her longing for clear structure and purpose—and for something truly *hers*—has only sharpened. Her challenge: not to be absorbed into others' plans, but to imagine a new role that's self-chosen and deeply satisfying. She dresses sharply, often in tailored jackets, as if structure might return through her wardrobe.

Paul

A former emergency room nurse and senior administrator, contemplative by nature but forged in decades of nonstop crisis response. He's now decompressing, searching for balance and disciplined reflection. He speaks slowly, with long pauses—as if weighing each word before release—and still carries the habits of someone who held lives in his hands.

Samuel

A retired philosophy professor who moved to Santa Fe at his wife's urging for adventure. Though done with academia, he misses stimulating conversation and wants to engage ideas that matter in a circle of peers. His New York accent has softened but persists—just like his appetite for deep conversation. He's the quiet skeptic-turned-seeker, eager to stretch both his thinking and his sense of contribution.

Alicia

Newly widowed and recently retired from a high-level corporate role in the athletic apparel industry. Raised in South Central L.A. and still strikingly athletic, she brings both warmth and power to the circle. Her energy is lean, focused, and fast-moving—as if momentum might carry her through the fog of loss into something entirely new.

Endnotes

1   Stanford Center on Longevity, *The 100-Year Life Is Here. We're Not Ready,* https://longevity.stanford.edu/the-new-map-of-life-initiative/.

2   Ellen J. Langer, *The Mindful Body: Thinking Our Way to Chronic Health* (Ballantine Books, 2023); Ellen J. Langer, *Mindfulness 25th Anniversary Edition* (Balance, 2014); Ellen J. Langer, *Counterclockwise: Mindful Health and the Power of Possibility* (Ballantine Books, 2009).

3   Charles M. Johnston, *Intelligence's Creative Multiplicity* (The Institute for Creative Development Press, 2023), 51-57. Dr. Johnston explains the methodology briefly in *Intelligence's Creative Multiplicity.* See also a useful explanation in the brief posthumous publication of *Parts Work* (The Institute for Creative Development Press, 2024).

4   C. Otto Scharmer, *Theory U: Leading from the Future as It Emerges* (The Society for Organizational Learning, 2007), 403.

5   C. Otto Scharmer, *The Essentials of Theory U: Core Principles and Applications* (Berrett-Koehler Publishers, 2018).

6   Scharmer, *The Essentials of Theory U*, 10, 12.

7   Scharmer, *The Essentials of Theory U*, 9.

8   C. Otto Scharmer and Katrin Kaufer, *Presencing: 7 Practices for Transforming Self, Society, and Business* (Berrett-Koehler Publishers, 2025), 15.

9   Scharmer, *The Essentials of Theory U*, 163.

10   Scharmer and Kaufer, 56, 57.

11   Scharmer and Kaufer, 57.

12   Barbara Bradley Hagerty, *Life Reimagined: The Science, Art, and Opportunity of Midlife* (Riverhead Books, 2016), 7, 134, 135.

13   Hagerty, 136.

14   Hagerty, 137.

15   Hagerty, 125–127.

16   Hagerty, 127, 128.

17   Hagerty, 127.

18   Marc Freedman also wrote a book titled Prime Time (1999). I did not discover it until late in my writing process, well after my title was set. I am grateful for his early vision, and his valuable contributions to this field.

19   C. Otto Scharmer, "Entering 2025: Meeting the Future in the Moment. What Is Ours to Do?" *Field of the Future Blog,* January 30, 2025, https://medium.com/presencing-institute-blog/entering-2025-meeting-the-future-in-the-moment-what-is-ours-to-do-6e6e19925238.

20 Donald A. Schön, *The Reflective Practitioner: How Professionals Think in Action* (Basic Books, 1983); Chris Argyris and Donald A. Schön, *Organizational Learning: A Theory of Action Perspective* (Addison-Wesley, 1978).

21 Richard Pascale, Jerry Sternin, and Monique Sternin, *The Power of Positive Deviance: How Unlikely Innovators Solve the World's Toughest Problems* (Harvard Business Review Press, 2010).

22 Pascale et al. 19–52.

23 Pascale et al. 83–120.

24 The author created this list. It is wholly original and not produced by *ChatGPT*. The context of the story showing the use of ChatGPT is intended to illustrate how readers can use an AI tool live in a study group to enrich the conversation.

25 An original guide designed by the author is available in the Sourcebook in the section referring to chapter 9. The context of the story showing the use of *ChatGPT* is intended to illustrate how readers can use an AI tool live in a study group to enrich the conversation.

26 Scharmer, *Theory U: Leading from the Future as It Emerges*, 192.

27 *The Presencing Institute Toolkit* is available for free use under a Creative Commons license: https://www.u-school.org/resources.

28 Scharmer and Kaufer, 12.

THE SOURCEBOOK

THE SOURCEBOOK CONTENTS

Sourcebook for Chapter 1

Retirement Freedoms, Reframed

You can find plenty of books telling you what you should do with your retirement. This list shows what people actually tell me when they bump into freedoms they didn't see coming. Read it like postcards from the road ahead — and feel free to scribble your own when they find you.

1. **Freedom to Set Your Own Pace**

   "I didn't realize I can stop rushing."

   Without back-to-back meetings or deadlines, you can embrace a slower, more intentional rhythm of life, savoring each moment.

   ____

   ____

   ____

   ____

2. Freedom to Define Success

"I didn't realize I no longer have to measure my worth by promotions or paychecks."

You can let go of external metrics and focus on fulfillment, relationships, or personal growth. Reflection: "What new criteria for success could I explore?"

____

____

____

____

3. Freedom to Unlearn Work Habits

"I didn't realize I could stop being 'on' all the time."

You no longer need to check emails obsessively, multitask constantly, or operate in high-stress mode. Reflection: "What old habit might I like to let go of?"

____

____

____

____

4. Freedom to Reclaim the Daylight

"I didn't realize I can enjoy the sunshine any day of the week."

After decades indoors during prime hours, you can now savor long walks, gardening, outdoor meals without a time limit, or simply sitting in the sunshine—Just sitting. Try: Find one new thing to savor.

____

____

____

____

5. Freedom to Challenge Old Roles

"I didn't realize I don't have to be the expert anymore."

Letting go of the need to always have answers frees you to be an explorer, learner, collaborator, or simply a participant. Ask: "What roles might I want to let go of?"

6. Freedom to Embrace Imperfection

"I didn't realize I can let myself try—and fail—at new things."

The high stakes of a professional career often leave little room for experimentation. Prime Time offers a safe space to explore without judgment.

7. Freedom to Redefine Productivity

"I didn't realize I can be productive in ways that feed my soul."

Productivity shifts from meeting corporate goals to creating meaningful experiences—writing poetry, cooking for friends, mentoring, or interacting with other people in unexpected ways.

8. Freedom to Break the Weekly Cycle

"I didn't realize weekends and weekdays can be the same now."

Schedules are no longer tied to the traditional workweek. Remember Maggie Smith quipped in *Downton Abbey*: "What's a weekend?"

---

9. Freedom from Career-Driven Relationships

"I didn't realize I can choose relationships that bring me joy, not just professional value."

The transactional nature of workplace relationships gives way to authentic connections.

---

10. Freedom to Question Authority

"I didn't realize I can trust my own judgment now."

After years of working under hierarchies, you can rely on your own wisdom and intuition without second-guessing.

---

11. Freedom to Say 'Enough'

"I didn't realize I don't need to keep striving for more."

You can find contentment in what you already have, letting go of the endless pursuit of recognition, promotions, wealth, or excess accumulation.

12. Freedom to Revisit Forgotten Pleasures

"I didn't realize how much I missed playing, laughing, or simply being."

Work culture often sidelines joy and spontaneity; Prime Time lets you rediscover them.

13. Freedom to Own Your Time Completely

"I didn't realize I can spend an entire day on something I love."

You now have the gift of focusing deeply on what brings satisfaction, without interruption.

14. Freedom to Care Without Guilt

"I didn't realize I can be fully present for loved ones."

You can give undivided attention to family or friends without the nagging pull of work obligations.

15. Freedom to Leave a Legacy Beyond Work

"I didn't realize my legacy could be about who I am, not just what I did."

You can focus on the values you treasure, the memories you create, and the impact you make on your community.

16. Freedom to Let Go of the Hustle

"I didn't realize I don't need to prove myself anymore."

You can step away from the relentless striving and focus on simply being present.

17. Freedom from Noise

"I didn't realize how much silence I craved."

You can find peace in quiet moments, free from the constant ping of emails, meeting chatter, and workplace buzz. Reflection: What quiet moment did I savor this week?

18. Freedom to Explore Unconventional Paths

"I didn't realize I can pursue things that don't make sense to anyone else."

Without pressure to justify yourself, you can follow passions or ideas that others might find impractical, unconventional, or even eccentric.

19. Freedom from Commuter Mindset

"I didn't realize I don't need to rush to the next thing."

The professional's state of perpetual motion can give way to the freedom to pause and reflect.

20. Freedom to Trust the Emerging Future

"I didn't realize I don't need to have everything figured out."

Letting go of rigid plans opens space for serendipity and surprise. Reflection: What unexpected spaces might I open up for my own *Prime Time*?

____

____

____

____

These freedoms aren't instructions or new expectations. They are simply invitations to widen your awareness. Which ones might be calling to you?

Sourcebook for Chapter 2

Virtuous and Vicious Circles

Overview: A small shift in mindset can set off a virtuous cycle that transforms the trajectory of post-60 life, just as Brian Arthur's concept of *increasing returns* helps explain success in technology and economics. Here's how it can work for *Prime Time.*

The Old Mental Model
(Vicious Cycle of Traditional Retirement)

For decades, people have been conditioned to think of retirement as "freedom from work" rather than "freedom for contribution" or "freedom to create a new and rewarding life." This old assumption leads to a vicious circle of decline:

1. **Expectation:** Retirement means stepping back, relaxing, and avoiding new challenges.
2. **Reality:** Without challenge and purpose, mental and physical engagement decline.
3. **Outcome:** Less engagement leads to loss of curiosity, increased isolation, and a shrinking world.
4. **Reinforcement:** A disengaged life leads to declining energy, which seems to confirm the false belief that retirement is about slowing down.

5. **Result:** The cycle feeds on itself, leading to stagnation, a sense of irrelevance, or depression.

This is the traditional retirement trap. Once inside it, the cycle keeps pulling you downward unless you disrupt it.

The New Mental Model
(Virtuous Cycle of Prime Time)

A single mindset shift—*seeing retirement as a launchpad rather than a rocking chair*—can trigger a *positive cycle* of increasing engagement and vitality.

How a Small Shift in Mindset Becomes a Self-Reinforcing Loop

1. **New Belief:** Instead of thinking *"Retirement is the end of my productive years,"* think *"This is my moment to redefine my sources of joy and my contribution."*

2. **First Action**: Take on one meaningful challenge—volunteer, start a project, mentor, learn something new, try something you've never done before with a beginner's mind.

3. **Initial Benefit**: A sense of purpose and engagement creates renewed energy and excitement.

4. **Reinforcement**: This new energy leads to more opportunities (social connections, creative ideas, intellectual growth).

5. **Upward Spiral**: A virtuous cycle of lifelong learning, contribution, and expanding possibilities continues to build upon itself. Curiosity grows, stimulation sparks more excitement, and satisfaction spreads outward.

This is the Prime Time launchpad—once you step onto it, every choice lifts you into greater vitality and possibility.

Action Step: Try mapping your own cycles with the Worksheet on the following page.

SOURCEBOOK FOR CHAPTER 2

Circles: Fill-in-the-Blanks Worksheet

(Make as many copies as you need)

THE OLD MODEL – Vicious Circle

[**Instructions:** *Fill in how you have operated in the past. This isn't 'bad,' it's simply about recognizing contrasts with the new alternatives you can create.* Each time you fill out this form, you are practicing how to break the old cycle and strengthen the new one.]

1. **Expectation:**

2. **Reality:**

3. **Outcome:**

4. **Reinforcement:**

5. **Result:**

THE NEW MODEL – Virtuous Circle

[**Instructions:** *Now record how you wish to move forward. Start with your new belief or assumption you would like to adopt. Then decide on one small step, your First Action. As life gives you feedback, fill in items 3-5. Finally, make notes on what you learn, then start a new form and try again.*]

1. New Belief:

2. First Action:

3. Initial Benefit:

4. Reinforcement:

5. Upward Spiral:

Sourcebook for Chapter 3

List of Characters

Himari

A recently retired medical administrator from San Francisco, now building a life in Santa Fe. After years of structured service, she longs for purpose that is personally meaningful—not just socially sanctioned. She grew up in the shadow of her parents' courage after surviving a U.S. government internment camp in World War II, and now carries their resilience into her own search for belonging. Calm on the outside, she's quietly determined to forge a next chapter with substance and grace.

Shirley

A laid-off design team manager who thought she had one more year to plan. Fiercely independent, shaped by a lifetime of figuring things out on her own, she now feels unmoored. Joining this group is a bold but frightening step toward learning how to trust others at eye level and to stop going it alone. A devoted solo hiker, she's most at home in the wildest parts of the mountains—but she instinctively knows she can't navigate this next terrain alone.

Martina

A former Secretary of State in the Midwest, now returned to her deep-rooted New Mexico family. Her days are slower now, but her longing for clear structure and purpose—and for something truly *hers*—has only sharpened. Her challenge: not to be absorbed into others' plans, but to imagine a new role that's self-chosen and deeply satisfying. She dresses sharply, often in tailored jackets, as if structure might return through her wardrobe.

Paul

A former emergency room nurse and senior administrator, contemplative by nature but forged in decades of nonstop crisis response. He's now decompressing, searching for balance and disciplined reflection. He speaks slowly, with long pauses—as if weighing each word before release—and still carries the habits of someone who held lives in his hands.

Samuel

A retired philosophy professor who moved to Santa Fe at his wife's urging for adventure. Though done with academia, he misses stimulating conversation and wants to engage ideas that matter in a circle of peers. His New York accent has softened but persists—just like his appetite for deep conversation. He's the quiet skeptic-turned-seeker, eager to stretch both his thinking and his sense of contribution.

Alicia

Newly widowed and recently retired from a high-level corporate role in the athletic apparel industry. Raised in South Central L.A. and still strikingly athletic, she brings both warmth and power to the circle. Her energy is lean, focused, and fast-moving—as if momentum might carry her through the fog of loss into something entirely new.

Sourcebook for Chapter 3

Objections to Finding or Starting a Group

*A glimpse into the self-talk we slip into when
facing a new or uncomfortable challenge.*

Our six characters offer their own responses to
these common fears and hesitations.

ALICIA: **"I don't know where to find people like me."**

Response: Start talking about the book you've just started reading. Watch for who lights up when you talk about what you are learning. It might even be someone you just met, but if you feel a tiny spark of connection with them, take a chance. Remember, it only takes two to start a group.

SHIRLEY: **"But what would I say to them?"**

Try this: 'I'm thinking about getting a small group together to explore these ideas. Would you be interested?'

PAUL: **"I'm not a leader, I wouldn't know how to run a group."**

No problem: All the instructions for a host/convener are in the Sourcebook, so the group can more or less run itself. We certainly haven't needed a lot of "leadership" here, once we understood the basic ground rules and expectations. Most groups will find that they can be self-guided, once people agree to the basic behavioral norms. You don't have to be the "leader," only the host/convener—and an engaged participant like everyone else.

SAMUEL: **"But what if I put myself out there and no one is interested?"**

No worries. It only takes one more. A group begins when one person says, "Let's meet," and someone else shows up. Movements don't start with a crowd. They start with two or three. A well-known phrase in Christian Scripture says, "Where two or three are gathered…" That is enough. Two people say to each other: "This matters." And when they share their enthusiasm with others, more people show up. Even if it takes two or three "starts," that's OK. Go for it!

MARTINA: **"I don't know how to recruit people."**

Instead of *asking* people to join, *assume* they will. Say, "I'm starting a conversation group around these ideas." Then describe briefly what is most compelling for you personally. Say, "Our first meeting is [day & time, at___ (for example) my house, or wherever] Want to come?" People respond better to invitations with a clear plan than to a vague, open-ended suggestion.

HIMARI: **"But what if the group doesn't work?"**

Think like an entrepreneur. Tweak it. Persevere. Find one other person who is interested and try again with the two of you. Six isn't a magic number just because our story happened to have six. Start wherever you are. Perfect doesn't matter. Starting does. Dare to speak from your heart about it with others, and you will attract who you need. Trust the process, instead of trying to map it all out exactly ahead of time. *Just Do It!*

MARTINA: **Instead of asking, "Do I have what it takes to lead?"** I can say,

"I'll invite one or two people to explore together." Then I'll just start. The book itself will do the heavy lifting, so a convener doesn't need to feel pressure to "run" a group, only to participate authentically. It will be fun!

Sourcebook for Chapter 4

Prime Time Group Facilitator's Guide

A Note to Facilitators

Welcome! You already have what it takes to host this group. This Guide is designed to help you create the conditions for rich conversation, mutual support, and forward movement.

*You are **not** here to teach or lecture. Your job is to hold the space, keep time, and help the group stay aligned with its purpose. You're the host—not the sage.*

For your convenience, a printable Facilitator's Homework Guide is available for downloading at https://www.MarieMorganPrimeTime.com/homework-guide. It gathers the weekly assignments in one place so you don't have to flip through the book during meetings.

Section 1 – Principles for Every Meeting

(These suggestions build on the Group Norms listed elsewhere—here we re-emphasize a few essentials and underline the nature of this facilitation role. The group should feel free to add or adapt these Group Norms as you discover what works best. This is your list, not bestowed by the Facilitator Gods on High.)

1. You Are Not the Teacher

- Your role is to invite participation and hold the structure.
- Avoid summarizing the chapter for anyone—the point is to explore *implications*, not reteach the content.

2. Everyone Reads Beforehand

- This is **not** like a casual book group where half the people "meant to read it" but try to fake it.
- We're here for serious commitment to our own personal growth—not just social time. Social connections are a valuable outgrowth—they're not the main purpose.

3. Create and Protect Safety

- Confidentiality is absolute.
- A rephrase of the Golden Rule: *Listen to others the way you hope to be listened to.*
- No eye rolls. No "helpful" sarcasm. Everyone's story is valid.

4. Respect Time and Flow

- Agree on time limits and use a visible time signal—options include:
  - A kitchen timer that dings gently (or loudly if you're feeling theatrical).
  - A small desk bell.
  - A bright sticky note waved silently like a small victory flag.
- If the facilitator is speaking, another member should track their time.

5. Keep a Supportive Spirit

- Commit to being each other's *best fans*. Whatever a person's goal or calling, support it 100%.

6. Encourage Flexibility

- Exercises can be adapted — participants may elaborate or diverge if it deepens insight and respects time.

Section 2 – Opening and Closing Moments

Opening Moments (5–10 min)

- Quick check-in: each person shares one word *or* one sentence about where they are today.
- Brief reminder of group agreements.
- Take turns reading one quote from *Prime Time*.
- Allow one minute of silence to let it sink in.

Closing Moments (5–10 min)

- Each person shares one takeaway or insight from the discussion.
- Appreciation Round: Each person in turn receives at least one appreciation, focusing on their quality or effort — not on the speaker's feelings.
  - Example: "You did a great job of naming your uncertainty without apologizing for it."
  - Example: "I appreciated how you stayed curious even when challenged."
  - The receiver simply says, "Thank you." (No "*Aw, shucks*" allowed.)
  - *See* Ellen Daniell, *Every Other Thursday* (Yale University Press, 2007), chapter 16 on the power of appreciation and suggested format.
- Preview next week's chapter and exercise.
- Homework assignment (specific to that week).
- End with appreciation — always close on encouragement.

Section 2.5 – Regarding Food

If the group decides to have food or refreshment, the host can set out cups and water, but a volunteer "host" should manage everything else. Keep it simple — no need to overcomplicate. This is not a Julia Child club, and no one is inviting the James Beard Foundation.

Section 3 – Before the First Meeting: A Checklist for Hosts

- Confirm date, time, and location — make sure everyone knows how to find the meeting location.
- Confirm which chapters to read in advance.
- Make sure everyone has downloaded the "gift note" mentioned in the Foreword.
- Have the Group Norms page printed or posted where all can see.

Section 4 – Suggested Sessions/Weekly or Biweekly Plan

Session 1 – Combining Chapters 1, 2, 3: "Our Stories and Starting Points"

- **Purpose:** Share personal experiences with the themes in the first three chapters (loss of structure, invisibility, longing for meaning, etc.).
- **Timing:** Each person shares 10–12 minutes, plus 1-2 minutes each for reflections.
- **Facilitator tip:** Gently keep pacing so all voices are heard.
- **Outcome:** Everyone knows each other's starting points and core issues.
- **Homework:** Write out your personal polarities to bring next week.
- **Optional:** Discuss anything from the Introduction that feels important to the group's shared starting point.

Session 2A – Chapter 4: Inner Character Work (Part 1)

- **Timing:** If four or more members, you may need two meetings — allow about 30 minutes per person, including debrief. Short breaks in between.
- **Sequence:** Draw straws or sign up for who goes first, second, etc.

- **Who guides**: Consider having a member with a coaching gift take Marie's role from Chapter 4; the facilitator does not have to do this.
- **Recognize:** Everyone is self-conscious at first — everyone. It gets easier.
- **Going deeper:** Reference the "DIY Inner Character Work" section in the <u>Sourcebook for Chapter 4</u> for additional guidance and follow-up. Remind the group that each person is responsible for their own boundaries, and saying, "I'd rather not go there" is always acceptable, no questions asked.

Session 2B – Chapter 4: Inner Character Work (Part 2, for a larger group)

- Continue sequence from Session 2A until all members have completed the exercise.
- Same tips and pacing apply as in Part 1.

Session 3 – Chapter 5: Listening for What the Future Wants

- **Stretch:** Encourage deep listening and allow silence without awkwardness.
- **Optional:** Order Otto Scharmer's book ahead to supplement discussion.
- **Homework:** Specific to the chapter, encourage journaling observations.

Session 4 – Chapter 6: Curiosity, Passion, and Self-Efficacy

- **Getting personal:** Share real-life examples from the Exercises homework.

- **Accountability + Support:** Set up check-in partners (optional) to track progress on personal goals suggested by the Exercises.
- **Update:** Check in on Morning Practice progress or obstacles (optional).

Session 5 – Chapter 7: Superpowers Revealed

- **Purpose:** Help people name and claim their Superpowers without false modesty or comparisons.
- **Optional:** Take an extra week before this session to interview former colleagues to help discern your Superpowers.
- **Getting personal:** Allow time for participants to share what they learned. Asking for feedback is optional but encouraged. ("Is this how you see me?" "Do you see something I don't?")

Session 6 – Chapter 8: The Future Belongs to Those Who Invent It

- Include personalized discussion of "Cultivating the Entrepreneurial Mind."
- Review self-assessment results. Each person commits to growing one element of that mindset.
- **Accountability:** Renew check-in partners to revisit progress in pairs. (Optional)

Session 7 – Chapter 9: Crystallizing Your Calling

- This Session can be multiple meetings. This is where timing could shift to meet each group's needs and wishes.
- As participants begin experimenting in the real world with projects, research, volunteer opportunities, etc., consider

meeting every 3 or 4 weeks to allow time for action between check-ins.

- Note the process that the characters used in Chapter 9 and try something similar in your group, adapting to individual differences.

- Some groups meet less frequently, but for six months or more, for idea stimulation and mutual encouragement, as each member tries out various involvements and activities in the community.

- At ongoing meetings, take the opportunity to review highlights of previous chapters. E.g., "How are we doing with Open Mind in these new situations?" "Are any of my inner characters rearing their heads to try to take over when situations get challenging?" "How well am I keeping my curiosity alive?" "Is Morning Practice helping me listen to my future from *liminal space*?"

- Members could choose to take on an assignment at each meeting, bringing at least one topic or area from a particular chapter where they identify a "growing edge," pose questions, and report progress.

- Check in at https://www.MarieMorganPrimeTime.com for updates on how others are finding new opportunities, staying motivated when inevitable discouragements hit, and to share your success stories.

Session 8 – Chapter 10: Our Collective Calling (Final Meeting)

- Explore the group's shared vision and discuss possible collective actions or cultural contributions.

- If the group is interested, explore what it might look like to evolve into an *Island of Coherence* group. See *Presencing* by Scharmer and Kaufer (listed in the Additional Reading section) for further insight and practical guidance on this important initiative.

- Two or three members from a group might take up a special project together. If so, plan on a major presentation to the remaining group, including key lessons learned and new ideas generated.
- Some "alumni" of *Prime Time* groups become facilitators for new groups forming.
- As mentioned above, https://www.MarieMorganPrimeTime. com can be a rich resource for what is emerging.

Reminder

The printable Facilitator's Homework Guide is always available at https://www.MarieMorganPrimeTime.com/homework-guide.

Thank you for saying yes to hosting.

Your willingness to hold the space makes all the difference.

Sourcebook for Chapter 4

A Daily Morning Practice by Otto Scharmer
[A duplicate from Chapter 4]

(Allow 10–30 minutes)

- Rise early (before others), go to a place of silence that works for you (a place in nature is great, but you also may find other places that work for you), and allow your inner knowing to emerge. [Keep liminal space alive by not opening your phone.]
- Use a ritual that connects you with your Source: this can be a meditation, prayer, or simply an intentional silence that you enter into with an open heart and open mind.
- Remember what it is that has brought you to the place in life where you are right now: Who is your Self? What is your Work? What are you here for?
- Make a commitment to what it is that you want to be in service of. Focus on the outcome that you want to serve (the larger whole).
- Focus on what you want to accomplish (or be in service of) on this day that you are beginning right now.
- Feel the appreciation that you are given the opportunity to live the life that you have right now. Empathize with all of those who have never had all of the opportunities that led you to the

place you are now. Feel the responsibility that comes with those opportunities, the responsibility that you have to others, to all other beings, to all of nature—even to the universe.

- Ask for help so that you don't lose your way or get sidetracked. Your way forward is a journey that only you can discover. The essence of that journey is a gift that can come into the world only through you, your presence, your best future self. But you can't do it alone. That's why you ask for help.

SOURCEBOOK FOR CHAPTER 4

A Presencing Practice in Stillness

EQUUS: 3 Keys to Innovation, Creativity, and Transformation

by Kelly Wendorf [used by permission]

As a coach I learned that if I wanted to ensure long-term, measurable, and meaningful change for my clients, I had to provide experiential processes and opportunities for them. These processes allow for the body to kinesthetically process the cognitive understandings that are arising and translate them into neurological shifts. That is when behaviors change and where new possibilities emerge.

Over the years I've found that it is not in the 'doing' part of the experiential processes that the magic happens. It's in the 'being' part. To oversimplify—when properly facilitated, the being informs the doing, and the doing informs the nervous system.

But why is the secret sauce in the *beingness**? Much has been written and researched about accessing collective intelligence through presence and beingness—from Peter Senge to Joseph Jaworski to Johann Wolfgang von Goethe. Many visionaries, from entrepreneurs, to scientists, to spiritual practitioners, speak about *dropping into presence* to become what George Bernard Shaw calls "a force of nature"—a field through which we drop our conventional and often reactive way of thinking, and immerse ourselves in something larger that is intricately connected to all life.

Presencing opens the door to greater intelligence. Regardless of if it is made explicit or implicit, when experiential processes deliberately bring presencing into the mix, they deliver transformative results. Similarly, when we deliberately bring presencing into our daily lives, we operate from a more optimal creative and transformative place.

So how do we do that? It is not as simple as just sitting down cross-legged in meditation for 10 minutes a day. While that may make you more "beingness-prone" throughout the day, presencing needs to be cultivated and invited. Here are three ways to support yourself (and your team) to be more innovative and creative.

Silence –

Silence is not an absence of noise, <u>it is a presence</u>. Think about a time in your life when the silence was so powerful that it stopped you in your tracks. Maybe you were in a snow field, a mountain top, or up early before the kids. Or maybe like me, it pounced on you in the middle of utter chaos, because miraculously your habit to react to the noise had ceased. Silence is the emptiness of our usual way of being, seeing, thinking, and reacting. Sometimes we enable it, sometimes it grabs us from behind, sometimes we stop and notice it.

Silence—the outbreath before the inbreath, the pause between notes, the whitespace of a painting, the momentary hover over a flower, the fullness of emptiness—is everywhere and always available. Hence, find opportunities throughout your day to pause and be in silence, or pause and notice the silence that is already there. Find micro-moments in an empty elevator on your way to work, at a stop light, as you walk out to get the paper early in the morning, to pause and take in the presence of silence. It will drop you in to receptive states of being that will inform every other part of your day.

Kairos –

The ancient Greeks used two words for time: *chronos* and *kairos*. The former refers to chronological or sequential time, and the latter signifies a time lapse—a moment of indeterminate time in which everything happens. *Kairos* embodies the notion that there's a right time to embark on something or that some things take time to evolve. While chronos is quantitative, *kairos* has a qualitative, permanent nature. Chronos is a stopwatch, i.e. "you have 15 minutes to complete that task". Kairos is a calendar, i.e. "this project will take the time it takes to evolve and fully reveal its success".

The time it takes for an apple to ripen, happens in *kairos*. The arc of time to build a relationship, happens in *kairos*.

"To everything there is a season, and a time to every purpose under the heaven," Ecclesiastes assures us. In other words: relax, it's taken care of. We don't have to be the person at the control panel every second of the day. We can pause, we can let the Greater Mechanism at work handle things. Kairos, meaning "the right or opportune moment" (i.e., the supreme moment), begs the question—right for whom? Therein lies the key, for the rightness is governed by something more universal than any individual idea of a deadline. That "something" is the collective intelligence of all life.

Modern life provokes us to move frantically in chronos all day long. Find ways to lean back and trust *kairos*. Let events unfold sometimes without meddling and micro-managing. If mired in a project that keeps you creatively hemmed in, push away from the desk and take a walk. Let *kairos* drive for a while. In that spaciousness and ease a more creative and inspired intelligence will avail itself to you.

The Space In Between –

If you look at nature, you'll see it not only uses form to manifest itself, but it uses space as well. The right space between trees determines a forest's well-being. Animals of prey will space themselves in the herd so that if they must take off together to escape a lion, they can do so without crashing into one another. In nature, space is a connector, enabling thriving, not necessarily a distancer. Much information is communicated across space--whether it be the call and response of two ravens, or the way we are inspired by the stars in a night sky. Whether it be physical space, or emotional, mental or psychic space, deliberately taking space and working with space allows you to access a greater field of information only made available in 'the absence of form'.

Give more space between projects. If designing a workshop, give more space between events or exercises. Give your kids more space. Give yourself a break and give yourself space from your constant pushing and prodding. De-clutter your home. Give yourself more time to run errands or walk down the hall in your office between meetings. Have entire days without technology or a to-do list and just let the day unfold, navigating only by what delights you.

A Cautionary Note

All of this sounds wonderful, doesn't it? So here is my cautionary note. All things innovative and creative encounter *resistance*. It's just the physics of creation. And resistance smells silence, kairos and space a mile away. It stays up all night and works all day to trace where presencing might be brewing. When you start orienting your life towards more presencing, know that you will start to push against some comfort zones. This is because you are changing your neurological habit patterns.

Be confident that resistance will come to sabotage you in your weakest moments. And it will sound like this: "I don't have the time", "I don't like how hot it is outside", "My partner is so annoying", "I don't have enough money", "I'm not good enough".... It will not show up as obvious resistance to beingness...no, no, that would be way too apparent. It will be a parade of seemingly reasonable and rational judgment calls, ideas, and plans designed specifically to derail you. The trick is that you need some form of presencing to be aware of this scam; otherwise you'll just believe the thoughts and react accordingly. Slow down, turn your attention towards your inner landscape and notice what's going on in there. If you notice a flurry of "rational" mental ruminations, it could be time to hang out with some silence, *kairos* or space.

*[For clarity in the context of this book, I substituted *presencing* for "beingness" throughout this essay.] -MM

Kelly Wendorf can be reached at:
https://www.equusinspired.com/inquire

Our custom-curated approach to breakthrough learning is used in our Coaching, EQUUS Academy Online Courses, Workshops, Retreats, and EQUUS Experience® Sessions

Sourcebook for Chapter 4

Shirley's List of Polarities

This list is offered as a sample of one person casually jotting down her inner polarities as they occur to her. No editing for form is intended. Yours should be equally quick and informal. Give the polarities names when you can.

1. My desk is messy, but I wish it was neater. Names: Messy Desk / Neat Desk –

2. Plan Ahead / Be Organized and Be Spontaneous / Wait until the last minute and go with the flow.

3. I suddenly remember one from college. My mother wanted to take me at Christmas of my freshman year to buy a new winter coat. She said I could pick it out, but then when I chose a daffodil yellow wool, she pulled out one in navy. 'You'll get tired of that." She said, gesturing to the yellow coat. "Pick one that will last longer, one you'll never tire of." I stood my ground, because the yellow one felt like me, not her. She relented. After all, she had told me I could pick it out.

   To this day, I have an inner voice that thrives on drama — my artist self, I suppose. But I have this voice that occasionally argues for the more conservative choice. Go for what's safe, that won't offend, that will last forever without controversy. I'll call them Drama Self and Careful Self.

4. <u>Do Everything</u> for my kids vs. <u>Let Them Figure</u> it out for themselves and grow up more self-sufficient. Am I being selfish? Or wise?

5. When we were looking for a house in Santa Fe, there was one I fell in love with and then there was one that was more traditional Santa Fe style. The latter was better resale, my husband reminded me. My inner characters were <u>Movie-Set House</u> vs. <u>Suburban Practical House</u>.

   If it were just me, I'd have picked the first one, but if it were just me, I could never keep it up by myself. I acknowledged that my <u>Drama Self</u> wasn't always my most reliable inner advisor.

6. Doing my dream—my new project as an independent, solo worker? Or find some colleagues and do the dream as a group. This one scares me to death, because I've never been willing to risk asking if others would join me in my brilliant ideas. The Inner Characters names are <u>Work Alone</u> vs. <u>Trust the Group</u>.

Sourcebook for Chapter 4

D.I.Y. Inner Characters / Liminal Space Work

In chapter 4 you can observe and study how Inner Character work is done with a facilitator/guide. But for readers who want to experiment with practicing this on their own, here is additional guidance.

You may feel awkward at first, but it can be done. You will need a journal at hand, and a completely private room with no interruptions for at least an hour. Set up your space with three moveable chairs, arranged in a triangle facing each other.

Most important, you will need your highest level of self-awareness. This is because you will need to "observe" yourself simultaneously as your own "facilitator/guide" while you also take the part of each character. That means embodying your Liminal Space (your most centered self) and your two (or sometimes three) characters who represent your chosen polarities.

I have practiced this process with myself alone in my living room many times over the years. It can be valuable when you find yourself ruminating on inner debates about life's issues. To begin, I suggest you re-read chapter 4 in *Prime Time* several times. Notice the "choreography" of when the person moves to a different chair: what is going on with their conversation when they move? The more vividly you picture yourself in the room and "see" the characters they describe, the more clearly you'll observe how the process works.

It is common to get stuck and not know what to say next, or feel unsure where to take the dialogue. When this occurs, simply return to your Liminal Space chair. Sit quietly for a minute. Then, in your centered voice, *ask out loud* "Who in the room has something to say?" Sit quietly for a while and see if a small voice begins to want to speak from one of the polarity chairs. As soon as you sense that nudge, sit in that chair and speak aloud. The voice will usually be grateful to speak, and your momentum will return. Remember, from your character's chair, you always direct your words back to your Liminal Space chair, never to the other polarity character.

Take your time. At some point you will sense you have learned enough for one day. You can always return and resume the conversation, but before you leave your quiet room, record as much as seems helpful in your journal. Note what transpired, what you learned, and any unaddressed questions. Close by sitting in your Liminal Space chair, collecting your full sense of centeredness and balance, and repeat the simple gesture that anchors the experience. This is the "you" that you take with you back into your daily life.

Here is a review of the guidelines described in chapter 4:

1. Choose a polarity you wish to begin with.
2. Starting in your Liminal Space chair, describe out loud who is sitting in one of the other chairs. Imagine yourself for a moment as a play director—how does that person look? Age? Gender if that is relevant? Clothing? Distinguishing qualities? As much detail as you can. Give them a name if one comes to you. Then do the same with the character in the other chair.
3. Still in your Liminal Space chair, ask the characters who would like to speak first, then move to that chair. Feel and assume the posture and position that character embodies. Begin speaking. Look back to your Liminal Space chair as you speak. That is always where the characters direct their comments.

4. Remember these primary choreography rules:
   a. Never voice a character's thoughts and feelings without sitting *in their chair*.
   b. Every conversation is between Liminal Space and one character; the other characters *never* address one another.

5. Liminal Space remains in the driver's seat of your life. Other characters are not allowed to "take over" or dictate what should happen. Liminal Space interviews the others to draw out their feelings and opinions, so those concerns are respected. When a character *feels heard*, they are more willing to cooperate with a new path. Let them know you appreciate their desire to keep you safe, even if a new path seems to frighten them.

A CAUTION: This method is designed for adults who are relatively healthy psychologically. If this process starts to take you to a place that worries or scares you, and you no longer feel that your full, centered Liminal Space self can safely handle it, stop and seek professional help. **This method is not a substitute for psychotherapy.** A therapist will understand your goal of wanting to grow your centered, balanced self so that you can chart a new life in retirement and can help you achieve that goal.

For additional guidance, see **Parts Work**: *Culturally Mature Identity, Relationship, and Leadership: A Method*, by Charles M. Johnston, MD (2024). The book includes chair diagrams. The Kindle edition is inexpensive. From the Amazon description: "*Parts Work* engages the various aspects of our human complexity like characters in a play….it helps us access and apply the whole of ourselves as systems with…depth and nuance….The method provides the most reliable approach currently available for realizing [a] cognitive 'growing up.'"

Quick Steps for DIY Inner Characters / Liminal Space Work

Here's a simple summary you can keep nearby while you practice. It's meant to jog your memory, not replace the full instructions.

1. **Choose a polarity.**

   Pick two (or sometimes three) inner characters who represent opposite pulls.

2. **Start in your Liminal Space chair.**

   Describe aloud who is sitting in each chair — their look, age, qualities, even a name.

3. **Ask who wants to speak.**

   Move to that character's chair, feel their posture, and speak aloud — always directing words back to your Liminal Space chair.

4. **Follow the choreography.**
   - Never voice a character unless you're sitting in their chair.
   - Characters never talk directly to each other — only with Liminal Space.

5. **Return to Liminal Space.**

   When stuck, sit quietly in your Liminal Space chair, ask who has something to say, and wait for a nudge.

6. **Close the session.**

   Record notes in your journal. End in your Liminal Space chair, *anchor* the sense of balance with your chosen gesture, and carry that centeredness with you.

Sourcebook for Chapter 5

Why Islands and Circles of Coherence Matter

*Circles of coherence restore our agency by
focusing attention, listening deeply, imagining
together, and creating patterns that endure.*

In *Prime Time* we have talked a lot about *Islands* or *Circles of Coherence*. Let's step back and reflect on *why* they matter and what they can look like. Otto Scharmer and Katrin Kaufer, in their latest book *Presencing* (2025), write:

Given the forces of disruption surrounding us today, and the sensed loss of agency so many of us feel, "…we have found that the concept of *islands of coherence* can help us to refocus on where the real opportunity is—in *our very own agency*—that is, in our capacity to act."

That sentence captures why I return to the phrase so often. When the world feels fragmented, circles of coherence give us a living example of what it means to create order, hope, and possibility together. Here are four ways this shows up in practice:

- **Alignment of Attention and Intention**

  Why it matters: When people point their attention in the same direction, even briefly, new energy becomes available.

  What it can look like: A group that begins every gathering with a moment of silence, each person bringing to mind shared purpose—say, supporting one another's next calling. The room feels different afterward: more grounded, less scattered, more able to act together.

- **Generative Listening and Dialogue**

  Why it matters: Most of us rarely feel truly heard.When listening is deep and generous, fresh insights arise that no one could have forced.

  What it can look like: Imagine someone in your circle telling a story of disappointment. Instead of rushing to fix it, the others lean in, pause, and ask questions that draw out what really matters. The speaker walks away lighter, with a new idea in hand.

- **Co-imagining and Co-creation**

  Why it matters: None of us can design the future alone. But when people sketch possibilities together, even tentative ones, confidence builds.

  What it can look like: Three or four people brainstorm a neighborhood project. One has the practical know-how, another the connections, another the creative spark. The project takes shape only because their imaginations intertwine and create synergy.

- **Ecosystem Governance**

  Why it matters: Coherence is not just about warm feelings—it is about creating ways of organizing that can last and ripple outward. "Coherence" literally means sticking together.

  What it can look like: A circle of retired professionals rotates facilitation and keeps a shared journal of key insights. Over time, that simple structure makes the group resilient, and others begin forming circles modeled on theirs.

Scharmer and Kaufer also remind us that coherence is strengthened by three essential kinds of connection. First, *downward to the land and the power of place*, rooting us in the soil, the waters, and the non-human world that sustains life. Second, *horizontal to one another and to the social and natural ecosystems* that shape our existence, so we do not forget our non-negotiable interdependence. And third, *upward to the highest future potential,* the possibility that depends on us to notice, imagine, and bring into being.

Finally, remember that coherence does not begin with a group—it begins with the self. *Our own self is the smallest unit of an island of coherence.* Each of us decides, moment by moment, where we place our attention. That placement is our freedom, our necessity, and our responsibility.

Journal Prompt: Finding Your Own Island of Coherence

Take 10 minutes to sit quietly. Recall, reflect, and write down your responses to these three questions:

1. *Downward connection* — Recall a place in nature (a garden, a trail, even a window view) where you feel most grounded. What happens in you when you return your attention there?

2. *Horizontal connection* — Think of one relationship—human or non-human—that brings you back to life when you feel scattered. What makes that connection restorative?

3. *Upward connection* — When have you glimpsed a future possibility that felt larger than yourself, but also quietly dependent on you to help bring it into being? What moves in you at that moment? Allow your *liminal space* to enter and confirm.

Write a few sentences about each. Then step back and ask:

If my own self is the smallest island of coherence, what one shift in my attention would make that island stronger right now?

A heartfelt note:

The book *Presencing* by Otto Scharmer and Katrin Kaufer (Berrett-Koehler, 2025) is itself a remarkable exploration of islands of coherence—and much more. If this discussion has sparked your interest, consider their book a rich companion to *Prime Time*, offering a broader context for these practices and a deep dive into the emerging future that calls us all.

Sourcebook for Chapter 5

Circles of Coherence Guidelines

"When a complex system is far from equilibrium, small islands of coherence in a sea of chaos have the capacity to shift the entire system to a higher order."

—Ilya Prigogine, Nobel Prize-winning chemist

This tool from the Presencing Institute is a guideline for how a small group (4–7 people) can start to build the capacity to listen for coherence in a volatile, uncertain, complex, and ambiguous (VUCA) world. By connecting around attention, intention, and agency, participants create space to explore what is emerging— within themselves and between them. The practice involves deep listening and reflective dialogue.

Sequence

Step	Time	Process
1	5 min	Welcome – Introductions Each participant shares name, location, and answers: • What are you noticing in yourself about how you are showing up in this moment?
2	5 min	Stillness • Centering together: pause, soften gaze, sit quietly.
3	25 min	Share personal context (5 min per person). Choose a question from each area: Attention: • Where is your attention focused now? • What is the quality of your attention? Intention: • What do you feel called towards? • What is clarifying in your intention? Agency: • What internal/external forces hold you back? • What supports give you strength? • What next step (even small) can you take now?
4	10 min	Mirroring • After sharing, pause and let stories resonate. • Notice what arises (mind, heart, body). • Share an image, feeling, drawing, or gesture.
5	7 min	Final Thoughts • What struck you in what you shared/heard? • What insights did you gain? • How will you carry this forward into the coming weeks?
6	3 min	Journaling on your own • Note thoughts, practices, inspirations you want to explore.

7	5 min	Closing • Is there a shared inquiry to continue? • Set the next time/place for the circle.

Attribution: Adapted from Presencing Institute's "Circles of Coherence Guidelines." Licensed under Creative Commons Attribution-ShareAlike 3.0 (CC-BY-SA 3.0).

Sourcebook for Chapter 6

The Three Doors in Liminal Space

Curiosity, passion, and self-efficacy form a hidden symmetry. Each arises from one of the great gateways of the human spirit:

- Curiosity flows from an **open mind**—the willingness to let go of what we think we know and to be surprised.
- Passion flows from an **open heart**—the ability to care deeply enough to be moved.
- Self-efficacy flows from an **open will**—the spaciousness to step forward and say, "I am willing, and I can."

But these qualities don't fully awaken through effort alone. They are not simply personal traits or skills to be mastered. They do not emerge from ego, nor from "willpower." They become transformative only when we allow ourselves to enter **liminal space**—that threshold place where old patterns no longer hold, and the new has not yet come fully into being.

In such moments, curiosity shifts from mere interest to wonder, because we have loosened our grip on certainty. Passion deepens from personal intensity to resonance because we sense that something larger needs our care. And self-efficacy expands from confidence into trust, because we realize we are participants in a greater unfolding.

Seen in this light, curiosity, passion, and self-efficacy are not three separate capacities to develop in isolation. They are **three doors that open together** when we pause in liminal space. And when they open, they connect us to Source—the deeper current of life that wants to move through us.

Take a few moments to reflect for yourself. Recall a time when your *mind* was genuinely surprised or opened to a new way of seeing. Remember when your *heart* was stirred so deeply that you felt called to act. Bring to mind an experience when your *will* felt aligned with something larger than yourself, and you trusted your ability to step forward. Notice how these three moments weave together in your life story.

Now imagine yourself again at the threshold of what's next. Rather than searching for answers, simply allow curiosity, passion, and self-efficacy to rise like doors slowly opening. What begins to stir in you as you pause there?

And as you do this, recall what you learned in Chapter 4. At the close of the inner character work, you practiced anchoring the sensations of liminal space and centered presence in your body with a simple gesture. Let yourself return to that gesture now. Resume your centered posture. Feel how the anchor gesture grounds the experience in your whole being—not just in your thoughts.

By reinforcing it again now, you are strengthening your body's memory of what it feels like to stand open in mind, heart, and will, ready to be guided by Source. Some call this *standing meditation.* Name it whatever helps you remember to return to it.

Sourcebook for Chapter 7

An Expanded List of Potential Superpowers

You've already explored your potential Superpowers in the main text of this book. This expanded list is here to help you see your strengths more clearly, offering new angles and examples that might spark recognition. You don't need to see yourself in any of these *exact* scenarios; they're here to jog your memory and help you name what you've already done in your own way.

Sometimes a true Superpower is something you take so much for granted that you barely notice it — until you realize that other people have been surprised or impressed by how easily you do it. As you read, picture yourself in these roles now, not just in a former workplace. Which ones feel like second nature? Which ones make you light up just imagining them? Note them in your journal and watch for patterns.

Deeply Connecting with People

1. **Empathy that Unlocks Insight**: Instinctively sensing the emotions, needs, and unspoken truths in others, often before they're voiced.

   Example: Sitting with someone in grief and knowing the right moment to speak — or to stay silent.

2. **Bridge-Building Mediation**: Guiding people from tension to understanding without anyone losing face.
   Example: Helping two feuding neighborhood associations find a shared plan for a community garden.

3. **Teaching that Transforms**: Making complex concepts not just clear but life-changing for the learner.
   Example: Showing a beginner painter how to see light differently — and watching their work leap forward in a single afternoon.

4. **Storytelling that Sticks**: Using vivid narrative to inspire action or change perspective.
   Example: Sharing a childhood memory that moves an audience to join a conservation project.

5. **Natural Networking**: Spotting connections others miss and making introductions that matter.
   Example: Introducing two local artists whose joint exhibit draws national attention.

Making Things Happen with Precision

6. **Orchestral Organizing**: Bringing clarity and momentum to a project with many moving parts.
   Example: Coordinating dozens of volunteers to transform an empty lot into a thriving pocket park.

7. **Elegant Problem-Solving**: Finding not just any solution, but the one that feels inevitable once revealed.
   Example: Redesigning a farmers' market layout so it doubles foot traffic and triples vendor sales.

8. **Unshakable Advocacy**: Rallying others to a cause with moral conviction and persistence.
   Example: Leading a petition drive that protects a historic building from demolition.

9. **Hands-On Restoration**: Bringing beauty and function back to what was broken or neglected.

   Example: Repairing a century-old carousel so children can ride it again.

10. **Tenacious Perseverance**: Staying the course on a goal despite delays, setbacks, or resistance.

    Example: Completing a five-year effort to restore native plants to a degraded wetland.

Seeing and Creating Differently

11. **Visionary Artistic Sense**: Seeing patterns, color, or form in ways that invite others to see anew.

    Example: Creating a mural that transforms how a neighborhood feels about itself.

12. **Design Thinking with Heart**: Marrying beauty, utility, and human need in one elegant solution.

    Example: Designing public benches shaped to encourage conversation between strangers.

13. **Trailblazing Innovation**: Generating ideas that open entirely new possibilities.

    Example: Inventing a low-cost water filter for households living off the grid.

14. **Masterful Craftsmanship**: Bringing skill, patience, and artistry to every detail.

    Example: Hand-carving a ceremonial table from reclaimed wood for a tribal council.

15. **Curatorial Story-Weaving**: Selecting and arranging objects, ideas, or experiences to create meaning.

    Example: Assembling a pop-up exhibit that tells the story of a town's immigrant roots through artifacts and personal letters.

Working Brilliantly with Ideas

16. **Investigative Research Mastery**: Following a trail of questions until you uncover the pivotal fact or hidden pattern.

    Example: Tracing the forgotten origin of a folk song and reintroducing it to a festival stage.

17. **Deep-Dive Expertise**: Applying a lifetime of specialized knowledge to new, fertile ground.

    Example: Using decades of botany experience to advise a community food forest project.

18. **Strategic Vision-Mapping**: Seeing the whole chessboard and charting the best moves ahead.

    Example: Designing a ten-year plan that brings back a local river's health.

19. **Insatiable Curiosity**: Asking questions that reveal possibilities others miss.

    Example: Learning beekeeping from scratch, then showing a neighborhood how to start backyard hives.

20. **Data Storytelling**: Turning numbers into narratives people can act on.

    Example: Creating a simple, powerful chart that convinces a town to switch to renewable energy.

Inspiring and Relating with Ease

21. **Contagious Encouragement**: Infusing others with confidence and enthusiasm.

    Example: Training with a friend for their first 5K and cheering them across the finish line.

22. **Grounded Leadership**: Guiding people toward a shared goal while keeping trust intact.

    Example: Leading a diverse volunteer crew to complete a mural without a single flare-up of conflict.

23. **Listening Between the Lines**: Hearing what's unsaid and inviting the truth forward.

    Example: Hosting a circle where someone finally shares a story they've carried silently for decades.

24. **Wry, Disarming Humor**: Using wit to open hearts and lighten heavy moments.

    Example: Telling a perfectly timed joke that shifts a tense meeting into problem-solving mode.

25. **Graceful Diplomacy**: Steering sensitive conversations to resolution without bruising relationships.

    Example: Helping two nonprofit leaders merge their programs while preserving both missions.

Leading with Vision and Values

26. **Visionary Imagination**: Painting a picture of what could be so vividly that others lean in to help make it real.

    Example: Inspiring a town to plant 1,000 trees in a year.

27. **Compassion in Action**: Turning care into tangible help where it's needed most.

    Example: Organizing meal deliveries for neighbors recovering from surgery.

28. **Stewardship with Foresight**: Protecting resources, traditions, and landscapes for future generations.

    Example: Leading a campaign to save a historic lighthouse from erosion.

29. **Adaptive Agility**: Thriving in change and helping others do the same.

    Example: Reimagining a community festival when weather cancels the outdoor venue.

30. **Resilient Rebound**: Recovering quickly from setbacks and showing others it's possible.

    Example: After a flood damages your home, leading an effort to rebuild the neighborhood stronger than before.

Emerging Superpowers in Purposeful Giving

31. **Strategic Giving**: Moving from scattershot donations to focused investments in causes that align with your values and long-term vision.

    Example: Choosing to direct all major giving toward restoring native habitats in your state, then tracking measurable progress each year.

32. **Skills-Infused Philanthropy**: Pairing financial support with your unique expertise to multiply impact.

    Example: Funding a sustainability initiative and also advising its leaders on coalition-building, using your deep networking skills.

33. **Collaborative Funding Leadership**: Bringing donors and doers together to tackle shared goals.

    Example: Hosting a series of small salons where philanthropists and grassroots organizers meet to shape a joint climate action plan.

34. **Systems Change Advocacy**: Using your influence and resources to shift the conditions that create problems in the first place.

    Example: Supporting a local food bank while also helping launch a policy campaign that addresses root causes of food insecurity.

35. **Mentoring the Next Generation of Givers**: Guiding younger family members or community leaders to align their giving with purpose and integrity.

    Example: Inviting your grandchildren to help choose and research an annual family giving project.

Reflection Prompts – Focusing the Lens

Prompt #1—The Effortless Excellence Test

From the Expanded List, circle any Superpower descriptions that feel even loosely familiar. Then ask yourself:

- Which of these do I do so naturally that I hardly notice I'm doing it?
- Which of these draws consistent, unsolicited praise or surprise from others?
- Which of these energizes me instead of draining me? Look for one or two that check all three boxes—they may be strong candidates for your true Superpower.

Prompt #2—Translate the Inspiration into Your Own Story

Pick one or two items you circled. Without worrying about matching the example exactly, write down a time when you did something *in your own way* that fits the spirit of that Superpower. Be specific — what happened, who was involved, what impact it had. Did anyone around you seem surprised or impressed by how well you handled it? That reaction can be a powerful clue.

Prompt #3—The Good vs. Gifted Distinction

Think of a skill you use well but without much spark — something you can do competently but that doesn't light you up. Then, beside it, describe a time you used one of your true Superpowers at a level that felt exceptional. Notice the difference in your energy, the effect on others, and your own satisfaction. That contrast can help clarify what belongs at the center of your *Prime Time*.

SOURCEBOOK FOR CHAPTER 8

Entrepreneurial Mindset Self-Assessment and Development Guide

USE THIS GUIDE TO SHIFT FROM JOB-SEEKER TO OPPORTUNITY CREATOR.

Introduction: This tool is not a scientific test but a reflective aid. It will help you see where your current mindset aligns with entrepreneurial thinking, highlight areas for growth, and suggest small experiments to build confidence. It is designed to nudge you into reflecting on less familiar assumptions and mindsets, practicing Open Mind, and shifting toward creating opportunities instead of only applying for predefined volunteer roles.

Self-Assessment: Entrepreneurial Mindset

For each statement, rate yourself on a scale from **1 to 5**, where:

- 1 = Strongly Disagree
- 2 = Somewhat Disagree
- 3 = Neutral / Sometimes True for me
- 4 = Somewhat Agree
- 5 = Strongly Agree

Section A: Opportunity Recognition & Vision

1. I actively notice unmet needs, problems, or inefficiencies in my community.
2. I see problems as potential opportunities rather than obstacles.
3. I can generate multiple ideas for how to create something new or improve existing situations.
4. I believe it's possible to *design my own role* rather than waiting for a position to be created.
5. I am excited by the idea of bringing a new idea, service, or project into the world.

Section B: Risk Tolerance & Comfort with Uncertainty

6. I am comfortable making decisions without having all the information upfront.
7. I can take calculated risks without feeling a paralyzing fear of failure.
8. If I try something and it doesn't work, I see it as a learning experience rather than a failure.
9. I can handle ambiguity and uncertainty without needing constant structure or security.
10. I believe that *taking action* is more important than waiting for perfect conditions.

Section C: Initiative & Proactivity

11. I don't wait for permission — I take the initiative to start projects on my own.
12. I actively seek out ways to improve or create value rather than waiting to be assigned tasks.
13. I am willing to test new ideas before I feel completely "ready."
14. I take ownership of my own success rather than expecting external systems to create my opportunities.

15. I am willing to invest time and energy into *creating something new*, even without guaranteed success.

Section D: Resilience & Adaptability

16. I am comfortable changing course if something isn't working.
17. I have the persistence to keep going despite setbacks, criticism, or slow progress.
18. I believe failure is just feedback, not a sign that I should stop trying.
19. I see challenges as opportunities to grow rather than as reasons to quit.
20. I have overcome past obstacles and found ways to move forward.

Section E: Persuasion, Influence & Networking

21. I can clearly communicate my ideas in a way that excites and engages others.
22. I am comfortable promoting myself or my ideas without feeling like I am "bragging."
23. I believe that *building relationships* is essential to success, and I actively cultivate my network.
24. I am open to asking for help, mentorship, constructive criticism, or collaboration.
25. I understand that influencing others (whether clients, funders, or partners) is a key entrepreneurial skill.

Scoring & Interpretation

- **100-125** – Strong entrepreneurial mindset. Focus on refining specific skills like sales, networking, or execution strategies.
- **75-99** – Solid foundation. Identify where you scored lowest and develop those areas.
- **50-74** – In transition. Work on building confidence in opportunity recognition, resilience, and risk-taking.
- Below 50 – Likely job-holder mindset. Begin by expanding how you recognize opportunities and by developing initiative.

Developing Your Entrepreneurial Mindset: Small Experiments

If you scored low in an area, try these **small experiments** to develop your mindset:

If you scored low in...	Try this...
Opportunity Recognition	Write down 3-5 unmet needs or inefficiencies you notice daily. Practice brainstorming possible solutions.
Risk & Uncertainty	Start a "test" project—something small with a little uncertainty but no major consequences if it fails.
Initiative & Proactivity	Take action on one small idea without over-planning. Experiment with moving forward without waiting for perfect conditions.
Resilience & Adaptability	Reframe a past failure as a learning experience. What did you learn, and how can you apply it now?
Persuasion & Influence	Pitch an idea to a friend or colleague and see how they respond. Practice speaking about your ideas with enthusiasm.

Additional Small Experiments

1. **Volunteer in a new role** – Choose a volunteer position that requires creative problem-solving or leadership, rather than routine tasks.

2. **Host a small event or workshop** – Teach something you know well, and assess the interest and engagement of attendees.

3. **Create a low-cost product or service** — such as offering a one-time paid consultation, writing a short guide, or designing a small group coaching session.

4. **Attend an entrepreneurial networking event** – Engage in conversations with business owners and observe how they discuss opportunities and challenges.

5. **Test a micro-business idea** – Try selling a product, offering a local service, or launching a community initiative on a small scale to experiment with market demand.

6. **Offer to solve a problem** – Identify a small problem for a local nonprofit, business, or group and propose a creative solution.

7. **Practice reframing challenges as opportunities** – Each day, write down one obstacle you faced and how it could be viewed as a steppingstone to something new.

Next Steps

1. **Reflect on your assessment** – Where do you want to grow?

2. **Choose one experiment** – Start today with a small action to build your entrepreneurial mindset.

3. **Journal your insights** – Track what you notice about your thinking patterns and behaviors.

This guide ©2025 is part of the **Sourcebook** in *Prime Time*: *A Bold New Narrative for Life After 60 – And a Roadmap for Reinventing Your Future, by Dr. Marie Morgan ©2026.*

There's no wrong place to begin —
momentum builds no matter where you start.

Sourcebook for Chapter 9

The After-Action Review

Instructions: This exercise is designed to help you find clarity in your quest to develop or discover a new context for practicing your Superpower. After you have participated in a volunteer or paid experiment, answer each question below *in writing*. When you have captured as much detail as you wish, set it aside for 2-3 days, then read your notes through as if you were seeing them for the first time. Look for patterns, as well as unasked questions that might help you further understand what you have—or have not—learned from the experience.

1. **What was planned?** Did someone brief you on what to expect? If you created the experience yourself, what did you think would happen?

   ____

   ____

   ____

2. **What actually happened?** Describe specific experiences for later reference. (Use additional pages as necessary.)

   ____

   ____

   ____

3. **What went well?** List what went well and the criteria you used for each item you evaluated.

____

____

____

4. **What could have gone better?** Describe your preferred outcome.

____

____

____

5. **How did it *feel*?** Capture your subjective feelings as accurately as you can. If you were to do this three days a week for a year, how might you feel?

____

____

____

6. **What might you have done to achieve a better outcome?**

____

____

____

7. How did the overall experience benefit:

—The people present?

____

—The larger group or community?

____

—Yourself?

____

8. **Was there an adverse effect on anyone?** What do you learn from this?

____

____

____

9. Sometimes a new experience has a certain "glow"—like falling in love. **Can you imagine how this situation might feel over a longer time period?**

____

____

____

10. **How did the situation align with your curiosities, passions, and sense of purpose?**

____

____

____

11. **How do you feel about how you "fit" into the overall situation, especially with the people involved?**

____

____

____

12. **In what ways did the situation utilize your Superpowers?** Be as specific as possible. What might have been different that would have allowed them to be utilized more fully?

____

____

____

13. Describe your overall conclusions at this time. (You may enter other conclusions here later.)

____

____

____

14. Record any additional thoughts or observations not covered by the above questions.

____

____

____

The Clearness Committee:
A Trustworthy Circle, Not a Clever Technique

Once you have read Parker Palmer's work or heard him speak, you know how deeply he honors the inner teacher in each of us—the belief that every person carries a source of wisdom that, if listened to, can guide with surprising clarity. This is the same conviction we have been practicing throughout this book: learning to listen to our personal future, especially in liminal space, where ordinary distractions fall away and deeper knowing can emerge.

The Clearness Committee was developed by the Quakers in the 1660s as a way of supporting that listening. Its power comes not from brilliant advice but from the humility of a circle that holds your dilemma with reverence, discipline, and care.

Let's be clear:

This is *not* a coaching session.

It is *not* a place to brainstorm ideas or share what has worked for others.

It is *not* a Mastermind.

It is *not* about diagnosis or expertise.

The Clearness Committee is an act of trust. One person—the *focus person*—shares a real, complex dilemma. A small group surrounds them with attention and silence, asking only open-ended, honest questions. No nudging, no suggestions, no "have you thought of…?" questions. Just curiosity, reverence, and presence.

This may sound simple, but it is profoundly difficult. Even experienced facilitators can struggle to resist giving advice. I once introduced the method to a circle of professional consultants. Despite clear guidelines, a few simply could not hold back their opinions. It was frustrating—and instructive. The discipline of *not knowing* is harder than it looks.

That is why I do not include step-by-step instructions here. Instead, I encourage you to absorb the tone of this practice from Parker Palmer himself. His way of teaching conveys the responsibility and restraint needed to protect the space where an inner teacher might be heard.

✦ Recommended Resources

Before gathering your own Clearness Committee, start here:

- Parker Palmer on the Clearness Committee (short talk) https://www.youtube.com/watch?v=t_J6RE5_5R4 (*If this link ever changes, search YouTube for "Clearness Committee Parker Palmer."*)

- Written Instructions from Parker J. Palmer, "The Clearness Committee: A Communal Approach to Discernment." Center for Courage & Renewal. Available at: https://couragerenewal.org/library/the-clearness-committee-a-communal-approach-to-discernment/

- Parker J. Palmer. *A Hidden Wholeness: The Journey Toward an Undivided Life.* Jossey-Bass, 2004. See particularly Chapter VIII for the Clearness Committee discussion. https://couragerenewal.org

- Or simply try a Google search for "Parker Palmer Clearness Committee" for a multitude of additional resources.

The Clearness Committee only works when participants
trust that the focus person has what they need
within them. When the circle can hold back its own
wisdom, that deeper wisdom can finally be heard.

Sourcebook for Chapter 10

Ways We Are Already Changing the Narrative

*Culture does not change in a single stroke. It
shifts when people like us, quietly and steadily,
live a truer story the world cannot ignore.*

You may not realize it yet, but by embracing the invitations of *Prime Time,* you are already helping to reshape the cultural story about aging. Here are six practical ways your personal growth translates into collective impact:

1. You use new language.

When you describe yourself in terms of passion, curiosity, or reinvention—rather than retirement or decline—you subtly reset the expectations of others.

2. You model new behavior.

Every time you take a class, mentor someone, or start something that hasn't been done before, you plant a different story about "elders" in someone else's mind.

3. You build collective identity.

By seeing yourself as part of a *Prime Time* cohort, you help create a visible wave of people redefining what it means to age. You're not just living differently—you're also showing that we are doing this together.

4. You frame aging as developmental and intergenerational.

You embody the idea that this stage of life is about growth, not decline, and that what you model now will shape the expectations of younger generations.

5. You create shared meaning.

Whether in conversations, small groups, or on social media, when you reflect aloud about this stage of life, you help normalize *Prime Time* as a vibrant, evolving season.

6. You help the movement grow.

When you recommend this book, share your story, or invite others into conversation, you keep the energy moving outward. Each action, no matter how small, strengthens the collective momentum—like a virtuous circle, where one person's step inspires another's.

Journal Prompt: Amplifying the Signal

Which of the six ways of changing the narrative feels most alive for you right now?

How might you amplify that signal this week?

When you act, you add your strength to the larger current.

And together we amplify this signal: **We are not fading—we are beginning as never before.**

*The story is already changing because you are
living it—roots taking hold, ripples widening
on water, wings lifting in great migration.*

ADDITIONAL READING

A gift to my readers

This list highlights books that have informed and inspired the ideas in *Prime Time*. While the three subcategories overlap, I hope they serve as a helpful guide for your own browsing. Some titles are classics—intentionally included lest we forget—while others reflect emerging science on health, longevity, and purpose. And some I have found personally meaningful.

All are offered to deepen your exploration of life after 60.

Discernment, Listening, and Purpose

Angeles Arrien. *The Four-Fold Way: Walking the Paths of the Warrior, Teacher, Healer, and Visionary.* HarperSanFrancisco, 1993.

Arthur C. Brooks. *From Strength to Strength: Finding Success, Happiness, and Deep Purpose in the Second Half of Life.* Portfolio, 2022.

David Brooks. *The Second Mountain: The Quest for a Moral Life.* Random House, 2019.

Beatrice Bruteau. *Radical Optimism: Practical Spirituality in an Uncertain World.* Sentient Publications, 2002.

Chip Conley. *Learning to Love Midlife: 12 Reasons Why Life Gets Better with Age.* Avid Reader Press, 2024.

Chip Conley. *Wisdom at Work: The Making of a Modern Elder.* Currency, 2018.

Barbara Bradley Hagerty. *Life Reimagined: The Science, Art, and Opportunity of Midlife.* Riverhead Books, 2016.

Joseph Jaworski. *Synchronicity: The Inner Path of Leadership.* Berrett-Koehler, 1996.

Marie Morgan. *Prime Time: A Bold New Narrative for Life After 60 — And a Roadmap for Re-Inventing Your Future.* Delgado Street Press, 2026.

Peter M. Senge, C. Otto Scharmer, Joseph Jaworski, and Betty Sue Flowers. *Presence: Human Purpose and the Field of the Future.* Doubleday/Currency, 2004.

Parker J. Palmer. *A Hidden Wholeness: The Journey Toward an Undivided Life.* Jossey-Bass, 2004.

Parker J. Palmer. *Let Your Life Speak: Listening for the Voice of Vocation.* Jossey-Bass, 2000.

Parker J. Palmer. *The Active Life: A Spirituality of Work, Creativity, and Caring.* Harper & Row, 1990.

Parker J. Palmer. *To Know as We Are Known: Education as a Spiritual Journey.* HarperSanFrancisco, 1993 (rev. ed.; orig. 1983).

Daniel Quinn. *Ishmael: An Adventure of the Mind and Spirit.* Bantam/Turner, 1992.

C. Otto Scharmer and Katrin Kaufer. *Presencing: 7 Practices for Transforming Self, Society, and Business.* Berrett-Koehler Publishers, 2025.

David Spangler. *The Call: Discovering Why You Are Here.* Riverhead Books, 1996.

David Whyte. *Fire in the Earth.* Many Rivers Press, 1992.

David Whyte. *The House of Belonging.* Many Rivers Press, 1996.

David Whyte. *Where Many Rivers Meet.* Many Rivers Press, 1990.

Self-Care, Self-Management, Health and Mindset

Peter Attia. *Outlive: The Science and Art of Longevity.* Harmony, 2023.

James Clear. *Atomic Habits: An Easy & Proven Way to Build Good Habits & Break Bad Ones.* Avery, 2018.

Nancy Copeland-Payton. *The Losses of Our Lives: The Sacred Gifts of Renewal in Everyday Loss.* SkyLight Paths, 2009.

Ellen Daniell. *Every Other Thursday: Stories and Strategies from Successful Women Scientists.* Yale University Press, 2006.

Sanjay Gupta. *Keep Sharp: Build a Better Brain at Any Age.* Simon & Schuster, 2021.

Kasley Killam. *The Art and Science of Connection: Why Social Health Is the Missing Key to Living Longer, Healthier, and Happier.* HarperOne, 2024.

Ellen J. Langer. *Counterclockwise: Mindful Health and the Power of Possibility.* Ballantine Books, 2009.

Ellen J. Langer. *Mindfulness: 25th Anniversary Edition (orig. 1989).* Balance, 2014.

Ellen J. Langer. *The Mindful Body: Thinking Our Way to Chronic Health.* Ballantine Books, 2023.

Anne D. LeClaire. *Listening Below the Noise: The Transformative Power of Silence.* Harper Perennial, 2009.

Cyn Meyer. *The Rewire Retirement Method: From Aimless to Amazing.* Prominence Publishing, 2024.

David Steindl-Rast. *Gratefulness, the Heart of Prayer: An Approach to Life in Fullness.* Paulist Press, 1984.

Going Deeper (on topics raised in this book)

Chris Argyris and Donald A. Schön. *Organizational Learning: A Theory of Action Perspective.* Addison-Wesley, 1978.

W. Brian Arthur. *Increasing Returns and Path Dependence in the Economy.* University of Michigan Press, 1994.

W. Brian Arthur. *The Nature of Technology: What It Is and How It Evolves.* Free Press, 2009.

Albert Bandura. *Self-Efficacy: The Exercise of Control.* W. H. Freeman, 1997.

Marc Freedman. *Encore: Finding Work That Matters in the Second Half of Life.* PublicAffairs, 2007.

Marc Freedman. *How to Live Forever: The Enduring Power of Connecting the Generations.* PublicAffairs, 2018.

Marc Freedman. *Prime Time: How Baby Boomers Will Revolutionize Retirement and Transform America.* PublicAffairs, 1999.

Howard Gardner. *Changing Minds: The Art and Science of Changing Our Own and Other People's Minds.* Harvard Business School Press, 2004.

Lynda Gratton and Andrew Scott. *The 100-Year Life: Living and Working in an Age of Longevity.* Bloomsbury, 2016.

Charles M. Johnston. *Intelligence's Creative Multiplicity.* The Institute for Creative Development Press (ICD Press), 2023.

Charles M. Johnston. *Necessary Wisdom: Meeting the Challenge of a New Cultural Maturity.* ICD Press, 1991.

Charles M. Johnston. *Parts Work: Culturally Mature Identity, Relationship, and Leadership—A Method.* ICD Press, 2024.

Ryan Levesque. *Return to Real* (forthcoming, January 2026). Check online for the most up-to-date subtitle and publisher information.

Richard Pascale, Jerry Sternin, and Monique Sternin. *The Power of Positive Deviance: How Unlikely Innovators Solve the World's Toughest Problems.* Harvard Business Review Press, 2010.

Ilya Prigogine and Isabelle Stengers. *Order Out of Chaos: Man's New Dialogue with Nature.* Bantam Books, 1984.

C. Otto Scharmer. *Theory U: Leading from the Future as It Emerges.* The Society for Organizational Learning, 2007; Berrett-Koehler, 2009.

C. Otto Scharmer. *The Essentials of Theory U: Core Principles and Applications.* Berrett-Koehler, 2018.

Donald A. Schön. *The Reflective Practitioner: How Professionals Think in Action.* Basic Books, 1983.

Bradley Schurman. *The Super Age: Decoding Our Demographic Destiny.* Harper Business, 2022.

Martin E. P. Seligman. *Authentic Happiness: Using the New Positive Psychology to Realize Your Potential for Lasting Fulfillment.* Free Press, 2002.

Peter M. Senge. *The Fifth Discipline: The Art and Practice of the Learning Organization.* Doubleday/Currency, 1990.

Stanford Center on Longevity. *The 100-Year Life Is Here. We're Not Ready.* https://longevity.stanford.edu/the-new-map-of-life-initiative/ Accessed Nov. 14, 2025

M. Mitchell Waldrop. *Complexity: The Emerging Science at the Edge of Order and Chaos.* Simon & Schuster, 1992.

Acknowledgments

*Self-publishing is a misnomer. No one
person can produce a book.*

In collaboration with **Delgado Street Press**—who helped me assemble so many disparate people and functions into a linear process and a real, live product—I am grateful for:

Essential Collaborators

Bessie Gantt, my editor, for reading my mind when I couldn't, and shaping my ideas into a clearer, stronger form.

Kelly Notaras and Jill Esplin at KN Literary, for finding Bessie for me.

Lil Copan, for reviewing my first draft and showing me how major revisions could lead to a usable book.

Rhonda Douglas at ResilientWriters.com, for helping to keep me focused during those early writing months.

Chandler Bolt and his team at SelfPublishing.com, for pointing the way, mapping the moving parts, and managing production to make it real.

Ray Brehm and his "all the tech in one place" PubFunnels crew, for designing a seamless structure for my online presence.

Carrie Jareed at AVirtualExecutive4U, for coordinating all the details in my PubFunnels account.

Stephen George and the crew at Twin Flames Studios, for producing the audiobook.

Kristi Burns, my narrator, for not only becoming my voice but also bringing my six characters to life.

Paul Brodie, for leading the official launch with strategy and perseverance.

Roxanne Darling, for website design, tech help, tough love as my brand-police, and for overall encouragement as a friend.

Michael Woods of Bardacke Allison Miller LLP, for clear and generous guidance on intellectual property law and for giving me added confidence as I brought this work into the world.

Berkeley T. Merchant, MBA, co-founder of Delgado Street Press, for making the chaos linear, offering reality checks, and for superhuman patience.

Informal Support Team

The Hearts & Minds group—faithful companions since 1995—Bruce Hazen, Darcy Hitchcock, David Lacka, Marsha Willard, and Sharon Buckmaster, who listened well and always gave thoughtful feedback.

Steven Freemire, who read the manuscript and offered invaluable suggestions about his specialty—the men in my audience.

Mike Seely, who helped me see how invaluable—and initially invisible—Superpowers really are.

Mimi Koehl, who shared the accumulated wisdom of the *Every Other Thursday* group and asked me timely and remarkably clarifying questions.

Jeanne Crouch, for both content ideas and encouragement along the way.

Sara Eisenberg, who read the manuscript with a discerning and generous eye.

My husband and partner for three decades, who dodges the spotlight whenever possible but offers steadfast support always.

Guides Who Lit the Path

Charley Johnston, M.D., Peter Senge, Otto Scharmer, Antoinette Klatsky, Ryan Levesque, Alexander John Shaia, Sharon Daloz Parks, and Annette Weyerhaeuser. Lifelong gratitude to Mrs. Svane at Berkeley High School, circa 1960—from her precision and rigor came a gift still mysterious: words arrive, I catch them.

I am indebted to all the people I interviewed who willingly shared their dreams and their frustrations, especially those unnamed who inspired the six composite characters.

I thank Santa Fe itself—its landscape and its remarkable community of people—for shaping this book in ways I may not realize.

I am grateful as well to Yosemite, whose immensity and sacred presence have stirred me since childhood—wild inspiration for the cover of this book.

And to you, the reader—this book comes fully alive in your hands; your reading completes the circle of its making and carries its purpose into the world.

With immense gratitude,

Marie Morgan

Santa Fe, New Mexico

About the Author

Marie Morgan has spent her professional life helping others ask better questions—about their work, their leadership, their inner lives, and now, about a new purpose in their later years. A longtime leadership coach and spiritual mentor, she has spent five decades guiding others through life's thresholds and turning points.

She earned a doctorate at the convergence of psychology, spirituality, and adult development and is a lifelong student of transformation. Her work weaves together rigorous scholarship, inner practice, and people's lived experience. The idea for *Prime Time* crystallized after a day of interviews with three different retirees—each accomplished, yet unable to name the unsettling problem they were facing. She realized a book could give people a starting place: language to name their struggle and a roadmap to help them chart a new path.

Marie created *Prime Time* as both a guidebook and an invitation: to live boldly, offer what only each person uniquely can, and reshape the culture of aging from the inside out. She writes for the curious, the dissatisfied, and the restless who suspect that retirement isn't the end of their story but the opening scene of a new one. It breaks her heart—and makes her angry—to see talented, generous people put on a shelf by consumer culture, told to "kick back" while the world desperately needs their wisdom and life experience. Writing *Prime Time* reignited her calling: after recent years in art-making and gallery life, she realized she wasn't using her Superpower—seeing and calling forth the potential in others.

Marie shares her Santa Fe home with her husband and a cream Golden Retriever—surrounded by her own paintings and sculpture, and a 3-D model of I. M. Pei's East Building of the National Gallery of Art, her metaphorical cathedral. It has been reported that a California state flag—honoring her birthplace—can be seen flying from her front porch.

Still emerging, Marie is less interested in legacy than in the living edges of reinvention: the questions still unfolding, the work still unfinished. She hopes readers will wake up to how great their Superpower is—and find or create places to put those gifts to work in ways that bring joy to themselves and benefit to others.

To learn more about her work and the growing Prime Time community, visit https://www.MarieMorganPrimeTime.com